JOHN BERCOW

JOHN BERCOW
Call to Order

SEBASTIAN WHALE

Biteback Publishing

First published in Great Britain in 2020 by
Biteback Publishing Ltd
Westminster Tower
3 Albert Embankment
London SE1 7SP
Copyright © Sebastian Whale 2020

ISBN 978-1-78590-558-2

10 9 8 7 6 5 4 3 2 1

A CIP catalogue record for this book is available from the British Library.

Set in Bulmer

Printed and bound in Great Britain by
CPI Group (UK) Ltd, Croydon CR0 4YY

For Dan, to whom I owe this book, and Boo, to whom I am eternally grateful.

CONTENTS

PREFACE

At just after nine on 3 August 2019, my editor and good friend Daniel Bond sent me a message. 'Has Bercow had a biography?' he asked. 'You should write it.'

For reasons known only to himself, Dan was spending his Saturday night researching for a podcast with John Bercow (evidently, he was yet to stumble across Bobby Friedman's biography from 2011). Sitting at home in north-west London, I thought over his proposal, 'I would 100 per cent do that,' I replied. 'Maybe I could look into it.' Within two weeks, I had been commissioned.

If you think Brexit elicits controversy, try asking people for their views on John Bercow. The afternoon he announced his resignation, on 9 September 2019, I had consecutive interviews for this book with two Conservative MPs whose offices were just four doors apart. In the first meeting, the MP, a former minister, described Bercow as an extremist. The next MP, seconds down the corridor, told me Bercow was *the* great reforming Speaker.

Bercow has been not only one of the most eccentric characters in our national life but also one of the most contentious. In many ways, he was the Speaker for the times: divisive, polarising, abrasive. For better or worse, he was undoubtedly one of the most consequential.

While I had no preconceptions about his character before writing the book, I did have a few personal observations about Bercow. I found some of his interventions self-indulgent, I thought there had been signs of bias – particularly in his latter days – but I was clear on this: his being in the chair created theatre. For the first time, the Speaker was often the story. He was another factor; an unknown quantity. For lovers of political drama, he was a star turn.

Bercow is not the first politician, nor will he be the last, to go on a 'journey'. But his is one of the more notorious. Just how did a former member of the ultra-conservative Monday Club – and secretary of its Immigration and Repatriation Committee – become the darling of the liberal left? How could an ardent Eurosceptic, who would challenge his professors at the University of Essex over the UK's membership of the Common Market, end up not only voting Remain at an EU referendum but even helping to choreograph the resistance to a no-deal exit?

Such is his political voyage that many of Bercow's former enemies on the left now count themselves as admirers. Take Linda Bellos, who remembers Bercow as being 'outrageous' and 'appalling' from their time together on Lambeth Council, and now regards him as a 'forthright man of honour'. Conversely, his one-time comrades on the Conservative student right have scarcely a good word to say about him personally or professionally.

This remarkable transformation has been the source of much speculation. Plenty of people have wondered whether Bercow's changing political outlook is primarily down to his wife, Sally, who also went on a notable journey from right to left. Others point out that his political beliefs often mirrored those that were in the ascendancy, such as Thatcherism in the '80s and centrism during New Labour's heyday.

A word that crops up time and again about Bercow is 'mercurial'. 'I'm not sure you're ever seeing the real person,' one of his contemporaries at the Federation of Conservative Students told me over lunch. 'Maybe Boris Johnson comes into this category. They develop layers on top of whoever they really are in order to cope with, or project themselves through, life.'

For this book, I spoke to more than 140 people from across Bercow's life. For many of his friends, the notion that he could bully someone is well beyond their comprehension. To them, Bercow is a thoughtful, humorous and kind man. For those who have incurred or witnessed Bercow's wrath, they cannot fathom how other people are unable to see what to them is self-evident.

Many of those who have a deep hatred for Bercow – a real, visceral hate – had run-ins with him at some point during their careers. Over time, the resentment had grown strong and they were more than motivated to try to throw him under a bus. One Conservative MP had even hired an investigator to look into his dealings. Meanwhile, many opposition MPs wilfully buried their heads in the sand over some of the more concerning claims about Bercow's behaviour in lieu of his 'progressive' values. In other words, a selection of vengeful MPs would stop at nothing to bring him down; others were willing to back him come what may, sacrificing their principles on the altar of Brexit. In these muddied waters, Bercow was able to cling to a life-raft and survive for as long as he did.

Two months before publication, I had my rucksack stolen at Waterloo Station. Inside was my laptop and everything related to the book. I had most of it backed up and a kind man got in touch to say he had found a booklet on a road next to the station. I mention this because some people close to me asked if foul play had been at hand. I can categorically confirm that it was some chancer at Waterloo Station and had nothing to do with the former Speaker. But such is the air of conspiracy that surrounds Bercow that usually sensible people were indulging themselves in silly, unsubstantiated and left-field theories.

While writing, there were days when I found myself feeling sympathy for Bercow. His was a complicated and challenging childhood. During his early years in the Commons, he was subjected to some unacceptable abuse. Other days, as he stood up for backbenchers and revitalised the House of Commons as a place of scrutiny, I would be rooting for Bercow, cheering him on.

But there were other occasions when empathy would be replaced by anger. An anger based on his alleged treatment of others. An anger at those who protected him. An anger at those who appropriated causes to suit their political vendettas. An anger at people's refusal to see him as anything other than their own projection of what they wanted him to be.

Bercow did not contribute to this book. Towards the end of the process, he was given the opportunity to comment on and fact-check certain anecdotes. Unless explicitly stated otherwise, the information comes from the research and interviews conducted over a period of five months. This book is my attempt at a balanced look at a complex man.

Not long after I was commissioned, it emerged that Bercow had written his own memoir. I believe my book offers different perspectives on the same story, shedding light on what was going on behind the scenes, and giving a voice to some of those who, for various reasons, have not been able to articulate their views. It must also be said that Bercow's book did prompt some people, who otherwise had stayed silent, to reach out.

This is the story of John Simon Bercow, the son of a taxi driver from north London, and the 157th Speaker of the House of Commons.

ACKNOWLEDGEMENTS

For this book I am indebted to a number of people. Dan, whose idea this was in the first place, and whose faith in me inspired me to go for it. Kevin, Georgina and Sally, who selflessly picked up the slack without any reservation while I was off work. John Johnston, who not only helped me stand up a couple of stories but also provided valuable advice throughout. Simon, Nitil, Adam and Mike, who gave me the all-clear to pursue my own project. Shivani, who helped with research early on. Andy, without whose close friendship and generosity I would not have been able to finish this book. Boo, who I leaned on more than I ever have, and who supported me, as she always does, right the way through. Nick and Sally, who backed me to the hilt. To the rest of my family and friends, particularly Lucy, Jeremy and Luke, whose positive encouragement was a source of great energy. And Olivia, whose patience and guidance helped me get over the line. Finally, I would like to thank every person who gave up their time in order to contribute to this book. Without you, there would be a series of blanks left unfilled.

CHAPTER ONE

DON'T CALL IT A COUP

'If you're going to shoot somebody, make sure you kill them.'

Fewer than ten people knew of the plan. Among them were David Cameron and George Osborne, although the Prime Minister and the Chancellor were not intimately involved. That way, they could avoid some of the shrapnel should the plot to oust John Bercow blow up in their faces.

Osborne was against the idea. The Conservatives were about to enter into a general election campaign, and the master strategist felt it would be an unnecessary distraction. He, unlike Cameron, was largely tolerant of the Speaker, if not full of admiration. Osborne, arguably the shrewdest political operator on the Conservative benches at the time, would tell colleagues: 'Bercow ran a bloody brilliant campaign to be elected Speaker, and hats off to him. You may not like him, but he won all those votes, he knew how to get elected.' A former minister explains: 'George always admired politicians being politicians in that sense, which not everybody does.'

A select group, including William Hague, the Leader of the House, and Chief Whip Michael Gove, had been preparing for three to four weeks. On the final evening of the 2010–15 parliament, the government would table a motion calling for the Speaker's re-election in the new parliament to be put to a secret ballot. The House would debate and vote on the amendments to the motion the following day. By that stage, Labour MPs from far-flung constituencies would be back in their seats campaigning, while their Conservative equivalents were on a three-line whip to stay in Westminster for a meeting with Lynton Crosby, the Australian election strategist. By launching a last-minute ambush, the Tories felt they could get the proposals over the line.

Remarkably, a key plotter behind the scenes contends that the idea was put to them by a Labour MP. 'It was suggested by Natascha Engel,' claims the schemer. Engel, who would go on to become a Deputy Speaker after the subsequent election, was one of fifteen MPs to nominate Bercow for the Speakership in June 2009. Her opinion of Bercow would wane significantly over the years, however. Engel, who lost her North East Derbyshire seat after the 2017 election, denies involvement in the coup and says she has no recollection whatsoever of tipping off the plotters about moving to a secret ballot.

The plan had to be top secret to avoid it being leaked. A Cabinet minister at the time says: 'We only discovered we were planning to do it at the last moment. Cabinet members didn't know. It was planned in No. 10.' If Bercow got a sniff of what was happening, he could swiftly neutralise the threat. 'Natascha told me in advance that Bercow was incredibly capable,' says a source involved. 'She said: "You can't give him any opportunity," and that's why we launched it as a surprise.'

It has become customary for incumbent Speakers to regain their position unopposed following a general election, after the House agrees to the question that they 'do take the chair of this House as Speaker'. If the motion was challenged, MPs would head to the division lobbies in the usual fashion, with their votes made public. Much to the chagrin of Bercow's more eager Tory critics, his Speakership was not contested after the 2010 election. But the Conservatives, now vexed after more than five years of Bercow's jurisdiction in the Commons, wanted to take him on.

While moving to a secret ballot was not guaranteed to get rid of Bercow, the thinking was that MPs would be more likely to vote against him if their vote was cast in private. The proposed policy is not, in and of itself, controversial: Deputy Speakers, chairs of select committees and new Speakers are all chosen by secret ballot. The controversy stemmed not just from the last-minute timing but from the methodology. The government was appropriating a report by MPs into the re-election of a Speaker for its own ends, and without due consultation of the chair of the committee that produced it, Charles Walker.

The Procedure Committee, then chaired by Conservative backbencher Greg Knight, first called for the House to vote on whether the Speaker should be re-elected by a secret ballot in 2009, and reiterated this view in an October 2011 report. In February 2013, under the chairmanship of Walker, an ally of John Bercow who was the only Conservative MP to nominate him for the Speakership, the Procedure Committee produced another report calling for MPs to be given a say on the matter, while also recommending that the status quo be maintained. Ministers failed to allocate any parliamentary time to discuss the report until the evening of 25 March 2015.

The plotters – who bristle at their efforts being described as a coup – insist that moving to a secret ballot was a long overdue update to the procedures of the House. 'It made perfect sense, it was the right thing to do and of course it was also something that a lot of people wanted,' one of those involved explains. But by moving on the last day of the parliament, they were more likely to successfully push the changes through and lay the ground for disposing of Bercow when MPs returned in May.

The Conservatives, who had now been in coalition government with the Liberal Democrats for almost five years, knew the move could spark hostility from various quarters of the Commons. But, for reasons we shall go on to explore, Cameron's party felt the referee was no longer playing straight.

*　　*　　*

William Hague decided he had to inform Bercow personally before tabling the motion. 'He's just too fair-minded for this kind of stuff,' says another plotter. 'I said to Hague, "Whatever you do, if you feel you have to go and see Bercow, wait until the Scottish Labour MPs have got on the plane to Glasgow or Edinburgh."'

Hague met Bercow in his office at 5.30, more than an hour earlier than originally planned (a source cites 'diary clashes' for the meeting being brought forward). After outlining what was taking place, Hague, Bercow would later claim, told him that MPs would be given a free vote on the motion. The motion was tabled at 5.45.

The Speaker, one of the most astute political brains in circulation, read between the lines. He immediately got on the phone to Rosie Winterton, Labour's Chief Whip, and Angela Eagle, the party's shadow Leader of the Commons. 'Honestly, if they had told him half an hour later, we wouldn't have been able to stop them. They told him, he phoned me, and I ran down to see William Hague,' Eagle says.

Eagle, a diminutive but forceful figure, burst into Hague's office around the corner from the Speaker's chair, deep in the ventricles of the Palace of Westminster. The Labour frontbencher walked past his staff and into Hague's study, where he was talking to his political team. She stared at one of his advisers, pointed at the door and declared: 'Get out.'

A source close to Hague says: 'The leader's office has thin wooden doors, and she proceeded to harangue William for about twenty minutes. Rosie was then doing the same thing to Gove at the other end. It was a shambles from start to finish.' Staff in the leader's office would later joke about the Labour frontbencher leaving behind an 'Angela Eagle-shaped hole' in the entrance door.

Eagle recalls:

I just basically stormed in and said: 'What the hell do you think you're doing?' William is normally a very nice, affable person. We had quite a lot in common in terms of our love of politics – and the House – and he was so sheepish. You could tell in his body language that he'd been told to do this, and he'd sort of gone along with it against his better judgement and not fought it. He knew everything I was saying was correct.

Fortuitously for the Labour Party, there was a vote in the Commons soon after Eagle had confronted Hague. Winterton and her team immediately put out an edict that all MPs must be in Westminster the following day, and they managed to stop many MPs from setting out for their constituencies.

Bercow also called his close friend Julian Lewis, the Conservative MP for New Forest East. 'He was in a state of some agitation,' recalls Lewis. At 6.30, Lewis rang Charles Walker. This was the first time that the chair of the Procedure Committee became aware the motion had been tabled. According to Lewis, Walker's response was largely 'unprintable'. The plotters' discourtesy in failing to brief him of their plans would prove fatal. 'I was extremely pissed off,' Walker admits.

David Davis, the Conservative backbencher who had stood for the party leadership in 2005, was scheduled to travel to Switzerland early on Thursday morning for a skiing holiday with his family. He was having dinner in the Adjournment restaurant in Portcullis House when Lewis and Walker approached. 'Do you know what they're up to?' Lewis asked. Davis was shocked. 'I thought that was wholly inappropriate and quite improper behaviour,' he says. He delayed his flight by a day in order to help marshal the resistance in the Commons, while his wife and kids went on without him.

Lewis returned to his parliamentary office, fired up his computer and began composing an email under the subject line 'An Unworthy Manoeuvre by the Leader of the House'. Unable to send one blanket email to all 650 Members, Lewis worked into the early hours sending out the same message to groups of MPs at a time.

The 469-word message, first delivered at 12.09 a.m., relayed the evening's events and focused on the 'astonishing' failure of ministers to inform Walker about their plans to use a report in his committee's name for this purpose. 'One need not be a particular admirer of the Speaker to realise that this is no way for decent people to behave,' he wrote. Lewis encouraged MPs to 'make the effort to attend and vote appropriately tomorrow, by rejecting the proposal to re-elect the Speaker secretly rather than openly'.

*　　*　　*

Thursday 26 March was to be the last day of Parliament before the 2015 general election. The Labour Party had a one-line whip for the final day's proceedings, where more rudimentary parliamentary discussions were scheduled to take place. Ed Miliband's party was firmly on an election footing, and the forty-one Scottish Labour MPs were up against it, with the SNP insurgent after the 2014 Scottish independence referendum six months earlier. They needed to get their feet on the ground. The plotters knew this.

'They'd twigged quite late in the day they were in trouble and they were going to have to go out canvassing for the first time in their constituencies for twenty years or something, so they were desperate to get back, and we knew that,' an insider says. 'There was a lot of planning, a lot of thought went into this process, when is the best day to do it, and there was total secrecy.'

The mood among Tory MPs was buoyant; at the last Prime Minister's Questions of the parliament, Cameron had outmanoeuvred Miliband by ruling out any VAT rise under a Conservative government. Labour MPs were heading back to their constituencies dejected by what had unfolded. 'We were all pretty miserable about having that dreadful PMQs and then going on an election,' recalls a backbench Labour MP.

That Thursday was also due to be William Hague's last day in the Commons after a storied 26-year parliamentary career, during which time the MP for Richmond in Yorkshire had served as Conservative Party leader and Foreign Secretary. Well-liked and admired across the House, the ebullient politician had few detractors.

His team had concerns about the Bercow plan. While another plotter insists Hague was keen on the idea, his aides wanted to hear more about the whipping operation to get the vote over the line, besides relying on Labour MPs being out of Westminster. One former aide says: 'I kept saying to William, "Have the whips got the numbers?"' The aide went to visit the whips' office, demanding to see spreadsheets with the names of MPs who were signed up to the plan. 'I was quite annoyed at the time that they didn't show me. It made me mistrust it.'

Sworn to secrecy, the whips involved with the coup had not informed some of the more vociferous anti-Bercow Conservative backbenchers, for fear of the plot leaking. The rest of the whips were briefed after the motion was tabled that evening.

To buy time, Bercow awarded three Urgent Questions to Labour MPs on Thursday morning after Business Questions. The first was to former Cabinet minister Peter Hain, who asked whether the 'public inquiry into undercover policing will examine files held by Special Branch on Members of Parliament'. The second, to Diana Johnson, focused on 'the publication of the Penrose Inquiry and its implications for the United Kingdom government'. The last was awarded to Sir Gerald Kaufman, who wanted a statement on the change to the day's business – in other words, for Hague to explain just what on earth he was up to. Setting the tone for what followed, Kaufman asked: 'Is [Hague] aware that this grubby decision is what he personally will be remembered for? After a distinguished career in the House of Commons, both as a leader of a party and as a senior Cabinet minister, he has now descended to squalor in the final days of the parliament.'

Peter Bone, the Eurosceptic backbench Tory MP, followed, adding: 'This is a bad day for Parliament.' Angela Eagle voiced many MPs' fury at the underhand measures taken by the plotters, asking:

Is not the truth that this is nothing to do with the Procedure Committee's report and everything to do with the character of the Prime Minister? It is a petty and spiteful act because he hates his government being
properly scrutinised, thanks to this reforming Speaker. The Leader of
the House should be ashamed of himself for going along with it.

Hague was under pressure from the moment he stood up at the despatch box. Facing a barrage of criticism, he argued that three factors had
prompted the decision to lodge the motion overnight. Firstly, parliamentary time had been freed up due to there being no amendments to legislation for consideration coming back from the House of Lords. Secondly, a
report from the Procedure Committee the previous week had requested
an amendment to the Parliamentary Standards Act 2009 before the disso-
lution of Parliament. And thirdly, it was therefore the view of 'government
business managers' that other outstanding matters, such as the re-election
of the Speaker, should be considered at the same time.

Jacob Rees-Mogg, who hailed Hague's various political successes, expressed 'deep sadness' that his career 'should end with his name being
put to a bit of parliamentary jiggery-pokery'. Philip Davies, the MP for
Shipley and the embodiment of an independent-minded Conservative,
said Hague would regret going along with the 'student union politics' of
the whips' office. David Davis revealed he could have supported moving
to a secret ballot were it not for the 'mean-spirited' way the government
had gone about its business.

Stewart Jackson, a long-time ally of Davis who would later serve as
his chief of staff in the Department for Exiting the European Union, was
sitting nearby. The MP for Peterborough was a vehement opponent of
Bercow. 'It's the only time I ever had a row with David Davis,' he recalls.
'On the one hand, I thought it was shabby. I thought the way it was done
at the last minute – the last sitting day – it was badly handled.'

But he adds: 'I sat in the Chamber with DD and I said words that you
wouldn't say in church on a Sunday about Bercow. I told DD: "Look, I'm

a backbencher, I can vote the way I like but, on this occasion, I'm backing the government."'

* * *

By the time the debate started at 12.17, Hague had taken a beating. MPs who might otherwise have been relied upon were queuing up to criticise the move. 'William was under pressure. Even though he was one of the main organisers, he went off the idea during the course of the debate,' says one of the plotters. 'He's too nice a bloke, you could see it, he would get more and more uncomfortable and he basically lost his nerve.'

Hague, turning to the senior whips, said: 'I think we should pull this.' Gove resisted, replying: 'No, we're going to hold firm here, William, stick to this. We're going to see this through. We're going to have the vote, win or lose.'

A source who worked for Hague at the time argues that the whips had failed to do their jobs properly by not securing enough people prepared to speak in favour of the motion. Only a few honourable mentions, including Tory backbenchers David Nuttall, Graham Stuart and Michael Fabricant, handed Hague a lifeline. But Labour's Kevin Barron, the chair of the Standards Committee – Parliament's watchdog – was another to take aim. 'We have a bad enough reputation now; this motion sullies it further.'

All the while, of course, Bercow was watching from the chair. He had done all he could to allow opposition MPs sufficient time to return to Westminster by granting the three Urgent Questions.

If the government's position looked precarious, it was dealt a hammer blow when chair of the Procedure Committee Charles Walker rose at 12.44.

Addressing Bercow, Walker said: 'The report should not be about you, Mr Speaker, and it is becoming about you. I fear that the government have wanted it to become about you. It should be about the position of Speaker.'

He outlined the chronology events, capturing the underhanded nature of the government's position. In the preceding days, he had spoken to Hague and his special adviser, as well as Hague's Lib Dem deputy, Tom Brake. 'All of them would have been aware of what they were proposing to do. I also had a number of friendly chats with our Chief Whip yesterday, yet I found out at 6.30 p.m. last night that the Leader of the House was bringing forward my report,' he said.

His voice starting to crack, Walker concluded: 'I have been played as a fool. When I go home tonight, I will look in the mirror and see an honourable fool looking back at me. I would much rather be an honourable fool, in this and any other matter, than a clever man.'

Labour MPs rose to their feet and applauded. Graham Brady, the chair of the 1922 Committee of Conservative MPs, patted his colleague on the back. Bercow, with tears in his eyes, and his mouth quivering as the adulation continued around the House, eventually called for order.

If there was any chance of the motion passing, Walker had just obliterated it.

At 1.17 p.m., the motion was put to the House.

One of the many idiosyncrasies of the Commons is how votes are announced. Once MPs have been through the division lobbies, the results are given to tellers, two MPs who represent each side of the question – aye and no. The tellers representing the victorious side stand to the right as they face the Speaker's chair and announce the result. When Labour's Heidi Alexander and David Hamilton ventured to the right, opposition MPs broke out in applause. The government had been defeated.

Bercow, visibly moved, coughed and struggled in vain to contain a smile. The government had lost by twenty votes. Bercow was handed the count after the numbers were announced. 'The ayes to the right 202. The noes to the left 228. So, the noes have it, the noes have it. Unlock,' he announced. He focused his gaze on Hague, his eyes occasionally narrowing. Engel, by staying in her constituency, had abstained.

Members of Parliament and House staff were watching the events unfold on a monitor in the front office at Speaker's House. Ed Davey, the Liberal Democrat Energy Secretary, was also there and was taken aback by the extraordinary scenes in the Commons, with Bercow's eyes filling with tears. 'Have you ever seen anything like that?' he asked one of the staff present.

To this day, Brake supports the substance of the motion put forward. The problem, he suggests, was that the issue became conflated with Conservative angst towards Bercow: 'The House chose otherwise because they did see it as being a direct attack on John Bercow.'

A former Cabinet minister, on the other hand, says: 'That was outrageous executive overreach.' They allege that one of those involved said they did so to 'take one for the team'. 'It showed that it was an effort from on high to get rid of the Speaker. That was quite wrong.'

Eagle agrees: 'There was enough outrage in the Tory Party about the sheer impropriety about what they were doing that we beat them.'

Davis, who helped orchestrate the government defeat, says he has been in Bercow's good books ever since, though he notes: 'It wasn't done because he was a particular friend; he's quite difficult to be friendly with, actually. He's quite a prickly character at the best of times. He's almost formal when you're talking to him in private. It's really quite strange.'

Immediately after the defeat, the recriminations began in earnest. The whips insist that Hague should not have tipped off Bercow more than an hour before originally scheduled, but one source with knowledge of the plot maintains that the plan was doomed from the beginning: 'The idea should have been killed at birth. [Cameron] wanted to do one last thing before the House rose. Instead, a long and glittering career for William was ended with the whole House haranguing him and him trying to defend something that was indefensible.'

One of the schemers went to see Cameron in No. 10. 'Sorry, David, we didn't quite pull it off,' they told the PM. Cameron is said to have replied that the move was 'worth trying'.

The plotter remembers:

I didn't tell him about William Hague, I didn't want to land William in it, I thought the reason was that Hague tipped off Bercow an hour and a half too early, but it didn't seem to be very helpful to create a row between Cameron and Hague going into the election campaign.

A source close to Hague says:

> The whips promised No. 10, DC and William that they could deliver the votes. The regret was, if we were going to do a coup or a putsch on [Bercow], one, we should have done it in a way that did more damage than just trying to get a secret ballot on the re-election of the Speaker, which was a shit end result; or we should have done it in a way that was not informing the Speaker the night before.

No. 10 decided that Gove was largely to blame. A former aide to Cameron says:

> People were pretty fucked off about it because the optics looked really, really bad. If you're going to do it, you need to execute it properly. It looked like we were playing games at a critical time for the country before going to the polls. We were really pissed off with Gove about it at the time ... It was classic Gove playing parliamentary games and messing up.

The plot was indeed poorly executed. But it was doomed to fail from the start: the measure itself was limp, its motivations transparent and ultimately success would not have guaranteed Bercow's ousting. A lot of political capital was expended in the process – not least the sullying of Hague's reputation – and it came as the Tories were entering into a general election campaign. Changing the rules surrounding the re-election of the Speaker is not a malicious endeavour: taken in isolation, the changes are themselves not wholly unsound. But the coup was never about correcting a procedural abnormality; it was about a political vendetta against a Speaker whom the upper echelons of government felt was biased against them.

The failed manoeuvre was significant for other reasons. Bercow's death stare was telling; he had been a thorn in the side of the government for many years, but he was now even more emboldened to curtail executive excesses. This would have implications for successive governments and would go on to define his Speakership. It also exposed the level of support Bercow held among the Labour benches (his critics would argue that it showed how in hock to the opposition he was at this point).

Either way, the plotters, ironically, had shored up Bercow's position. A Cabinet minister who was not involved with the manoeuvre concludes: 'If you're going to shoot somebody, make sure you kill them.'

Bercow's and Cameron's relationship continued to sour after the election. It is only Gove who recovered some semblance of a cordial relationship with Bercow, after initial years of hostility.

The move clearly riled Bercow, and it wasn't soon forgotten. During an appearance before students in November 2017,[1] his displeasure was still on show. Branding Hague's failure to tell Walker of his plan a 'monstrous parliamentary discourtesy', he argued that the whole event was 'hugely to the discredit of the government', adding: 'As far as whether it was Cameron, Hague or Gove is concerned, I'm pretty clear in my mind it came from the top.'

Bercow saved most of his animosity for Hague, however:

The best Leaders of the House in history recognised it's their duty to be the House's representative in the government. And William Hague should have said: 'This is ridiculous and discreditable, and I will have no part in it.' To his great discredit, he didn't take that attitude; he was happy to act as David Cameron's agent, and it was a display of malice and incompetence on an industrial scale. Put very simply, Hague made a mess of it on his last day in Parliament. Sad, sad, sad.

With a characteristic rhetorical flourish, Bercow added: 'I know I do tend to be rather gentle, restrained and understated in these matters. One of these days, I'll tell you what I really think.'

The botched plot was the culmination of more than a decade of aggravation between Bercow and the top brass of the Conservative Party. By the time of his election as Speaker on 22 June 2009, Bercow was an isolated figure on the Tory benches. He had travelled a long way from his younger years on the Conservative right; a place he called home for the best part of three decades.

CHAPTER TWO

PLANTING SEEDS

'I just thought he was a pompous little arse.'

Members of the Labour Party travelled to Bournemouth at the end of September 1985 with a cloud hanging overhead. The miners' strike, called by the National Union of Mineworkers under Arthur Scargill against the National Coal Board, had ended on 3 March. Militant, the hard-left faction, had taken control of Liverpool City Council and set an illegal 'deficit budget' as part of the rate-capping rebellion that Lambeth Council, led by 'Red Ted' Knight, was also engaged in.

The 1985 conference is best known for Labour leader Neil Kinnock's barnstorming address inside the Bournemouth International Centre, in which he challenged Militant activists and supporters head on. Warning that 'impossible promises don't win victories', the Welshman declared:

> I'll tell you what happens with impossible promises. You start with far-fetched resolutions. They are then pickled into a rigid dogma, a code, and you go through the years sticking to that, outdated, misplaced, irrelevant to the real needs, and you end up in the grotesque chaos of a Labour council – a Labour council – hiring taxis to scuttle round a city handing out redundancy notices to its own workers.

Derek Hatton, the deputy leader of Liverpool Council and one of the

spiritual figureheads of Militant, was caught on camera shouting: 'Liar.'
Eric Heffer, the Labour MP for Liverpool Walton, staged a walkout. He
ended up on a balcony overlooking Bournemouth Pier, while being pursued by the press.

The United Nations had proclaimed 1985 as the International Youth
Year, and in recognition of this focus, the Labour Party allowed every
constituency party to bring along a young person to conference, in addi-
tion to their normal delegate. This increased audience further fuelled the
atmosphere around the conference hall. David Wilson, who was studying
for his A-levels, was thrilled to go along as a representative of his Devizes
constituency.

Aggravated by a string of heated arguments between different Labour
factions inside the conference hall, Wilson returned to his hotel. Outside
the restricted area, he was confronted by a group of young Conservative
activists sporting branded T-shirts and posters. They were members of
the Federation of Conservative Students (FCS), who had travelled down
to Bournemouth to distribute leaflets with the approval of Conservative
Party chairman Norman Tebbit. 'We went down as a group in a minibus
just to wind them up,' says a former member.

Wilson remembers: 'It was the arrogant swagger of they were in charge,
they were the Thatcherites. They had that self-assurance that only young
Conservatives can have. After a day of listening to Militant picking fights
with Neil Kinnock, I wasn't in the mood to have a reasoned argument.'

Wilson barked at the group to 'bugger off'. 'Oh, that's not a very
cogent political argument,' responded one of the activists, who was short
at around 5ft 6in. His name was John Bercow. 'I remember at the time
thinking, "You pillock,"' says Wilson. 'But it taught me a lesson, which is
it's best not to resort to abuse, it's better to win the argument.'

While Wilson says he 'squared up' to Bercow, that was as far as it went:
'It was only a very minor skirmish.' Years later, their paths would cross
again when Bercow, then Speaker, addressed the David Cairns Foun-
dation in memory of the former Scottish Labour Party politician, who

died in May 2011. 'He gave a very touching tribute to David, so all was forgiven,' says Wilson. 'But at the time, I have to say, I just thought he was a pompous little arse.'

Certain factions of the FCS, in some respects, were Margaret Thatcher's Praetorian Guard, although they were to the right of the UK Prime Minister. Bercow had long been a cheerleader for the Iron Lady. Along with Enoch Powell, the PM was one of Bercow's two political heroes. His connection to Thatcher went back several years earlier, when the then Leader of the Opposition had played a key role in his journey to the Conservative Party.

* * *

Margaret Thatcher was due to give one last stump speech before polling day on Thursday 3 May 1979. It was in her constituency of Finchley, a north London seat that she had represented for twenty years. John Bercow, then aged sixteen, was a student at a local comprehensive, Finchley Manorhill, where he would take his O-levels later that year. He went along to hear Thatcher speak at the Woodhouse School between North Finchley and Friern Barnet.

Bercow had to listen to the address over the Tannoy due to the hall being so packed. After Thatcher had finished, he pushed his way to the front so he could collar her on the way out of the venue. He introduced himself and informed the Conservative leader of how inspired he was by her speech. 'Mr Bercow, are you a member of the Young Conservatives?' Thatcher inquired. 'Well, no,' Bercow replied.

'But you most assuredly should be. Do you know Roy Langstone?' Thatcher asked.

'I'm afraid not.'

'He is my agent for the Finchley and Friern Barnet Conservatives. A first-class man. 221 Ballards Lane. Mr Bercow, you must go there, by arrangement, to see him. He will see you all right.' After a few months,

Bercow heeded Thatcher's advice. He signed up to the Conservatives in Hendon North, before joining the Finchley Young Conservatives.[1]

Bercow will often cite the Winter of Discontent as a catalyst for his political interest. 'Streets unswept, sick people untreated, dead people unburied. I thought that this was no way to run a country,' he says.[2] His political journey, however, long predated the winter of 1978–79.

His father, Charles Bercow, known as Charlie, bore a significant influence on Bercow's thinking. The son of a Romanian Jew named Jack Berkowitch (the family would later Anglicise the name to Bercow) who moved to Britain in 1900, Charlie was one of four children. Growing up in Hackney, east London, Charlie had wanted to train as a barrister, but his parents wanted him to leave home and contribute to the family upkeep. Bercow would describe his father as an 'intelligent' guy from a working-class background who never had the opportunity to go to university.[3] Like his father, Bercow had once held aspirations to become a barrister, only to abandon them over concerns about funding. 'That short-term debt shouldn't have stopped me qualifying for the Bar and practising at it,' he told an interviewer in 2009. 'My only major regret is that I would have liked to have been a barrister. Partly because I have no private money … I decided not to pursue it.'[4]

His mother, Brenda Bailey, grew up in Huddersfield. She also came from what Bercow describes as an ordinary background. The daughter of a single mother, she left school and worked as a junior reporter on the *Huddersfield Examiner* before moving to London, where she worked part-time as a legal secretary. In the late 1990s, she received a degree in English Literature from Middlesex University, aged sixty-nine. Her entry, Bercow would comment, was delayed by more than half a century. Brenda's determination and work ethic would have a lasting impression on her youngest child.

Charlie served in the RAF during the Second World War, along with his brother, Ralph, who was an officer in Bomber Command. When he met Brenda in the 1950s, the pair bonded over a mutual love of the arts. Charlie was a member of The Lodge, a Jewish theatre group, while Brenda would continue to work as a supporting actress into her eighties, with roles at the Royal Court Theatre in London, among others. In 2013, she played an extra in the Channel 4 series *London Irish*, described as '*Girls* meets *Father Ted*'. A report in the *Evening Standard* said that Brenda took a liberal view on the profanities in the six-part show. 'She absolutely loved it and said it's exactly what Channel 4 should be doing,' said an insider. 'But she also warned, "My son's a bit stuffy, he might not like it."' Brenda herself wanted to stay quiet about the role. 'Brenda doesn't want to speak to anyone about it,' said her agent. 'She's happy to do her thing and stay in the background.'[5]

Brenda converted to Judaism at a reform synagogue before marrying Charlie at Edgware District and Reform Synagogue on 13 December 1956. At twenty-seven, Brenda was nine years her husband's junior. They had their first child, Alison, in 1960. Three years later, on 19 January 1963, John Simon Bercow was born at the Edgware General Hospital.

After the war, Charlie worked for the London County Council in an administrative role before joining his brother Ralph at Bercow Motors, a car business in Warren Street, just south of Euston in London. 'Dad was asked to join it as a junior partner and he did and he was very proud to do so,' says Bercow.[6] There was a falling-out in the family as Solomon Bercow, one of the four brothers, took issue with not being brought into the business. Bercow Motors moved to Colindale in north London after the council announced that it was restricting parking by putting yellow lines near the showroom, and it folded in 1974, a few years after Ralph's death from cancer in 1969. 'Although in many ways Dad was a very good dad, he wasn't really a good businessperson,' says Bercow. Charlie was too risk-averse to thrive as an entrepreneur. With the oil crisis hitting the sale of cars, the business went downhill.[7]

Charlie, who had also suffered from ill health, would later become a minicab driver. 'There was a period of very modest success and then a period of no success. We lived a modest lower-middle-class lifestyle,' Bercow says.[8]

Bercow's first experience of running for high office came in the school council elections at Frith Manor Primary School in Woodside Park, situated on the western side of North Finchley, a traditional middle-class area with a large Jewish population. Aged nine, Bercow stood on a platform of improving school dinners. 'A rather questionable manifesto as the quality of the school dinners was not that bad, I quite liked them and there was no prospect of me being able to do anything about them,' he recalled at the seventieth anniversary of the school in November 2009.[9] John Davies, another student at Frith Manor, also believes Bercow was telling untruths about the state of the school meals, noting: 'He obviously developed his political acumen early.'[10]

Derek Wyatt, an ex-Labour MP and a former England rugby player, is a fellow Frith Manor alumnus. Located next door to Inglis Barracks, a military installation that closed in 2007, Frith Manor's intake was composed of army kids and a good smattering of middle-class parents. 'It had fantastic teaching,' recalls Wyatt. 'Miles better than anywhere that I went subsequently.' One teacher in particular brooked no disobedience: during his time there, Bercow found himself 'expelled with some insistence' from the school choir by music teacher Tim Geaney.[11]

Bercow's first real election success came in his final year, aged eleven. Seven candidates stood in a mock poll on the eve of the first of two elections in 1974, in which Ted Heath was running against Labour's Harold Wilson. The poll was the brainchild of deputy head John Stringer, who wanted pupils to understand how democracy worked and what their parents would be voting on that week. Bercow was one of three Tories on the ballot.

Many of the pupils produced banners with abstract pledges in keeping with their age; Nicola Crowther, described as the 'most popular girl in school', vowed to be the 'best, the whole best and nothing but the best', while Russell Beynon, a candidate for the Scottish National Party, declared himself 'The King'. The ever-precocious Bercow concentrated on the issue of the day: inflation. His banner, perhaps showing an awareness of his dad's business struggles, carried a commitment for 'cheaper food and petrol'. The candidates wore oversized rosettes on their person. Bercow, shorter than the rest, had a fringe hovering above his eyebrows and hair down to his shoulders. He finished second with sixty-three votes, behind Crowther, who won with eighty-five. She had told her fellow pupils: 'I can't think what to do about prices, but if you vote for me, I'll think harder.'

Brenda insisted on her children having hobbies, and the young John took judo lessons and was sent to the local Cubs, both of which he hated with a passion. He took more of a shine to tap-dancing, a skill for which he showed a decent level of proficiency. At the age of eight, he was introduced to tennis.

It should not be underestimated how talented Bercow was with a racket in hand. Ashley Fuller played Bercow in a tournament at Paddington Tennis Club in the Middlesex Championships. He had won his first game and had been told by his friend Stuart Bale, who would go on to become a professional player, that he was facing the no. 1 seed next. But when his opponent arrived, Fuller thought his mate was having him on. 'This kid comes up and he's about half my size, got long hair down to his waist, and I looked at my friends and I thought they were pulling a joke on me,' he says.

Fuller turned to his dad and said: 'This will be quick, don't worry.' He was correct: Bercow won 6–0, 6–0 in fewer than forty minutes. 'He absolutely slaughtered me. The thing with John as a young kid, we called him "the rubber ward". He never made a mistake.' Bercow would deploy high looping balls from the baseline that would pin his opponents back and run down everything from the back of the court. 'He just out-rallied us every single time.'

Bercow's opponents, who included Andrew Castle, another future professional, would try to take advantage of his height. 'I used to try and play short balls to bring him into the net, but when I did that, he used to drop-shot me all the time,' says Fuller. Bercow was the top-ranked tennis player in the country at under-twelve level, and a Middlesex champion. Despite his prowess in his age group, however, he was knocked out in the first round of the national championships.

The pre-teen could regularly be found at the clubhouse reading *The Times*. 'He used to talk politics with my mother and father until the cows came home. My dad would say: "He knows more about it than I do,"' recalls Fuller. 'I was going from *Beano* to *Spiderman* at the time, and there was John Bercow reading *The Times* newspaper.'

Bercow was coached by Bobby Wilson, a former top-ranking English tennis player who reached the quarter-finals of Wimbledon four times. 'When he was a junior, he disliked losing,' says Wilson. 'Occasionally he behaved so badly I had to inform his mother that if he behaved as badly as that again, I wouldn't coach him any further.' Wilson recalls Bercow getting 'very angry' and 'throwing his racket about'. 'It was just complete frustration that he couldn't beat me!' he adds.

Brenda Bercow came to watch all of her son's games, sitting with her knitting beside Fuller's mother. Winners of tournaments run by the Lawn Tennis Association would receive British Petroleum badges, which would be stuck proudly on the side of equipment and clothing. Fuller played Bercow the week after winning his first tournament, but he had yet to receive his BP badge. He had lost to Bercow twice more since their first encounter but came much closer after losing in three sets. When he came off, he realised that Brenda Bercow had sewn a BP badge onto his track-suit top. Joining forces, Bercow and Fuller won two Middlesex under-fifteen doubles championships.

At the age of fourteen, Bercow chanced his arm when he saw Australian tennis great Rod Laver practising on his own. He asked if he could help by collecting balls, and then began hitting with the eleven-time grand slam champion.[12]

The tide turned against Bercow as he entered his teens, with his diminutive stature proving a hindrance to his development as a tennis player. 'I grew and grew and grew, and sadly John didn't. I beat him at the next tournament we played at. From then on, I went on to bigger things in tennis and he went on to be a politician,' says Fuller. 'Once players started beating him, for him it was very tough.' Wilson agrees: 'When he played bigger youngsters, the height was quite a factor in his not improving any further. He had got the temperament to make the grade if he had been taller.' This was compounded by a bout of bronchial asthma, which forced him to take prolonged absences from school and disturbed his training.

'I was what was known at the time as a very determined hacker – very determined to get every last ball back,' Bercow says. 'But I lacked any great weight of shot and I don't think I was a talented shot maker. I was quite a terrier, but would I have made a competitive player professionally? No.'[13]

Fuller says: 'The thing about John that shone out was he was tiny, hugely confident – the most confident person you've ever seen – and had this long hair practically down to his waist. He had the most beautiful touch tennis.'

After forty years, the former doubles partners were reunited when Bercow addressed Roehampton Tennis Club, where Fuller was working as the in-house professional. 'We embraced; it was lovely. People have this hugely wrong interpretation of John. He is a highly intelligent, very, very nice guy,' says Fuller. 'He is also a very caring guy. He hadn't seen me for years and the first thing he asked me was: "How's your mum?"'

Bercow's love of tennis is well known. In 2014, he wrote a book called *Tennis Maestros*, in which he analysed his top twenty male tennis players of all time. No. 1 on his list was Roger Federer, his sporting idol, whose image is the screensaver on his phone.

'He is a tennis and Roger Federer nut,' says Barry Cowan, the former tennis player and commentator who helped Bercow with research on his book. 'It's great that he's as passionate about the sport as he is. Even in the busiest times, he would watch tennis, which I think is really important.' Cowan hits balls with Bercow, describing his game as relying on 'guile as opposed to power'. 'He had my tickets for the final at Wimbledon this year. He was obviously super-pumped, but it wasn't to be,' he says, acknowledging that Federer fell short in a dramatic five-set match against Serbian Novak Djokovic.

Such is Bercow's borderline obsession with Federer that a former employee recalls him crying after the Swiss suffered a loss. 'He was not in a happy place when it was happening. It was just at the beginning of the time when Roger was just starting to lose the odd match here and there,' says Emma Macey, who worked for Bercow between 2009 and 2010. This trend would worsen over the years. As we will discover in later chapters, Bercow's mood after a loss suffered by Federer or his beloved Arsenal Football Club would sour greatly.

Bercow continued to play tennis throughout his adult life, on weekends in south London with MPs including Chris Leslie. 'He is a bloody good tennis player,' Leslie says. 'He is very competitive, and he gets in the zone. It's not just a friendly match. He really, really wants to win.' Bercow thrashed Boris Johnson 6–0, 6–0, 6–0 during a game at the then Foreign Secretary's official residence at Chevening. Labour peer Michael Levy, a friend of the Bercows, says: 'He's a very determined competitive player and that reflects in his personality.'

Outside of tennis, Bercow was also showing signs of promise in the classroom. However, Frith Manor had the opportunity to put forward four candidates to be considered for one of the local grammar schools, and Bercow did not make the shortlist. A former classmate says Bercow would have warranted selection and claims the decision by Sam Unsworth, the headmaster, was in part related to Bercow's mother. 'It was openly known that they had rowed, and she had regularly been an irritant. As a result of that, I can remember John being excluded from the possibility of going to a top school,' says the classmate.

Bercow would go on to attend Finchley Manorhill, a comprehensive school in north London. Primary school proved a happier time for Bercow than what would follow.

CHAPTER THREE

BULLIED

'He was such a rabid little Tory twat.'

A group of teenagers were standing outside a laundrette one after-noon in Finchley, north London, when one of their classmates approached on his way home from school. The teenagers created a blockage on the pavement, and the boy was hurried inside the laundrette. Some of the group lifted him up while others opened a dryer. John Bercow was tossed inside, and the door was shut. The children laughed while Bercow, scared, was trapped.

Bullying at Finchley Manorhill was rife. 'It was a bullying sort of place, but he would have been the most bullied person. There are endless stories around,' says a former school friend who recounted the laundrette story. Bercow would often invite much of the vitriol on himself, according to his contemporaries. He would 'taunt' pupils who made mistakes while reading in class, says Julian Baker, a classmate of Bercow's from the age of eleven.

John was bullied because he was an idiot and he didn't know when to shut up. You know when you see a little dog and he's yapping at a load of Alsatians, that dog doesn't know that it's not an Alsatian, and it really should. There were times I'd say to John: 'John, just shut the fuck up, stop talking, mate.' And he didn't.

While Baker says Bercow was 'brilliant' and the 'star of every intellectual endeavour he put his mind to', the pair clearly were not on good terms. After Bercow failed to 'shut his face', Baker 'picked him up at the end of term and stuck him in the biology pond'. 'I'm not proud of that, but it was like, "You've got this coming, John,"' he adds.

Baker took issue with Bercow's politics, which he describes as 'slightly to the left of Genghis Khan', adding: 'I hated that John couldn't see what was going on. His politics was so divisive, and he was such a rabid little Tory twat.' Despite the strength of his words, Baker says he had a 'fondness' for Bercow. 'He wasn't vile, he was just smart and was running his mouth off when he should have shut his face. I didn't like the way that he would pick on other kids in terms of their shortcomings, intelligence or ability to read.'

Bercow has a pathological fear of bees and wasps, and fellow pupils would often guide them through the classroom window to see how he reacted. The phobia would follow him into adulthood. While dining at La Poule au Pot in Pimlico, south-west London, Bercow was seen hauling his jacket over his head in panic at the presence of a nearby wasp.[1]

Bercow would be picked on for his appearance; he was less than 5ft 5in. for most of his teenage years (he is now 5ft 6in. and, like many people under six foot, lays claim to an extra half-inch for good measure), suffered with severe acne, had greasy hair and was not afraid of baiting his peers by demonstrating his intellect, or undermining theirs. A former classmate recalls: 'He showed signs of being more interested in himself than interested in other people, showed some vanity, spoke over people, wasn't good at interacting. If he disagreed, his answer would be to yell back and then wonder why people yelled back at him. His emotional intelligence wasn't there.'

His answer to adversity would be to come out swinging. Sen Monro, an actor who was two years below Bercow at school, says:

He was always very smart. A lot of the other kids used to take the mickey out of him quite a bit. He was very forthright, very focused, extremely bright and his use of vocabulary was very good. If anybody would give him a hard time, he could be very cutting.

Bercow's troubles with acne would continue to plague him. During his time at Essex University, a student stuck a slice of pizza to a noticeboard at the student union with the caption 'Portrait of John Bercow'.[2] His skin is still slightly pockmarked to this day, and it would appear it has been a source of some insecurity. During his time on the shadow Education team between 1999 and 2000, when he was Employment spokesman, Bercow turned up to a meeting looking 'exceptionally red-faced', according to a source. One of the other members of the team asked: 'Have you been to the gym? What's the matter?' The source remembers: 'It took a while prodding him. It turned out he had a chemical peel.' Bercow says taunts about his acne made him feel 'very, very self-conscious'.[3]

Ahead of the 1999 Tory conference in Blackpool, Bercow visited a make-up artist at the nearby BBC studios before going on stage, to avoid appearing 'excessively pale'.[4] A source in the shadow Education team at the time says that prior to being introduced, Bercow asked for advice on how to wave to the audience. 'This was what was important to John,' says his colleague.

Bercow insists he has never been fazed by abuse over his height, though he does consider it 'really low-grade' to imply that a person is 'inferior because he or she is shorter'.[5] Alan Duncan, the former Conservative MP, used to jokingly refer to Bercow as 'Mr Speaker Hobbit' in the tearooms in the Commons. 'I gently point out that a hobbit is a friendly creature,' Bercow replied when informed of this nickname.[6] In his early days in the Commons, Labour MPs would heckle 'Stand up, stand up' when he asked a question from the green benches.[7] 'I haven't identified who they are, but I'm going to find out,' he said. He was also referred to as a 'large ego in a small suit'.

His height would be raised as an issue on his route to Parliament. 'I

remember once hearing that a selection committee had rejected me because one of its members said of me: "Nice chap, but a bit too young and
a bit too short." The person they selected was no older than me, but a bit
taller,' he says.[8]

One of his opening gambits on the lecture circuit from over the years is
a self-effacing anecdote about claims that he is the shortest Speaker in the
history of the House of Commons. Bercow would point out that former
Speakers Sir John Bussy (1394–98), Sir John Wenlock (1455–56) and Sir
Thomas Tresham (1459) are all believed to have been shorter than him.
'Although I do have to admit that this was true only after all three of them
had been beheaded,' comes the punchline.

While interested and friendly with girls at his school, he did not have
any girlfriends. Indeed, though he was known for his sharp wit and prolific tennis skills, Bercow was something of an isolated figure. 'He was very
unpopular. He had a small group who were not offended by him, but it
wasn't a very large group,' a classmate says.

The struggles were compounded by events at home, with Brenda and
Charlie divorcing when their son was a teenager. It is a life event that
Bercow has downplayed over the years, though others recall it differently.
'He was very heavily scarred by that,' says a former classmate, who would
receive briefings from a family who lived near the Bercows' home at 108
Southover in Woodside Park, North Finchley. 'We got a weekly if not
monthly update on the sad state of the marriage and also the break-up. It
was very acrimonious, and John would have retreated into his shell.'

Charlie would take out his anger on Brenda's corgi, Tibor. 'He was never
much interested in animals. When he got home and the dog was yapping
away, Dad found that annoying,' Bercow says.[9] He also recalls wet bank
holidays at home when his parents argued. 'I would hear raised voices, go
into the sitting room and appeal to them to calm down.' During couples
counselling, Charlie accused Brenda of having 'ideas above her station'.

On the rare occasions that Bercow has discussed his parents' divorce,
he would disagree with the assertion that it affected his character. 'I don't

recall it like that. I don't sense there was this difference in my behaviour before they were divorced and after,' he says.[10] But interviewed in *The Times* in 2014, he said the experience showed him life was not going to be easy:

> My parents divorced when I was fourteen. There was no question of me thinking that right was on one side and wrong was on the other. Their divorce reinforced my sense that a) you have to work very hard at relationships – because that's life – and b) that life was going to be a bit of a battle.[11]

As children of divorce will know, the separation of parents and all that comes with it can be a formative experience. While no two divorces are the same, the initial level of upheaval is bound to have had some impact upon Bercow, who had only just entered his teenage years. In November 2019, Bercow opened up about the experience, saying he did not enjoy his school days in part because of what was taking place at home 'I was distracted by my parents' break-up. I was at sea for a period. I've got some sad memories: terrible tensions between them, though much later they made up.'[12]

An ex-pupil at Finchley Manorhill says: 'The traits in him of being a loner and not being sociable, not having good skills in reading his peers, however much he may or not have approved of them, those traits would have been exaggerated by that personal family breakdown.' Bercow became appreciative of small gestures – a trait he holds to the present day. 'For John, it made a great deal of difference. It may have been a small act of kindness in a larger picture of hostility, among both his friends and his family,' a friend says.

After they separated, Charlie moved to Totteridge while Brenda, Alison and John lived on the Uxbridge Road in Stanmore. On 31 October 1986, Charlie died aged sixty-six after a sudden heart attack. He had watched his son graduate with a first-class honours degree but would never see

John go on to achieve higher office; nor would he meet three of his grand-children. John was just twenty-three when he buried his father at a Jewish cemetery in Cheshunt, north London.[13]

While Bercow had demonstrated a strong intellect from an early age, he was also underperforming at school. He was only enamoured by certain subjects, and teachers would have a hard time getting him to knuckle down. A school friend remembers:

> A small number of teachers recognised he was very talented intellectually and very curious. But converting that into him studying or wanting to make a go of it was quite difficult because he had the alternative interest in tennis at the time. He must have thought to himself: 'I'll go in that direction.'

Sen Monro says Manorhill was a school where 'you got out of it what you put into it'. 'If you were prepared to work, the teachers would reward you,' he says. Pupils would spend the first two years at the lower school on Finchley High Road, before moving to the Summers Lane building a mile and a half further up the road. Of Bercow, Monro adds: 'It was always fairly obvious that this guy was destined for really good things. With some of the smart kids at school, people could be quite hurtful, disparaging and say nasty things, as happened with John. He used to give as good as he got.'

Liz Walton taught Bercow for General Studies in sixth form. 'His eloquence, interest in politics and strong personality stood out even then,' she says. Walton did have the impression, however, that school 'wasn't an easy time' for the teenager.

Julian Lewis, who met Bercow years after he left Finchley Manorhill, says:

> One thing that is absolutely central to understanding John's character is that he cannot and will not tolerate being bullied by anybody. I remember him telling me how he would have run-ins with the headmaster of

his school. He just would not be bossed about, even if this endangered the prospects for his future career.

Charlie Bercow would urge his son to make the most of his school days, 'as they're the happiest days of your life'. Bercow disagrees with that assessment:

> Well, they certainly weren't for me. I bear no scar, physical or psychological, from my school career, and it was so-so. I was at state schools, primary and secondary, and my children are at state schools. They were reasonable schools, but not outstanding. I don't have any joyous recollection of my primary or secondary school career.[14]

A close friend of Bercow's says he has never opened up to him about his childhood. 'He's never really shared any of that,' the source says. 'From a modest start in life, John's always been the underdog. And it's his steel, his determination and his sense of purpose and being himself that is the key to understanding the person – the politician – that he became.'

Armed with this information, a lot more begins to make sense about John Bercow: his stern dislike of government seeking to bypass or ram things through Parliament, his propensity to get angry and retaliate to resistance – all these could have their origins in the playground of Finchley Manorhill. It explains how Bercow perceived his role: as defending the rights of the House of Commons against the bully boys in government.

The bullying he received may also have helped to foster a blind spot to an area of his character that threatened to derail his legacy as Speaker of the House of Commons.

As with most who go through such experiences, they are undoubtedly formative to who he would become as a person. It formed layers, an antipathy to the powerful majority and, one could argue, a sense of grievance. All of which led him down a very particular path.

CHAPTER FOUR

THE MONDAY CLUB

*'Maybe going to some of those little cliquey meetings
made me feel quite important.'*

O f all the things Charlie Bercow passed on to his son, his unique speaking style is one of the most notable. 'Dad spoke in paragraphs. Dad spoke very good English. Dad was probably rather mannered in his speech, as I am. Dad regarded it as a serious sin to split an infinitive or put a preposition at the end of a sentence,' says Bercow.[1] When an MP, Bercow would infuriate his colleagues by pulling them up on what he considered incorrect use of the English language. 'Split infinitive!' he would bark.

Bercow also took much of his initial political inspiration from his father. Charlie was a Conservative voter and an admirer of Enoch Powell. 'He was [a] right-wing Tory, and even though he was Jewish and must have been aware of the Cable Street battle, the Black Shirts, Oswald Mosley and all the rest, he was fundamentally very anti-New Commonwealth and Pakistani immigration,' Bercow recalls.[2]

His father would describe Powell, who had a steep fall from grace over his infamous 1968 'Rivers of Blood' speech, as a 'much-maligned man'. Bercow comments: 'I don't wish to speak ill of my late father, who was a good father, but I used to think that no Jewish person could be racist and that's not strictly true … He genuinely did fear that the large influx that had taken place by the '70s threatened social cohesion.'[3]

Charlie transferred a passion for Powell's politics onto his son, who had begun reading books by thinkers on both left and right, including Tony Benn, whom he would mimic. Bercow also tried reading some of Karl Marx's work, though he did not have much patience for the German philosopher. It was Powell who would capture his attention. 'I read about what a brilliantly educated man he was, I read books of speeches of his, and so on. My father tended to take the view "let him explore and find out things", but I wish he had said to me, "Hold back on that, son."'[4]

What Bercow was hearing at home did not overlap with the views of his teachers at Finchley Manorhill, who he felt were either broadly in support of James Callaghan's Labour government or Bennite critics of it. 'I disapproved of the Callaghan government. I believed the wealth of Britain came from the private sector and that the Labour government had lost sense of that,' he says.[5]

In his final year of school, Bercow, wearing a light blue shirt with a dark blue tie and a V-neck brown jumper, was in the audience for a re-cording of *Question Time*. After being chosen by presenter Robin Day, Bercow attacked Labour's Barbara Castle for criticising fellow panellist Willie Whitelaw, the Conservative Home Secretary, over economic policy. He also accused the former Labour MP of swapping the Commons for the European Parliament because Labour had no answers to Britain's problems. 'Mr Whitelaw was talking economic common sense,' he de-clared. This was not his first TV appearance. In 1975, aged twelve and with floppy long hair, he took part in BBC children's television series *Crackerjack!*, where he finished last in a race to scoop up four curtain rings using a broom handle.

By the time he left school in the summer of 1981, Bercow's politics were pretty well established. It was the year of the inner-city riots, which were sparked by antagonism between black youths and the police. Bercow says that Powell had convinced him that it was 'right to fear large-scale immigration'. The riots prompted him to conclude that the UK was 'in a politically explosive situation'.[6]

Aged eighteen, Bercow was retaking an A-level and coaching tennis part-time as he pondered his next move. In the meantime, he joined the Monday Club young members group. The organisation, named after the day of the week the founding members met for lunch, was formed in 1961 by four young Conservative Party members, and remained independent of the Conservative Party but affiliated with it. By 1970, eighteen MPs were members of the organisation, including Julian Amery, who would go on to become a Foreign Office minister. Six would serve in Ted Heath's Cabinet. Several modern-day Tory MPs have also been members, including Andrew Rosindell, the MP for Romford. Enoch Powell spoke on a number of Monday Club platforms and was invited as guest of honour to the annual dinner in 1968. He argued that it was due to the Monday Club that many were brought within the Conservative Party who might otherwise have been estranged from it.

The Monday Club was hardline about its concerns on Europe integration and, in particular, on immigration. The group advocated a more traditionalist social conservatism, while also being strong on law and order. Bercow, the son of a Jewish father and grandson of a Romanian immigrant, took a particular interest in its immigration stance.

Sam Swerling, a Westminster councillor who stood twice for Parliament as a Conservative MP, was chair of the Monday Club from 1980 to 1983. He describes Bercow as a 'very pleasant chap' and a 'hero worshipper' of Enoch Powell. 'He had distinctly right-of-centre or right-wing views. He was young, he wanted to make his way, he was ambitious,' he adds.

Gregory Lauder-Frost, a long-standing member of the Monday Club who is writing a book on its history, remembers Bercow as a 'bit of a weed':

He told us that he was a professional tennis coach and that he was an active member of the Finchley Young Conservatives. I wrote to the Finchley Young Conservatives to confirm that, or he wouldn't have got into the club. At that time, he was living in Mill Hill, from memory. He told everyone that he was very right-wing and pro-Enoch Powell. He was what he termed a hardline Tory.

Meetings of the Monday Club took place in committee rooms of the House of Commons and the House of Lords in the name of Tory MPs such as Sir John Biggs-Davison or Patrick Wall. Lauder-Frost recalls Bercow keeping himself to himself:

> I think there was a general feeling that he was something of a loner. He didn't really mix in very well. We used to hold regular meetings with speakers, and he would stand at the back of the room on his own rather than sit down with other people. We found that a bit odd.

Eleanor Dodd, who was secretary of the Monday Club women's group, turned to Lauder-Frost and commented: 'He's not really one of us, is he?'

Bercow did, however, become friendly with Harvey Proctor, then the right-wing MP for Basildon. In September 1981, Bercow was appointed secretary of the Monday Club's Immigration and Repatriation Committee, which was chaired by Proctor. The committee wanted an 'end to New Commonwealth and Pakistan immigration, a properly financed system of voluntary repatriation, the repeal of the Race Relations Act and the abolition of the Commission for Racial Equality'.[7] As secretary, Bercow would be responsible for capturing the exchanges during the meetings.

In April 1982, Bercow stood for election as a full member of the Monday Club's executive council, where he had sat as a representative of the group's young members. Running on an anti-immigration ticket, Bercow argued during a rally at Westminster Central Hall: 'The strengthening of our national identity demands a programme of assisted repatriation.'[8]

Bercow started at Essex University in September 1982 but remained a member of the Monday Club until February 1984, at which point, he later said, 'it became clear that there were a lot of people at the meetings who were really unpleasant racists and so I left'.[9] Lauder-Frost rejects claims that the Monday Club was racist. In 2019, he was fined £300 and ordered to pay £200 in compensation after being found guilty of a racially aggravated offence over social media to a 21-year-old British-Indian student, Isadora Sinha. On Facebook, he had told Sinha: 'You have no right to be in our country or arguing with a superior race.'[10]

The issue of the Monday Club has followed Bercow throughout his career. He has referred to his decision to join as 'bone-headed', 'utter madness' and one he will regret to his 'dying day'.[11] Bercow explains:

> I thought, at the time of the Brixton and Toxteth riots, that it would be very, very difficult to integrate the ethnic minority communities into mainstream British society. That is why I supported a halt to immigration and at one time I did support a programme of repatriation. But I ceased to believe in that more than twenty years ago.[12]

When Bercow is confronted about his previous membership of the group, he embraces the question wholeheartedly. He will speak in detail of his involvement and outline the timeline of his membership. He owns the answer, leaving no stone unturned. The most telling contribution he has given on this subject came in front of students at the Cambridge Union in October 2015. 'I've got one great regret in my political life, which I can't do anything about other than demonstrate that it's very much a feature of the past,' he said, referring to the Monday Club. 'I do believe myself, and I hope you do, in the Rehabilitation of Offenders Act. So, I hope that it would be accepted that it is possible for people to make mistakes in their youth and to recover from them.'[13]

He reiterated his position that once he realised how 'objectionable' some of the members of the club were, he 'jumped ship', adding: 'But it somewhat scarred me for many years. I think a lot of people on the left for a long time viewed me with great suspicion, although I think that's long since ceased to be the case. That was my error and I hope I've learned from it.'

Citing his actions in Parliament, Bercow championed his record on LGBT rights, equality and anti-racist policies.

I would like to think that these days, and for quite a long time, people would have been inclined to say: 'Well, John is certainly a supporter of equality. He doesn't have any racism in him, he doesn't have any sexism in him, he doesn't have any homophobia in him.' But did I make mistakes in the past? I most certainly did.

Bercow, as we shall discover, would indeed go on to become a champion of progressive politics. One might reasonably ask whether you can trace some of his activity back to a deep-rooted guilt stemming from his days in the Monday Club. The further away from this period he gets – both literally and metaphorically – the more pronounced his mortification. 'I am enormously and permanently ashamed,' he said in 2019.[14]

Bercow would also go on to renounce his one-time political heroes. 'Enoch Powell's views on immigration, race relations and repatriation were absolutely wrong,' he said in 2017.[15] Thatcher, for so long a totemic figure for Bercow, was also despatched. 'She was brave and gutsy, and she was in a male-dominated party ... But she was also profoundly wrong about a number of things; there were huge gaps in her record. Is she today a heroine of mine? No, absolutely not.'

Some may feel that his assertion that he left the Monday Club when he became aware of the views of some of its members doesn't stack up with his role as secretary of a committee that believed in the repatriation of immigrants, the repeal of the Race Relations Act and the abolition of the Commission for Racial Equality. Bercow was taking the minutes of the meetings, noting down what the attendees were saying. The clues were there in front of him. Not only that, but he stood for election to the Monday Club's executive council advocating the repatriation of immigrants.

As for why he joined the Monday Club, Bercow highlights attrib-utes that might have inculcated a natural predisposition towards more hardline politics. 'Possibly the fact that I was physically quite feeble, a relatively short little fellow, attracted me to that idea of a very authoritative and aggressive version of Conservative politics,' he says.

> I'm not saying that I had an inadequate Adam's apple, but I think that sometimes people who aren't fully formed and fully confident in themselves can be attracted to something which appears to give them a bit of meaning and a sense of purpose. Maybe going to some of those little cliquey meetings made me feel quite important.[16]

Given his experience at school, one can see how he might have been drawn to an authoritarian genre of politics, though others who have been bullied do not find themselves in such company. What is less clear is how Bercow ended up supporting the repatriation of immigrants, especially after attending a diverse school in north London. As a third-generation immigrant, perhaps Bercow found a sense of belonging in being able to pronounce on whether others had a right to live in Britain.

Another factor to consider is that, as Jewishness is matrilineal and his mother had converted at a reform synagogue, to some, Bercow was not considered an authentic Jew. To traditional Jews, he was not one of them; to those of different faiths or none, he was close enough to be counted as Jewish. In the summer of 1976, Bercow had his bar mitzvah, for which he took classes at Finchley Reform Synagogue under Rabbi Jeffrey Newman. Simon Morris, who would go on to become CEO of the charity Jewish Care, taught Bercow Hebrew. In an interview with the *Jewish Chronicle*, Bercow, aged twenty-three, said he had not been a practising Jew, 'but I am Jewish and proud of it'.[17]

Taking these factors all together, Bercow had not found himself at home in any particular group: he was unpopular at school, his parents had separated, and he lacked a formal identity. Having never truly fitted in, he found a group that could offer him solace.

Whatever his immediate reasons for joining the Monday Club, Bercow is undoubtedly hard on himself for his previous affiliation to it. He is not the first person to feel some semblance of anxiety towards the actions and allegiances of their younger selves. After stripping Powell and Thatcher of their 'hero' status, he listed in their place Martin Luther King, Mahatma Gandhi and Eleanor Rathbone.[18] All, of course, hugely worthy recipients of such an accolade. But the disparity with the previous incumbents could not be starker, and a degree of trying to atone for his past views seems to be in evidence.

Arguably, this overcompensation should be looked upon favourably. In an era in which politicians are hammered for their past indiscretions, Bercow has proactively accrued a body of work to dilute his flirtation with the far-right.

CHAPTER FIVE

FRESH START

'Anyone not on the left was antagonistic just for breathing.'

John Bercow was at a loose end. A combination of apathy, compla-
cency and distractions at home had led to him falling short of his
academic expectations. He was retaking an A-level while working as a
tennis coach, filling the rest of the void by dabbling in far-right politics
within the Monday Club.

Some of his colleagues at Finchley Manorhill had already started their
degrees. Shamit Sagar, who also attended Frith Manor with Bercow, had
arrived at the University of Essex in October 1981. Bercow, who had applied to the institution, went to visit Sagar one weekend for a taste of life
on campus. 'I was inspired by the place,' he later recalled.[1] He also grew
'mildly envious' of the life his friend was leading.

Essex, which had around 2,000 students, had a reputation for being
a hotbed of left-wing activism. The university also had an outstanding
reputation for his course of choice. As he bid Bercow farewell, Shagar
encouraged: 'Look, this is a great place to come if you want to study Government.'[2] Bercow later told a student audience: 'For those two reasons
– he'd gone and was enjoying it and I knew I wanted a university that had
a politics specialism – it really made up my mind for me.'[3]

Bercow signed up to the Conservative Association during his first
freshers' fair. At the time, the group only had fifteen members and was

chaired by Andrew Crosbie, who had arrived at Essex a year earlier. 'We hit it off straight away because he was very, very passionate about politics and a lot more experienced than I was,' Crosbie says.

The pair made for a formidable alliance. 'He had a lot of experience and contacts within the Conservative Party that enabled him to bring speakers down to the university and give us a little bit more of a profile, while I had the competitive spirit to put us on the map,' Crosbie explains. Bercow was quickly appointed vice-chair of the association. 'We became the second biggest political association on campus over the following two years,' says Crosbie.

Whatever unfulfilled potential Bercow had, he ensured it was put to good use at university. He speaks effusively about the 'magnificent seven', a group of lecturers who taught him for his Government degree during his time at Essex, including the late Anthony King, a renowned Canadian-British professor, and Professor David Sanders, who taught Bercow throughout his degree. 'He was an outstanding student. You're always desperate to get people to talk in small groups. John was always someone who could be relied upon to make not only a contribution but a powerful contribution,' Sanders says.

During his first year, Bercow was taught by Bob Jessop, a Marxist academic who had written a book called *The Capitalist State*. Despite harking from opposing political backgrounds, Bercow was 'seized by the almost uninterrupted eloquence' of the lecturer. 'I had a view of politics which was very different from Bob Jessop. But he was a hugely impressive lecturer,' Bercow remembered years later. The young student would think to himself: 'Gosh, this guy is incredibly organised and systematised in his thinking.'[4] For his part, Sanders recalls Bercow engaging with students from opposing ideological standpoints:

One was a social democrat type, there was also quite a radical Marxist guy in the class as well. To be honest, I could easily just set the three of them off against each other at the beginning of the class. If allowed, they would have just taken it over. But it was always very well mannered.

Justin Griffiths-Williams, a left-wing student, had one class with Bercow. 'He was confident and very, very able – brilliant. I wasn't remotely surprised that he ended up where he was; in fact, I even anticipated it. I thought: "Well, this guy is going to do something" because he was so eloquent, confident and all the qualities that he shows now,' he says.

Professor Michael Freeman, who taught Bercow Introduction to Political Theory, was another of the magnificent seven. 'He was very self-confident, which is a polite way of putting it. He was a very bright student … He talked a lot in class, perhaps a little too much; some of the other students found him a bit dominant,"' he recalls. 'I do remember, I had to restrain him a little in order to give other students a chance to speak.'

Bercow's university days also offered an early insight into his Euroscepticism. Professor Emil Kirchner taught him for a class on the European Community. 'It was indeed interesting in that he took a perspective that was more sceptical about the EC, as it was then,' he says. 'But he was always very courteous, probing, engaging. I found him a very intelligent student at the time.' Kirchner, who kept in touch with Bercow over subsequent years, notes that the Euroscepticism lingered for some time. 'He was very, very Eurosceptic, particularly around the time we had Maastricht in '92 and the euro and so on. Since the referendum, his views have somewhat changed, I would say.'

On campus, there were still residual elements of Essex's radical past. During the miners' strike of 1984, the government started to ship coal through the nearby port of Wivenhoe. Miners taking part in pickets camped in the dorms of sympathetic students and could often be found in the student union bar. 'The left were bringing miners into the university to sleep on floors. It did upset some of the students. Rather than being regarded as far-right extremists, we put forward some sensible things that appealed to the students who weren't that interested in politics,' says Crosbie.

Bercow, undeterred by the hostile atmosphere, would make addresses from the public squares in the university. 'He would simply start giving a speech. People would gather around him and the radical left would heckle him, and he would respond. That took an awful lot of courage to do that. He was very brave,' Sanders says. Kirchner also recalls Bercow taking an active interest in student politics:

> He participated in many rallies on the square. It was a tough time because in those days Essex was pretty much a left-wing-inclined university, the student body particularly. He revived and strengthened the Conservative student society with its activities. His role and constitution were quite essential for the revival.

Not everyone took kindly to Bercow's confrontational approach. One former contemporary says Bercow was 'pretty much universally despised' among the predominantly left-wing student body. 'He was always attacking left-wingers, gays and feminists,' they say. Another former student describes Bercow as a 'lightning-rod figure on campus', noting: 'He was very, very unpopular at the time.' Crosbie agrees that Bercow did not hold good relations with women's groups. 'They particularly didn't like him because they thought he was a bit pompous,' he says, adding: 'I never heard John ever say anything that I would have said would have been politically incorrect even today. He's just clear and passionate about what he believed in.'

When a safe space was set up for women on campus, there was push-back from some of the student body. 'There was an outcry from the Tories about it,' claims a former student. Some right-wing students decided to form the 'White Gentlemen's Club' in response. A leading figure in the White Gentlemen's Club was Stuart Millson, who would succeed Bercow as chairman of the Essex Conservatives and later join the British National

Party. Fellow students do not recall Bercow being involved in the White Gentlemen's Club, and a spokesperson says he had 'nothing whatsoever to do with the creation or running of that group, attended no meeting of it and absolutely did not support it in any way'. An ex-student says: 'I can't say whether John was involved or not, but I do know that he didn't condemn it.'

A friend at the time says Bercow 'wouldn't shy away from the argument', and on occasion would come across as an 'obsessive quasi-religious warrior'. The source adds: 'He had cult-like qualities in the way he was making the argument. The inability to listen even to the tiniest bit about what people are saying in response. Understanding where people are coming from would have been helpful.'

Essex had two watering holes: the university bar, also known as the Top Bar, which was the preferred haunt of Conservative-minded students, and the student union bar, which was dominated by the left. A former student says Bercow rarely frequented the latter. 'On the few occasions he went there he would have got himself stuck in a debate or argument.' Bercow himself explained: 'I eventually did become accustomed to going to the student union bar, partly because an early girlfriend at the university was keen on going there.'[5]

Whenever they did make an appearance, Bercow and Crosbie would receive a hostile reception. 'When we walked in, you would be greeted by boos and hisses,' Crosbie says. During their rare visits to the disco at the student union, the DJ would play '(We don't need this) Fascist Groove' by Heaven 17. 'It's a small university and the union bar and dancefloor were dominated by the noisy left,' says Crosbie.

On one memorable occasion, Bercow was sat having a drink with friends after making a speech at the student union. 'I thought [I was] behaving perfectly properly and minding my own business – and all of a sudden I felt a great sensation of being, to put it bluntly, soaked,' he said.[6] A woman had come up behind Bercow and poured a pint of beer over his head. It was recently reported by Popbitch that the person who poured

the pint over Bercow was Janet Pringle, the sister of former England crick-
eter Derek.[7] 'I have lived to tell the tale, and I bear no resentment. It was
all a very long time ago. She probably thought I deserved it,' Bercow said.[8]
A former student notes: 'It wouldn't put him off. The more pints he had
poured over his head, the more he would have felt that he was prosecuting
the good cause. Others might have thought, "I'll skip that bar next time."'
Crosbie adds: 'Anyone who wasn't in an acceptable society, in the Labour
Party or on the left was antagonistic just for breathing.'

Bercow also joined the Essex Jewish Society, though he did not spend
much time with Jewish students. Bercow was critical of 'some people in
the Jewish Society who, in order to maintain friends in the union, had to
pander to other people's social mores', adding that 'if people in the union
are put off supporting the Jewish cause because the Conservative Association supports it, that is not a very intelligent position'. He revealed that
he was summoned to a meeting of the Jewish Society to explain his views.
He turned them down, as he 'resented being put in the dock'.[9]

In February 1984, Bercow invited Cecil Parkinson, the former Cabinet
minister who resigned after it was revealed that his former secretary was
pregnant with his child, to speak at the university. A huge demonstration
prevented Parkinson from being able to enter the venue. 'I remember
seeing him being bundled into a car with students literally screaming for
his blood,' says Griffiths-Williams. The Conservative Association took
Parkinson out for dinner in Colchester instead. Months later, Bercow
invited him back for an open meeting for students from across the university, which he chaired.

Bercow also provoked backlash after he invited Teddy Taylor, a right-
wing Tory MP and former vice-president of the Monday Club, to speak
at the university. 'We declared it a closed meeting, which caused a bit of a
furore, but we had to because if it hadn't been then it wouldn't have been
a meeting at all. The police were there; that was pretty interesting,' says
Crosbie.

After standing uncontested, Bercow became chair of the Conservative

Association in his second year. 'We had to start having some policies and some sensible things, and that wasn't my forte. I was his enforcer, so I stayed as vice-chairman and made sure he was OK. I was the strongarm man and he was the thinker,' explains Crosbie.

The association expanded exponentially under Bercow's watch. By the time of his graduation, the group had withdrawn from the student union and grown to 207 members.[10] In his second year, he stood for student union president, narrowly losing to Labour candidate Maria Debono, in large part due to the alternative vote system favouring left-wing candidates, with second and third preferences flooding in for Debono. His manifesto included a pledge to 'protect the interests of all students, not just a minority of egotistical political hacks'.[11] On back page of the leaflet was a question to determine whether you were a Conservative: 'Do you like having fun, drinking, Clint Eastwood movies, making money, playing sport? Do you never wear sandals, men's earrings, dope pouches, Palestinian scarves, Oxfam coats?'

The vote illustrated how far the Conservative Association had travelled. 'Given the radical self-image and radical image that Essex had in the '70s, I think that was quite extraordinary. John played a huge role in that. He persuaded the student body generally that there are different ways of looking at the world,' says Professor Sanders.

Though Bercow thrived at Essex, he still proved a highly divisive figure. 'He wasn't hugely popular. He was a right-wing student in a very left-wing environment, which must have been quite testing for him,' says Griffiths-Williams. Crosbie adds: 'He is a strange chap. I liked him because I got on with him, but a lot of people thought he was a bit pompous, quite frankly. But that was John.'

Bercow received a first-class honours degree in Government. At his graduation in the summer of 1985, Bercow was proud to see his parents, Brenda and Charlie, in attendance. 'They had by then been long divorced, though fortunately they'd long overcome the period of bitterness. That wasn't a problem and I think they were both very proud and pleased for me,' Bercow said later. He picked them out when he went on stage to collect his degree. 'I felt a degree of gratitude to them because although neither of them had gone to university, both of them were very keen that I should, if I wanted to do so.'[12]

For Bercow, his student years were formative, and far happier than anything he experienced at school. 'I have consistently maintained that I got to university despite, and not because of, my attendance at that school. I had a few outstanding teachers, but there were serious problems in the state-funded service,' he told the Commons in 1997.

In July 2017, Bercow was announced as the new Chancellor of Essex University. 'Going to Essex University was a life-enhancing experience. It was something very special, and although it is thirty years next year since I graduated, there are aspects of my time there, including modules on my course, personalities among students and teachers, that I remember as well as if I'd encountered them yesterday,' he said.[13]

Bercow's path continues to cross with many of his acquaintances from university. Among his cohort at Essex was Ian Austin, the former Labour minister and subsequent independent MP. Griffiths-Williams, now a photographer, was tasked with taking pictures of Bercow for a 2019 interview with German newspaper *Der Spiegel*. As Chancellor, Bercow attends an annual event at Essex called The Court, along with local MPs, councillors and past and present professors. 'He's always very friendly, and he's always spoken very warmly about the teaching he received at Essex. That's obviously very gratifying,' says Professor Sanders.

Professor Kirchner says: 'He clearly stood out. I always thought he would go places, potentially into politics or the civil service, but not to the ranks of a Speaker or something like that.'

While at university, Bercow also expanded his horizons beyond the confines of Colchester. 'He would come back from mid-week trips to London and said that he had been speaking at some event with Harvey Proctor or some other acolyte from the far-right. This was a standard course of his week when he was at university,' says an ex-Essex student.

Bercow was making inroads on the Conservative student scene as part of a notorious group of activists who were on course for an almighty row with Tory Party HQ. A fellow Essex graduate says: 'Students get carried away with student politics, but he got very, very misguided.'

CHAPTER SIX

THE FED

'He was the kind of guy that would probably read Hansard at night.'

Mark Francois was sitting in a damp coffee shop opposite Bristol bus station. The windowpane was cracked, letting in an icy breeze. It was Saturday lunchtime early in 1986, and Francois was waiting to meet a member of the Oxford University Conservative Association and Young Conservatives. They had arranged to meet to talk about the upcoming elections for chair of the Federation of Conservative Students.

The FCS had gained something of a reputation. Famed for their raucous behaviour, members of the group had been embroiled in numerous controversies, many of which derived from their choice interests in foreign affairs. Staunch defenders of anti-Communist regimes and opponents of left-wing leaders, members travelled to Nicaragua to visit the Contras, sent a 'get well' card to General Pinochet of Chile, and produced posters urging support for the Mujahideen in Afghanistan against the Soviet Union. Some FCS activists, who staunchly opposed the African National Congress (ANC) in South Africa, produced 'Hang Nelson Mandela' T-shirts and badges.

Once described as having loyalist and Protestant views that made the Rev. Ian Paisley 'look positively middle of the road',[1] FCS members took a particular interest in Northern Ireland. In December 1985, all sitting Ulster Unionist MPs resigned in protest at the signature by Margaret

Thatcher of the Anglo-Irish Agreement, which granted the Republic of Ireland an advisory role in the governance of Northern Ireland. The following month, the FCS defied Conservative Party chiefs by sending nearly forty members to support Ulster Unionist candidates in the resulting by-elections.

The alumni of the FCS make for interesting reading. Among the list of former members include Paul Goodman, a future Tory MP and editor of the ConservativeHome website. Bercow's contemporaries included Robbie Gibb, Theresa May's former director of communications, and Douglas (Dougie) Smith, who would go on to work for Boris Johnson in No. 10.

Whether they were conscious of it or not, the FCS were the right's answer to the so-called 'loony left', with their confrontational tactics mirroring those of their supposed opponents. The National Union of Students were regular targets. Ahead of the union's 1984 conference in Blackpool, an FCS pamphlet laid bare the group's approach: 'As long as the NUS forces students into membership the only avenue or protest available is disruption.'[2] Activists used delaying tactics such as demanding that the conference should be conducted in Welsh. Guy Roberts, a student at Leeds University, provoked acrimony after he called NUS members 'red, fascist scum'. FCS members referred to each other as 'comrades' and wore jeans and other casual clothes contrary to the popular perception of young Tories.

One former member recalls: 'Nice people tended to have to flake off because they couldn't take the heat. Conservative student activists and graduates at that time tended to be not the standard home counties or comfortably off middle-class young people but much more working class or upper working class. Conservatively, it was atypical.'

FCS members did not read from the same hymn sheet, and the group was split into many factions. The largest groups, who had been at war for many years, were the libertarians, referred to as the 'sounds' or 'libs', on the right of the party, while those in the centre were known as 'wets'.

Bercow was associated with the libs, though his politics were more authoritarian and traditional. 'The libs tended to be a bit more working class, rowdy and rough. From that social point of view, although Bercow had these great affectations in his speech and so forth, because his father was a taxi driver, he socially, in a way, probably fitted in more with the libertarian faction,' says an ex-member.

Further factions were the 'trad' wing, which advocated a traditional form of social Conservatism, and a hard-right bloc, known as the '2.10 Group' (named after the hotel room in which they first met during an FCS conference). The 2.10 Group allied with the wets, as they 'hated libertarians more than anything else', according to a former FCS member. There was also a 'party' faction, composed of people who refused to define themselves other than by their love of the party.

By the start of 1986, the libs had a stranglehold on the federation, and their candidate, Bercow, was odds on to replace the outgoing Mark MacGregor as chair. The wets were looking for a candidate to stand against the libs. Perhaps surprisingly to some, Francois – who many know as a tub-thumping Brexiteer MP – was a member of the wets, the group espousing One Nation Conservatism.

There was never a strong chance of success, but the wets needed a representative and a voice in the campaign, and the student from Oxford wanted Francois to volunteer. 'Look, Mark, someone has got to do it,' he pleaded. 'We need somebody, Mark. You're going to lose, but somebody needs to fight the good fight.'

Reluctantly, Francois agreed to put himself forward. The pair shook hands and promised to keep in touch. The person who convinced him to stand headed back to Oxford. That man, according to Francois, was Nick Robinson, a leading light in the Young Conservatives who would go on to become the political editor of the BBC and a presenter on Radio 4's *Today* programme. Robinson has no recollection of this meeting taking place.

By this point, the future of the FCS was far from certain. The antics of its members were a continued nuisance for Conservative Central Office, who were trying to carve out a different image to appeal to younger voters. Nearly twelve months earlier, the Tory Party chairman had tried to shut down the organisation entirely after an infamous conference in Loughborough.

*   *   *

Andrew Rosindell boarded a bus in central London destined for Lough-borough. Then nineteen years old, Rosindell was apprehensive; he had been invited to the annual FCS conference despite not being a member. Rosindell was instead closely involved with the Young Conservatives, an-other Tory-affiliated organisation with a contrasting ideological outlook.

The Young Conservatives, which was led by the wets, was pro-European and Heathite in disposition; the FCS had developed radical policies that put them well to the right of Thatcher. The wets and libs were in constant battle for dominance of each organisation at a regional and na-tional level. 'There was a war going on, a massive war. It went on for years,' recalls Rosindell.

Around fifty FCS members were on the bus. At the front of the coach was John Bercow, who was greeting people as they entered. 'That's when he first spoke to me and that's when I first noticed him. He was always quite different. He was always up front and wanting to talk to people,' recalls Rosindell.

Rosindell, who would go on to become an MP in 2001 representing his native Romford, describes the young Bercow as 'outgoing' and 'quite engaging', but notes: 'I would say there was an agenda … He was some-one who believed he was going to go places and, therefore, he wanted to build up support and meet people. It's not a bad thing, we all do that in politics – but he was particularly ambitious, I would say.'

When Rosindell took a seat on the bus, Bercow approached and handed him a badge, which read: 'I support South Africa'. FCS members insist that the badge, which Rosindell still has to this day, was not an endorsement of the apartheid regime. But few would disagree that it sailed close to the wind. *The Guardian* described the badge as 'racist by implication'.[3] Both Rosindell and Bercow were accused of being linked with the 'Hang Nelson Mandela' propaganda, though no evidence has ever been found of either man wearing or sporting any of the material and both men denied it. 'The only reason they said he did and I did is because we're both MPs,' suggests Rosindell.

After he was selected as the Tories' candidate for Buckingham ahead of the 1997 election, Labour MP Brian Wilson called on Bercow to make it clear he deeply regretted the abuse heaped on Mandela by FCS members. 'I defy Mr Wilson to produce any statement abusive of Mr Mandela made or approved by me at any time. He will not do so, for none exists,' Bercow responded.[4] In November 2000, Bercow told the *New Statesman*: 'I never wore the shirt myself,' though in hindsight he admitted that he had been in a position of authority to change it, adding: 'It didn't help our case.'[5]

Bercow had first caught the eye of the Conservative Party faithful at the party's annual conference in Brighton in 1984. During an address to delegates, Bercow demanded the abolition of wage councils, action against exorbitant rates and more effort to achieve zero inflation. His speech was reported to have gained 'some of the loudest support' from attendees.[6] At the 1985 conference in Blackpool, Bercow called for the basic rate of income tax to be reduced from 30p to 25p in the pound. 'What we need in this party and in this country is a ringing reassertion of the essential tenets of Thatcherism, not their abandonment,' he declared.[7] He received a standing ovation at the following year's event in Bournemouth, after describing the Thatcher government as the most radical reforming Conservative government of the century. He announced to delegates: 'We have only just turned on the ignition key.'[8]

Such pronouncements from the podium at Conservative conferences were all the rage. In 1977, William Hague, then sixteen years old, had the audience in raptures with his critique of socialism. Thatcher would later tell him his speech was 'thrilling'. In 1984, Edwina Currie, then a Birmingham councillor, brandished a pair of handcuffs and waved them in the direction of Willie Whitelaw, the Home Secretary, while making a crowd-pleasing speech about law and order. Whereas few bother to enter the main auditoriums at Tory conferences these days, in the 1970s and '80s they offered a chance for activists to show some leg.

A former FCS member remembers Bercow as an amusing, hyper-articulate personality. 'When he did a speech, he became another character. He was the kind of guy that would probably read Hansard at night. Also, he was scrofulous-looking and absolutely hopeless with women. A frustrated character I guess.'

Though Bercow had pleased some with his musings, others took issue with the substance of what he was putting forward – or the lack thereof. 'He spoke in clichés quite a lot. We were quite a fanatical sect, and specific in terms of the things we were being fanatical about,' says a former FCS member. 'He would never say the difficult stuff in public; he always kept it to verbose generalities about "Isn't Mrs Thatcher wonderful", the joys of low taxation or something.' Others would also attest to Bercow holding back from some of the more controversial views of the FCS. 'We would always take the piss out of him in terms of the content because one of his things would be to say, "Oh, well, I make no apology for…" And then he would be making an apology for saying something that, in a particular context, wasn't very brave,' says a former FCS activist.

Another ex-member says:

He was always a good orator, he was always trying to ingratiate himself with people. I think he was always trying to compensate for his lack of height by being a bit of a show-off in terms of mimicry, in terms of his oratory, a bit of an oddball when it came to the way that he dressed and behaved and very sort of old-fashionedly pompous but obviously not from a wealthy background or anything. He was one of those people who tried to put on a demeanour of somebody who was old money.

*   *   *

On Monday 1 April 1985, 400 delegates arrived in Loughborough for the start of the FCS conference. The controversy came thick and fast, with delegates supporting a libertarian-led motion to remove Ted Heath, the former Prime Minister, as life patron of the federation. It was the overnight festivities, however, that gained the Loughborough conference its notoriety. Following reports of vandalism by FCS members, John Selwyn Gummer, the Tory Party chairman, called for an inquiry and announced that party grants worth £30,000 would be suspended, with ten-year expulsions a possibility. He also called for the separation of the FCS's Irish and Scottish sections. 'I have heard today of actions which took place last night which cannot anywhere or at any time be excused. Damage, hooliganism, and sheer vandalism are totally unacceptable,' Gummer told activists.[9] The fracas was all the more embarrassing for the party coming as it did only a day after Thatcher had called for a crackdown on football hooliganism.

The alleged incident took place at a party hosted by members of the Scottish FCS in an accommodation block at Loughborough University, where, the BBC World Service reported, fire extinguishers had been let off and windows broken. Other witnesses recall damage to doors and alike, while one says an FCS member had 'shat in the shower'. The popular press had a field day. Nick Robinson, who had been invited to Loughborough by senior members of the party, briefed the media on what had taken place.

There was some immediate discrepancy, however, as to the extent of the damage. Marc Glendening, the outgoing FCS chairman, described it as a 'trivial incident'.[10]

Rosindell says: 'It was all exaggerated ... There's rowdiness at every student event. People were drunk, people running around the corridors, I think a door got broken.' Another former member agrees, saying:

They [Central Office] were always looking for an opportunity to close us down, not unreasonably in retrospect. They hated us and we hated them. It was a culture war. At the conference, we had some bawdy people especially from Scotland and Northern Ireland. It was sort of like a political version of *Animal House*. People used to have late-night parties getting really drunk, singing Unionist songs and this sort of thing. The thing was massively exaggerated for political reasons.

No one recalls Bercow, who was elected to the FCS national executive committee during the conference, being involved in anything untoward that evening. 'Never. John was always responsible, I have to say. He was big on the social scene, but he had to do that to promote his ambitions,' says one attendee.

The newly appointed chair of the organisation, Mark MacGregor, held a press conference the following week at which he claimed that only £14 worth of damage had occurred, based on figures given to him by Conservative Central Office and the Leicestershire constabulary. Loughborough University had previously claimed around £1,400 worth of damage had taken place. The inquiry, which reported in June, found that claims of hooliganism and extremism were exaggerated. Gummer lifted the suspension of funds and no member was expelled.

*   *   *

Twelve months on from the events in Loughborough, in April 1986, delegates travelled to Scarborough for the FCS conference. Having successfully seen off Gummer's attempts to bring the FCS into line, which included ousting the organisation from Conservative Central Office, there was an air of triumphalism. Gummer had since been replaced by Norman Tebbit as chair of the Conservative Party, an idol as far as members of the FCS were concerned.

MacGregor, in his final speech as FCS chair, said:

The named individuals are back here, your national officers are still in charge of a growing and vibrant organisation and, most of all, our Scots and Irish comrades are still in the fold, fighting for the Conservative interest. I believe we have triumphed, comrades, we are back and we are back for good.[11]

David Hoile, FCS vice-chair and the hardline proprietor of its foreign policy stances, offered strong support for guerrilla fighters in Nicaragua, Angola, Mozambique and Afghanistan. Hoile, who was Rhodesian, also accused Sir Geoffrey Howe, the Foreign Secretary, of 'veiled support for a Marxist terrorist organisation' by calling for ANC leader Nelson Mandela to be released from jail. The FCS issued its manifesto, titled 'We the People', for the next general election, which included proposals to privatise British Steel, the National Coal Board, the electricity industry, the railways and the Post Office; abolish licensing laws; put an end to the common agricultural policy; and reduce the top rate of income tax to 20p.

A boisterous hustings was held to find the next chair of the FCS. During his speech, Bercow, the candidate for the libs, referred to Francois, the wets' candidate, as 'intellectually knee-high to a grasshopper'. Francois says: 'I can't remember what I called him, but it was equally flattering ... I gave as good as I got.'

Bercow was duly elected chair of the FCS by 197 votes to 123. Despite the libs' antipathy to the wets, Francois was invited to a party held by the faction in 'some rather dodgy backstreet club in Scarborough', which others note was the Glasgow Rangers Supporters Club. 'We challenge Mr Francois to come for a drink as our guest of honour tonight in our club. It will be really interesting to see if he's got the moral courage to turn up,' said Mark Dingwall, a member of the Scottish FCS.

Francois turned up at around midnight and knocked on an entrance door. He could hear someone mutter: 'Oh, fucking hell', but he was let in and treated like a 'long-lost hero'. Francois offered his congratulations to Bercow, and everything was running smoothly until an inebriated Scottish student approached Francois at around one o'clock in the morning.

'Are you wet?' the Scotsman asked.

Francois looked down at his clothes. 'Well, as a matter of fact, no,' he replied.

The student poured a full pint of lager over Francois's head. 'Well, you are now,' he said. The stunt, Francois was subsequently assured by embarrassed onlookers, was not premeditated.

Bercow had climbed through the ranks of the FCS and was now its chair. Many of the federation were already working for MPs, and he would be elected to Lambeth Council a month later. Being the head honcho of the group was another string to Bercow's bow, and one step further up the ladder. But it would not be long before his loyalties would be tested.

CHAPTER SEVEN

CUTTING TIES

'He knew this was going to happen to us and he kept us in the dark.'

In early September 1982, Harry Phibbs travelled to Moscow with 800 anti-nuclear leaflets on his person. The sixteen-year-old, a pupil at Pimlico Comprehensive in London, was arrested on arrival at Moscow Airport, where he was detained for twenty-four hours and interrogated by the KGB.[1]

This story ignited interest in Phibbs from elements of the UK media, particularly Alan Rusbridger, *The Guardian*'s diary reporter and future editor of the left-leaning paper. He tracked the exploits of the young Conservative, whom he referred to as 'Wee Harry Phibbs'. In August 1985, he reported on Phibbs's founding of *New Agenda*, the Federation of Conservative Students' new quarterly magazine. Speaking to Rusbridger about the publication, Phibbs, a member of the FCS's national executive committee, mused: 'I hope it's going to be banned by lots of university campuses.'[2] Its inaugural edition featured articles from Enoch Powell on embryo research and a praise of the Contras by FCS vice-chair David Hoile. Phibbs's combative editorship was about to bring him into conflict with John Bercow, who was attempting to rebuild relations with senior members of the Tory Party.

The relationship between the FCS and Conservative Central Office was a delicate ecosystem. The FCS was run out of 32 Smith Square in Westminster, which then served as the Conservative Party's headquarters. To carry out its work, the FCS received a £30,000 grant from the party each year.

Phibbs had gained a reputation within the FCS as a bit of an eccentric. When he disagreed with another member's argument, he would declare: 'Substantiate or withdraw.' When he directed the refrain at another FCS member who had got a female student pregnant, a wise hack heckled: 'He didn't withdraw, that's the whole point.'

In September 1985, Norman Tebbit replaced John Gummer as chairman of the Conservative Party. FCS activists, who shared a political affiliation with Tebbit, were thrilled. The autumn edition of *New Agenda* featured a picture of Tebbit above the phrase 'Britain's Future'.

It would be the front cover of its summer 1986 edition, however, that would bring the magazine into direct confrontation with the party chairman, test Bercow's allegiances to breaking point and, ultimately, help to bring about the demise of the FCS.

* * *

Not every member of the libs was signed up to John Bercow's candidacy for the FCS chairmanship. 'A lot of people were impressed by him; others, like me, were repulsed by him instinctively,' says one former member. 'I wasn't convinced you were ever really speaking to a real human being.'

Given he was involved with such a confrontational faction, some felt Bercow was unable or unwilling to say the difficult things in public. This diffidence fostered concerns about what his true beliefs were, and whether he was truly aligned with the deeply ideological group he had attached himself to, which just so happened to be the one in the ascendancy. 'John's views were pretty fluid, and they changed depending on what was going to advance his own career the most,' says another ex-FCS member.

So he had very traditional, old-fashioned, old-right views while they were convenient, and then his views changed into whatever was the most convenient for them to be at the time. Knowing what I know now and what he's been like since, I'm not sure he believes in anything other than his own ego.

As leading members of rival camps – wets and libs – Nick Robinson and Bercow were enemies. Robinson recalls: 'Bercow was Mr Articulate; he was a public face and he was closer to Tebbit Conservatism – traditional, right-wing, pro-Thatcher – than he was this new movement of libertarianism.' Over the years, Robinson has not commented on his time in student politics due to his position at the BBC.

Bercow did have an influential outrider in the shape of Mark MacGregor, the outgoing chair of the FCS, who had helped get him appointed to the organisation's national executive committee in 1985. MacGregor had originally wanted to run for a second term to the sabbatical role, which had a salary paid for by Central Office. However, his deputy, David Hoile, was also keen on running for the chairmanship. In the aftermath of the Loughborough conference and amid the continuing friction with party HQ, some found Hoile to be too risky a candidate; his pronouncements on foreign affairs had earned him and the FCS something of a reputation.

'MacGregor made Bercow the candidate to stop Hoile but also because Bercow would speak to these Tory toffs and ministers in a way that they expected to be spoken to,' says an ex-member. 'There was a recognition that fences needed to be mended, and it was felt that Bercow would be a good person to do that.' The race for the candidacy proved a divisive time. 'It was painful because some people were on Hoile's side, others on MacGregor's side. It was very difficult for everyone because we were all friends.'

As they had done since 1983, when factionalism allowed the wets candidate, Paul Goodman, to become FCS chair, the libs held a caucus to elect their new candidate. With the group split down the middle, every vote would count. Mike Simmonds, a student at Leeds University who supported Bercow, had got his dates wrong. Believing the caucus to be taking place the next day, he had to rush down to London. MacGregor and Douglas

Smith, FCS vice-chair, realised they would not get Bercow across the line without Simmonds's support. In a bid to delay proceedings, MacGregor relocated the vote to his flat in Tooting Bec, south London, where he lived with another FCS member, Russell Walters. Members of the caucus ended up waiting in the car park outside while MacGregor took a scenic route to buy time. When MacGregor eventually made his appearance, pro-Bercow supporters gave long speeches until Simmonds arrived at the eleventh hour. Bercow won the candidacy by a majority of one.

FCS members were already familiar with the Tooting flat, which had been the scene of a notorious orange-themed party to mark the Orange Order in Northern Ireland. By the time the last guest left, all three of the emergency services had been called out. Firstly, the fire brigade was called after gatecrashers were denied entry and set fire to the intercom system. Then the police arrived after neighbours complained about the noise of naked revellers in the swimming pool chanting political slogans into the early hours. Finally, an ambulance was summoned after a guest fell into a hole in the front garden.

Despite FCS activists having a strong ideological affiliation with Tebbit, they had clashed over the decision to send a delegation to support Unionist candidates in the January 1986 by-elections in Northern Ireland. Memories of the IRA bomb attack that killed five people at the Grand Hotel in Brighton during the 1984 Tory Party conference loomed large. Tebbit, whose wife Margaret was paralysed by the blast (Tebbit himself was also injured, though less severely), had taken MacGregor aside to try to convince him to abandon the plans, only for the then FCS chair to reply: 'Sorry, Norman, the tickets are booked.'

Bercow, who maintained good relations with both Tebbit and his deputy, Jeffrey Archer, was seeking to bridge the gap between the FCS and the party's higher-ups. His approach was undercut when Simon Morgan, the chairman of the Scottish FCS, organised a conference to mark the signing of the Anglo-Irish Agreement. 'It will be 100 per cent against the party,' a national committee member said.[3]

Phibbs, meanwhile, was putting together the latest edition of *New Agenda*. The main feature of the magazine was an interview with Count Nikolai Tolstoy, a British-born historian and author of *The Minister and The Massacres*, who had claimed that former Prime Minister Harold Macmillan was responsible in 1945 for ordering 40,000 Russian prisoners and slave labourers liberated by the Allies in the Second World War to be sent back to the Soviet Union. Tolstoy argued that some of the Cossacks committed suicide rather than return, while many were executed, and others sent to labour camps. The cover of the summer edition featured a picture of Macmillan beside the caption 'GUILTY'.

Tebbit, who was on holiday when news reached him of the coverage, was apoplectic. He was incandescent that the libellous claim had gone out on a magazine that carried the Conservative Party's logo. He was granted a High Court injunction to prevent the FCS from further distributing the magazine. Along with Hal Miller, a Tory Party vice-chairman, Tebbit issued a writ claiming damages from Phibbs and the publication's printers, Annagh Graphical.

Prior to the court order, Phibbs had as a precaution rolled out 2,000 copies. 'The magazine has gone around the country. There is nothing anybody can do about that,' he said. The printing of 1,000 other copies was cancelled.[4] Phibbs did, however, agree to remove the Conservative Party logo from future issues of the magazine. He said:

> As far as I am concerned, *New Agenda* is no longer the property of Tory Central Office. It is an independent publication, which does not receive party money but is funded by subscriptions, advertisements and donations. I will be taking legal advice and intend to battle against this all the way.

Tebbit recalls: 'The proposed publication of the actionable libel against the Earl of Stockton [Macmillan], we couldn't allow that to happen. He was not my favourite politician by a long chalk, but fair dos after all.'

At the heart of the dispute was a row about whether Phibbs had circumvented an agreement whereby Conservative Central Office approved each edition of *New Agenda*. Phibbs has maintained that this had never been the case, and previous publications had never been run past members of the party. However, Bercow accused his fellow FCS member of not submitting the magazine for approval. In strong words that caused consternation in FCS ranks, he called on Phibbs to 'cease his posturing'.[5] 'Mr Phibbs cannot claim to have published the issue with FCS approval,' he claimed. 'He flagrantly violated the rules that all party publications have to be scrutinised before distribution. I was not consulted about the publication in advance.' He also called for an emergency meeting of the FCS national executive committee to discuss Phibbs's membership.

An ex-FCS member says: 'To be fair, given the purpose of Bercow being there was to improve relations with the party machine, he probably shouldn't have backed *New Agenda*.' However, the activist says there was no need for Bercow to 'pile into Harry' in the media, which caused great unrest among FCS students: 'Bercow just doesn't know when to shut up. He can't not open his mouth and get high on his own rhetoric.'

After a meeting with Michael Dobbs, the chief of staff at Central Office and assistant to Tebbit (who would go on to write the *House of Cards* trilogy), Phibbs agreed to resign as editor of *New Agenda*. He apologised to Tebbit and vowed to recall as many as possible of the nearly 2,000 copies of the magazine that had been distributed. In return, the writ against Phibbs and the magazine's printers was dropped. In just a week, however, Phibbs returned as deputy editor of the magazine and Bercow's proposed emergency meeting was cancelled.

Bercow spoke with Tebbit during the FCS's half-yearly conference in Leicester. The party chairman, who was growing weary of the persistent controversy surrounding the FCS, said he was prepared to wind up the organisation unless it came into line. Bercow offered to resign, but Tebbit turned him down, arguing that instead he should try to bring the 14,000-strong FCS on board.

Bercow's position on the Phibbs affair drew stern criticism from inside the FCS. Fellow members of the caucus, including members of the national executive committee and regional chairmen, voted by sixteen to one to censure Bercow for 'selling out' and taking the side of Central Office.[6] He was also removed as leader of the libs and replaced by Phibbs and vice-chair Steve Nicholson. In a further provocation, two members of the FCS joined Tolstoy on a platform at a fringe meeting in the conference hotel in Leicester.

The furore over *New Agenda* ushered in the final days of the FCS. The fire was further stoked when activists sent a get-well letter to General Pinochet after an assassination attempt in September. Bercow branded the move 'utterly stupid'.[7]

Tebbit finally severed the Conservative Party's links with the FCS in November, resulting in the organisation losing its £30,000 grant and workspace at 32 Smith Square.[8] In its place was to be a new body called the Conservative Collegiate Forum, to be led by Peter Morrison, a deputy chairman of the party. Bercow retained his sabbatical salary from his chairmanship of the FCS and was tasked with improving the party's reputation on campuses.

Tebbit says the FCS was a cause of constant nuisance to the party. 'It was a bloody headache. It was the sort of thing that caused us embarrassment and undermined the work that we were trying to get done in the university sector to get reasonably minded Conservatives to come forward,' he recalls.

Nick Robinson, the former chair of the Young Conservatives, welcomed the end of the FCS. 'They were at that age where anything that outrages your opponents was amusing. It was about causing outrage; sometimes intellectual – "Let's privatise the money supply" – and sometimes deliberately, wilfully offensive,' he explains.

Many in the FCS felt that when push came to shove, Bercow sided with the Tory top brass over his fellow comrades. For the FCS members who had already harboured doubts about Bercow's allegiances, it was a case of vindication. But it was the way Bercow went about his condemnation that really got people's backs up. His failure to warn activists of the impending closure was the final straw. One says:

> Bercow knew that the closure was coming because he was hanging around in Central Office and ingratiated himself with Norman Tebbit. He managed to successfully swap sides at the time. He could have aligned himself with his comrades; he chose not to and aligned himself with the bit that would further his career.

Another argues: 'He used us to become the chairman and then we discovered he was parlaying with Tebbit and Archer, who created this new vehicle just for him.' A former member who counted Bercow as a friend says: 'He knew this was going to happen to us and he kept us in the dark, whereas if we had known it would have been possible to take some evasive manoeuvres or concessions.' A source who worked for Tebbit at the time says: 'What he did was to bend to the party machine and try to get the party machine's take accepted among the students, which I suppose gave one the sense that he was a bit of a careerist.'

Robbie Gibb had tried to play peacemaker between Bercow and Phibbs. 'He'd try to reconcile things. But it was quite soon after that the thing was closed down,' says an FCS member. Some of the more cynical elements of the FCS felt the episode was a microcosm of how Bercow would go on to carry out his political endeavours. 'He was quite willing to further his own career on the shoulders of others; he was quite glad to push down and kick away,' says one source involved.

Every Friday, members of the FCS in London would meet at St Stephen's Tavern near the Houses of Parliament. The Friday after the news broke, Bercow entered the pub to an 'incredibly frosty' reception, says one witness. Phibbs approached him and said: 'As far as I'm concerned, we are no longer friends.' Russell Walters and another FCS member took pity on Bercow and took him back to Walters's flat in Tooting. 'You weren't fundamentally wrong, but you went over the top. Do some good stuff and it will all be fine in the end,' they told him.

Former members of the FCS often speak with an element of embarrassment about the organisation's past activities. 'What you tend to find is, people who were in FCS don't put it on their CVs these days,' says a former member. Many politicians are keen to note, often holding back laughter, that the right-wing Tebbit closed the FCS down for being, of all things, too right-wing.

Two things can be true at the same time: it's possible both that the FCS was doing the Conservative Party's reputation some harm and ultimately deserved to be cut loose from Central Office and that Bercow, perhaps with nowhere else to turn, threw his old mates under a bus. Bercow was plainly a confrontational activist at this point with some choice views. His Monday Club links were not far behind him, and he provocatively went about winding up his opponents. But, as many members have attested, Bercow was never involved with some of the more extreme ideas that came out of the FCS. Indeed, in March 1992, Bercow won an undisclosed 'large sum' in libel damages against the *Southend Evening Echo* over claims that he supported the legalisation of heroin and incest – two viewpoints expressed on the fringes of the FCS. He was also a staunch Thatcherite, while many of the libs were somewhat more critical of the Prime Minister and yearned for a more radical policy agenda.

Both in the Monday Club and in the FCS, Bercow encountered other members who doubted whether he was a true believer. As he used to tell acquaintances, politics to him was 'meat and drink'. On this metric, he had proved successful; he was now in the good books of the Conservative Party chairman, had built up other relationships with key players in the party hierarchy, was a councillor in Lambeth and would soon stand in the upcoming 1987 election. To have stuck with his 'comrades' in the FCS against the party machine would have been harmful to his career prospects. Perhaps Bercow calculated that the closure of the organisation was inevitable and hoped that his allegiances would survive. Judging by the animosity that still lingers among many in the organisation, this was a false hope.

Activists consider his true crime to have been the strength of his condemnation of fellow FCS members. Once he had decided his views, he did not moderate them.

Politics can be a ruthless pastime. Bercow has accumulated so many enemies and detractors over the years in part because of the repeated instances when people felt duped or let down by him. By the time he would become Speaker, many were emboldened to try to bring him down. Old grievances had been allowed to fester.

Bercow's loyalty ultimately went to the party ahead of his affiliates in the FCS. It would not be the last time that he would sever ties with people he once called his allies.

CHAPTER EIGHT

ELECTIONEERING

'He was an extremist.'

Unbcknownst to them, Michael Keegan and John Bercow had a lot in common. Both had a burning desire to become Members of Parliament and a zeal for winding up left-wing activists. These shared enthusiasms would see them independently gravitate towards south London after graduating in the summer of 1985.

'We wanted to go and live in a borough that had the worst example of the hard left that we could possibly find. And there was only one borough in London that really ticked the box big-time and that was Lambeth,' says Keegan.

Lambeth had gained notoriety when 'Red' Ted Knight, the hard-left leader of the council, had refused to set a budget following the Rates Act 1984, which aimed to limit the budgets of local authorities, forcing the council to the brink of bankruptcy. In April 1986, the district auditor surcharged Knight and thirty other Labour councillors and disqualified them from political office for five years.

Lambeth, which included representatives of the so-called 'loony left', posed a tantalising prospect for young firebrands like Bercow and Keegan. Former members of the FCS recall Teresa Gorman, who became Conservative MP for Billericay at the 1987 election, approaching Bercow and other activists to run in Lambeth for this reason. Gorman had a property at 60 Hopton Road in Streatham, at which, according to multiple sources, she offered to put down would-be candidates as residents so that they could stand for election to Lambeth Council.

Bercow was registered as living at 60 Hopton Road on the electoral roll from 16 February 1986 to 15 February 1987. But former colleagues in the FCS say Bercow was sofa hopping and staying with his mother at the time, and indeed Bercow was also registered at his mother's address. 'He used [the Hopton Road] address in order to get elected and fight a seat on Lambeth Council. It was completely illegal, there's no doubt about that,' claims one former FCS member. 'It was quite openly discussed in those terms at the time. So there was no ambiguity about it,' says another. A spokesperson says Bercow 'straightforwardly rebuts the claim that he resided "illegally"', and stresses that he was 'correctly recorded in the electoral register as residing at 60 Hopton Road at the relevant time'.

By the time of his election, according to council minutes,[1] Bercow was living at 41 Tooting Bec Gardens, but he was not registered as a voter there on the roll that ended on 10 October 1985. Marc Glendening, who was working as Gorman's researcher, was also registered at the Hopton Road address, though he never lived there either and did not stand for the council. 'I have no recollection of Mr Bercow living in my house in Hopton Road,' Gorman said in 2009, when asked by reporters.[2] In a statement, Bercow's spokesman said: 'John did rent a property in Lambeth and he lived in the borough full-time after leaving university until 1993. In the mid-'80s, the electoral register was much slower at picking up the movement of people than it is today.'[3]

Gorman came under scrutiny for her property dealings at the turn of the millennium, when the parliamentary commissioner for standards, Elizabeth Filkin, investigated her over the registration of her property interests. Gorman was suspended for one month from the House of Commons for failing to declare that her husband, Jim Gorman, owned three properties in London when she proposed the repeal of the Rents Act in January 1990.

Prior to their election, Bercow, Keegan and James Hutchings, the third man in their triumvirate, would disrupt public meetings of Lambeth Council. They would position themselves in different parts of the room and attack Ted Knight over his stance on rate capping. 'How can this be for the good of the poor?' one would heckle.

On Thursday 8 May 1986, Bercow, then aged twenty-three, was elected to the St Leonard's ward of Lambeth Council. Despite the controversy over rate capping, Labour added eight seats to their previous tally of thirty-two, while the Tories trailed on twenty-one. Linda Bellos, the radical feminist and left-wing activist, had just taken over as leader of the council.

A breed of Thatcherite councillors was born out of the 1986 election, known as the Young Turks; a buoyant, self-assured group who were often the product of student politics. Bercow and Keegan, both members of the Federation of Conservative Students, were among them.

There was a vast chasm on the council between the radical left on one side and the Young Turks on the other. Somewhere in the middle was John Mann, a newly elected Labour councillor and future MP. 'Nobody was harder right-wing than John Bercow,' he says. 'He was just an extremist.'

Already an esteemed public speaker (Bercow would join Conservative Central Office's Speakers Panel in 1987), Bercow would enjoy using oratory to target his Labour opponents. He would use refrains such as 'My political scandal meter is reading "Maximum Bellos"', in reference to the council leader. Fellow Conservative councillor Graham Pycock explains:

> He was a very good debater; he'd have them in knots. What he would do would be to quote various aspects of Trotsky, Marx and Stalin and argue that various Labour members were getting the ideology wrong, and they'd all get upset. They would end up clearly disagreeing with each other on the ideology of the Marxist position they all took. He was very good, he always entertained.

Bellos, for one, enjoyed the exchanges. 'We used to shout "More, More!" when he was speaking. He was so appalling! I'm talking about being utterly Thatcherite and revelling in it,' she explains. 'I'm not convinced that he took himself seriously, actually. Especially as one knows him subsequently, he was being as outrageous and rightist as he could possibly be – more so than anybody else in the Tory group.' The council leader did admire Bercow's abilities, however. 'He was amusing and confident,' she concedes. 'I would certainly indicate my contempt. He didn't intimidate me, he made me laugh – I just thought it was outrageous right-wing shit.'

Mary Leigh, a solicitor, served as the Conservative leader on the council. As a group, the Young Turks were no fans of Leigh's leadership. She was from the less hardline, more traditional wing of the Conservatives. Bercow had enjoyed a decent relationship with Leigh prior to his election and had introduced her to his father, Charlie Bercow, shortly before his death in 1986. Bercow took umbrage, however, when Leigh gave an interview on a subject that he felt pertained to his brief, and he later confronted her over the phone. 'From there, it just went downhill,' she says.

The Young Turks began a sustained campaign to oust Leigh as leader. Keegan says he and Bercow were 'prime movers' in the plot. Leigh attributes Bercow's manoeuvres to their fallout over the interview, saying: 'Bercow was in it for himself; there was no reason for him to take umbrage with the fact I had given an interview that he thought he ought to have given.' She adds: 'He stabbed me in the back.'

There were objections to Leigh's leadership. 'She was not a good debater; she was not a good team leader; she had her favourites,' explains Pycock, who went from the front to the backbench under Leigh. 'She fell out with all the Young Turks. She didn't get on with them and they didn't get on with her; it was very much personalities.' Pycock was no fan of the ambush against Leigh, however.

I was the odd man out and I had a discussion with my branch, and I said: 'This is so bad, I'm going to resign the Conservative whip.' I wasn't prepared to be part of the coup, and I wasn't on Mary's side, either – I was disgusted with the way they were all behaving.

By the time of the annual meeting in September 1987, the plans were coming to fruition. After months of lobbying, Bercow lodged a vote of no confidence. The motion – which Pycock did support, despite his reservations – was defeated by one after Leigh used her casting vote.[4]

Leigh resigned and stood again for the leadership. Bercow was initially expected to run against her. In the event, however, he sat out the contest and instead became the youngest Conservative deputy leader in the country, with the Young Turks selecting one of their own, Hugh Jones, to run successfully against Leigh. Keegan says Jones was the more experienced hand to take over, having served on the council since 1982.

The next time Leigh and Bercow spoke was in 2003, when he rang to inform Leigh of the death of Bill Shelton, the former Conservative MP for Streatham, whom they both knew. 'Look, I'm sorry for what happened, it's all very unfortunate,' he said later in the call.

The Young Turks had a clear objective: to rid the council of socialism. But, according to John Mann, the Tory opposition was 'absolutely dreadful' at holding the council to account. 'Bercow epitomised them; they were people who wanted to come in, have the argument but not actually do the work.'

Bercow and Keegan became close in part because of the 'hostile and aggressive' environment in which they found themselves. 'Being a Conservative councillor in Lambeth in the 1980s was quite risky. You would regularly be shouted at or assaulted,' Keegan says. On one occasion, Keegan filled in for Bercow at a debate hosted by the Vauxhall Labour Party Young Socialists. Midway through, a man walked over to Keegan with a tin of white paint and poured it over him. Realising this presented an ideal photo opportunity, Keegan stayed put until press photographers from the *Evening Standard* and other outlets turned up. He later successfully sued the Vauxhall branch of the Labour Party Young Socialists in small claims court and had to instruct bailiffs to collect the money from the Labour Party HQ on the Walworth Road in Elephant and Castle.

During a more serious incident, Keegan had to have police positioned outside his house after left-wing activists wrote 'Tory racist scum' on what they believed to be the walls of his home (they had incorrectly inscribed it on his neighbour's). Simon Fawthrop, a black Conservative councillor, had 'Uncle Tom burn' written on the front walk up to his house, says Keegan. 'So the police thought: "Actually, whoever's doing this is quite serious that they intend to harm these people." I remember getting this police protection,' he explains.

Bercow and Keegan's eyes were never too far from the prize – becoming Members of Parliament. They put together lists of Conservative MPs by date of birth and the size of their majority to work out where safe seats would crop up in the future. 'We'd sit there with the *Times* guide and go: "Well, he's going to be seventy-two at the next election so he's likely to go" … It fascinated both of us,' Keegan says.

Bercow first met Tory MP Christopher Chope in 1984 at a meeting of potential Conservative candidates. When asked for his advice for how to be selected, Chope responded: 'You should get married.' 'That just reminds us, does it not, of how times have changed?' Chope later recalled.[5] With Chope's help, Bercow was added to the Conservative list of candidates in the spring of 1987. 'One of your qualifications then was that you regarded, as did I, Enoch Powell as a schoolboy hero,' he reminded Bercow in 2019.

Thatcher caught her own party off guard by calling an election for May 1987, when many had been preparing for her to go to the polls in October. As a result, the Tories were left scrambling for candidates in Scotland. 'The Conservative Party was essentially caught with its knickers down,' says Gary Mond, who had also made the Tory candidates list. The result was that those who became prospective candidates late on, including Bernard Jenkin and Liam Fox, two future prominent Tories, were 'parachuted' to Scotland to fill up the seats. Mond became the candidate for Hamilton, and Bercow for Motherwell South. 'I can remember him packing up and saying: "I'll see you in a month's time." And he literally disappeared up to Scotland. I remember thinking that was a really brave thing to do,' says Keegan. (Keegan himself missed out on the chance of running. He spent the 1987 election on the Thatcher battle bus travelling around the country, as part of the team organised by Harvey Thomas, a press adviser and conference organiser for the Conservative Prime Minister.)

Motherwell South was a chance for the 24-year-old Bercow to cut his teeth. He lived with Mond in a flat in Wishaw for the duration of the campaign, and the pair struck up an enduring friendship. 'We got on very, very well and we became friendly after that. We would speak to each other about the political scene in terms of seats that were coming up almost daily,' Mond says. It was never remotely possible that either man would win, but it offered an opportunity for a young up-and-comer to take one for the team with a view to securing a more winnable seat in the future.

Motherwell South was created in 1983 by the division of Motherwell and Wishaw, and had been won by Labour's Jeremy Bray at the previous election by more than 12,300 votes. In one piece of campaign literature, Bercow can be seen smiling outside the Ravenscraig steelworks with an accompanying statement declaring that the 'Conservatives recognise the crucial importance of the Scottish steel industry and have twice stopped the closure of Ravenscraig. We agree with the shop stewards that privatisation is not the issue here. Ravenscraig is now profitable and there is no question of it being closed.' Journalists at *The Herald* would later dig up the pledge when the steelworks were closed in 1992.[6]

Bray was re-elected with an increased vote share and Bercow slipped to third behind the SNP's James Wright, with the Tories picking up nearly 2,000 fewer votes than four years earlier. Such was Thatcher's unpopularity in Scotland that the Tories lost eleven seats, leaving the party with just ten MPs north of the border. After Bray's speech, Bercow was due to give his address. Showing an abrasiveness familiar to many who had encountered him on the student politics scene, he informed the crowd, composed mostly of Labour supporters, that Thatcher was on her way to another election victory. According to Bobby Friedman's biography of Bercow, Labour activists eventually picked up chairs and hurled them at the stage. 'John wasn't fazed at all,' Bob Burgess, the chairman of the local Conservative constituency association, told Friedman. 'He just took it in his stride; they had to rip the mic from him.'[7]

Bercow returned to London richer for what he had gone through. Two years on, it was his turn to help Keegan, who was putting himself forward to be the Tory candidate at a by-election in Vauxhall, triggered when Labour MP Stuart Holland resigned to take up a post at the European University Institute in Florence. Bercow and Keegan would spend evenings together practising speeches and bouncing ideas off one another ahead of the selection. Keegan, who was now working in banking at NatWest, was chosen as the Conservative candidate, and was up against Kate Hoey, a physical education teacher who had been imposed as a candidate by Labour's national executive committee, to some unrest at local level. For the campaign, Keegan was assigned a research assistant by the name of David Cameron, who was taking up his first job in the Conservative Research Department. It was here that Bercow met the future Prime Minister for the first time. 'I spent time with David because he worked for me, and John was my mate from the council who was coming to help with the canvassing and all the rest of it,' Keegan recalls. On 15 June 1989, Hoey won with 52.7 per cent of the vote, with Keegan second on 18.8 per cent.

By 1990, Bercow and Keegan had decided that they would not stand for re-election on Lambeth Council. 'We relished it because we thought this was so terrible that we've got to go in and do something about it. On the other hand, all of us felt, at the end of four years, "We've had quite enough of that,"' Keegan says.

In a copy of his CV from 1995, Bercow said he had 'exposed waste and corruption by the extreme left in control of the Council'. He also boasted that he had 'fought against left wing policies, double standards and dirty tricks campaigns by Liberal Democrat councillors'.[8]

Labour MP Dawn Primarolo had narrowly won in Bristol South at the 1987 election. It was because of this close result that Bercow put himself forward for selection as the Conservative candidate in what he would excitedly refer to as the thirteenth most marginal seat in the country.[9] As he had done in Motherwell South, Bercow impressed the local Conservative constituency association, and he secured the candidacy eighteen months ahead of the 1992 election, beating to the nomination contenders including Crispin Blunt, a future MP. Matters did become slightly awkward, though, when he turned up to a meeting at his agent Cora Stephenson's house and pinged the car of the chairman, Richard Eddy. At the age of twenty-seven, Bercow had only just passed his driving test.[10]

Unlike in Motherwell South, Bercow had a decent amount of time to campaign and get his feet on the ground. There was turmoil at the top of the Conservative Party, however, after Geoffrey Howe resigned from his position as Deputy Prime Minister over Thatcher's approach to Europe and the European Monetary Union. Michael Heseltine subsequently mounted a challenge for the leadership of the party. Bercow and Nick Gibb, his friend from the FCS and a candidate in Stoke-on-Trent Central, carried out a survey of prospective parliamentary candidates to sound out support for Thatcher. Of the 151 candidates contacted, 125 put their name to a statement calling for the beleaguered Prime Minister to achieve a 'resounding victory'. 'This survey is a massive vote of confidence in the leadership of Margaret Thatcher,' declared Bercow on 18 November 1990, a loyalist right to the end.[11] Four days later, Thatcher resigned. Bercow would go on to back John Major in the race to replace her.

In January 1991, Bercow told *The Guardian* of his long-established desire to become an MP and admitted that he was attracted by the idea of high office. 'And anyone who says they're not is a liar,' he declared.[12]

Bercow's abrasive approach to taking on his opponents, shown so vividly in Lambeth, was equally on show in Bristol South. 'I would say in '92 he excelled himself in developing a persona as a far-right Thatcherite,' recalls Primarolo. 'In Bristol South, he thought he was in with a shot to begin with. He wanted to run the campaign by trying to make me into the "wicked communist witch". He enjoyed himself.' Bercow tried to paint Primarolo, who would go on to serve as a Deputy Speaker while he was in the chair, as 'an extremist implanted by the Labour left'. Once more, his efforts would be in vain, as Primarolo romped to an impressive victory by nearly 9,000 votes. 'In fairness to him, he's changed,' she says.

> We all go on a journey, I suppose he'd say. I've heard him say it quite a few times when he introduced me as his deputy, he fought hard 'but the good people at Bristol South fought back'. My majority went from 1,500 to over 8,000. He makes a joke of it. In politics, people try and rewrite the past to explain that what they meant was what they might think now. But he doesn't; he's presented it as a journey. You've got to give him credit for that.

Not only had Bercow failed twice to become an MP; on both occasions he had lost more decisively than his predecessors. It was a trend he was determined to buck.

CHAPTER NINE

WORKING MAN

'I think of him above all as a very loyal and very kind man.'

Ken Clarke could not believe what his No. 2 had just proposed. 'We can't have him in the team,' the Chancellor said, shaking his head. 'It's crazy, it's completely off the wall, I don't want a right-wing loony here.'

Clarke did not have a good first impression of John Bercow. They first met in 1986 when Clarke, a minister in Margaret Thatcher's government, agreed to address an FCS event that Bercow chaired. During his speech, Clarke noticed that a 'large number' of delegates, the majority of whom were 'ragingly Eurosceptic', were wearing 'Hang Nelson Mandela' buttons on their lapels. One man was lying on the ground in a demonstration against the Anglo-Irish Agreement. Chomping away on a cigar in his south London home, Clarke says understatedly: 'Obviously it wasn't the best introduction to John.'

So when Jonathan Aitken approached him in early 1995 to say he was considering appointing Bercow as his special adviser, Clarke was not best pleased. 'You're talking about ten years ago,' Aitken told him. 'He's changed an awful lot since then, and not just got older, but his views have changed, he's nothing like as extreme as you think he is, he'll be all right.' Determined that his boss should be won over, Aitken arranged for the two to talk it out. 'You meet him for yourself; there's no reason to object to him,' he said.

Aitken had been appointed Chief Secretary to the Treasury in July 1994, after two years in the Ministry of Defence as Minister for Defence Procurement. Aitken, a former war correspondent, had joined the House in 1974 and had been seen by some as a potential high achiever. His talents were never given an airing under Margaret Thatcher, however, who took a different view of his capabilities. His first frontbench role came under John Major, eighteen years after entering Parliament.

Now a Cabinet minister, Aitken was entitled to have a special adviser, but he was not taken with the list of candidates suggested by Conservative Central Office. Malcolm Pearson, a businessman and a member of the House of Lords who would go on to lead the UK Independence Party, called Aitken. 'Would you consider looking at John Bercow?' he asked. Julian Lewis, who was working as deputy director in the Conservative Research Department, was recommending that his close friend be in the running.

Following Pearson's advice, Aitken agreed to interview Bercow in his office at the Treasury. 'I immediately rather took to him and liked him,' he recalls. 'Somebody else had said that he'd got a bit of a chequered past, but that didn't worry me; I believe in talent. I thought well of his brains and intelligence. I also thought well of his political position, which interestingly is not the one he has today.'

At the time, Bercow was working as an assistant director at Rowland Salingbury Casey, a public affairs company he had joined in 1988. In January 1994, he had been promoted to the board.[1] His employment at RSC came hot on the heels of his first job in 1987 working as a credit analyst at Hambros, the merchant bank. Peter Morrison, Tory MP for Chester, had put Bercow in touch with a friend at the bank, but the blossoming world of 1980s finance was not a good fit for the 24-year-old Lambeth councillor, whose interests lay elsewhere. His time at Hambros did not feature on the CV he submitted for the role of special adviser.[2]

RSC was a part of the American Rowland Group and was later acquired by Saatchi & Saatchi. (After the 1992 election, Bercow got involved with a new division created by the Saatchi brothers, Saatchi Government Communications Worldwide.)[3] His first boss was Leighton Andrews, who would go on to be a minister in the Welsh government. He remembers Bercow as a highly capable employee and a 'dry' Conservative. Andrews recalls Bercow being 'very down and upset' at the death of Nicholas Ridley in 1993, the former Thatcherite minister who was responsible for introducing the Community Charge, otherwise known as the poll tax. 'He regarded Nicholas Ridley as one of the old-school, original Thatcherites,' Andrews recalls.

Bercow got on 'pretty well' with his colleagues, his former boss says. 'Like a lot of people in politics, John had his own interests and there would be some things he would be happier working on than others. That's what you expect,' Andrews says. 'He'd come out for a drink and come to company events and so on. He played tennis with people who worked in the company and that sort of thing.'

Alison Clark, who was working as an account director at RSC, recalls Bercow as being 'quite a strange character' on first meeting. 'But as I got to know him better, I thought he was good. Consultancies in those days were full of a mixture of people. He clearly knew politics, he was well connected, and he was smart. But I haven't really come across a person like him before.'

Both Clark and Andrews recall Bercow's ability as a mimic, particularly doing impressions of Tony Benn and Ted Heath. Clark says that Bercow was also reading novels by Jane Austen and started imitating the characters. 'That's when he started speaking in this very old-fashioned way. It started as a piss-take, but it kind of stuck,' she remembers.

Bercow's connections with the Conservative Party made him an effective lobbyist, though it was well known that he had his eyes trained on a political career. In 1992, while still an account director, he stood for election in Bristol South. 'He was always going off to do events down there. It was an unwinnable seat. He was very active in the Tory Party and I thought he was quite right-wing,' Clark says.

Bercow took a gamble in applying for a job with Aitken. Special advisers are not allowed to stand as prospective parliamentary candidates. Given his desire to enter Parliament, it was likely that it would be Aitken who would lose out, should the opportunity have presented itself.

Special advisers have enjoyed increasing power and influence in Whitehall, which has only added to the intrigue and mystique that surround them. But in the mid-'90s, they had an altogether different status. 'They were really political aides, not quite the Tsar-like appointments they are now,' says Ken Clarke. Aitken adds: 'They were lower-level; their names were never known to anybody much outside the immediate circle.' Aitken himself had been a special adviser – then known as a political secretary – to Selwyn Lloyd, a former Chancellor and Leader of the House who would go on to become Speaker.

Aitken knew he had to win over his superior, and Clarke agreed to meet Bercow. 'I suspect I was very pompous and sort of patronising, I was literally lecturing him,' says the former Chancellor. Bercow tried to reassure Clarke that he was supportive of what the government was doing. Clarke, after deciding that there was no point in falling out with Aitken over the matter, agreed, but with conditions. 'Six months, see how it goes, but the first time I find he's leaked anything to the bloody newspapers, out,' he told Aitken.

Bercow was appointed on 10 March 1995, though there was some discrepancy over his exit from RSC. A report in *Private Eye* alleged that Bercow had left citing 'personal reasons' and saying he had no job to go to.[4] According to the magazine, RSC had negotiated a voluntary redundancy package for him. The lobbyists 'successfully got some of their money back', the *Eye* said, after the news emerged that Bercow had gone to work for Jonathan Aitken.

Clarke's doubts began to fade soon after Bercow's appointment. 'This guy was all right and we weren't having leaks, he wasn't causing any trouble,' Clarke says. Aitken, a staunch Eurosceptic, particularly remembers Bercow helping to write a political speech on the economic future of Britain, which hinted at what life would be like outside of the European Union. As part of his role, Bercow also tipped off the newspapers so that it got covered in advance of the speech being delivered. Not everyone, though, was completely taken with the 32-year-old. 'I did pick up that the civil service in the Treasury were rather hesitant about him. That didn't worry me at all,' Aitken says. 'They didn't say, "Don't have him," but they were more like, "Handle with care, Minister," it was that sort of thing. The Treasury has always looked down a bit on special advisers anyway.'

Aitken had long been a figure of interest to elements of the press. For eighteen months, *The Guardian* had been sniffing around his business links with Saudi Arabia, particularly during his time at the Ministry of Defence. Of particular intrigue was a stay at the Ritz in Paris in September 1993, which the paper alleged had been paid for by aides of the Saudi royal family. Although *The Guardian* had obtained a copy of the bill, Aitken insisted that his wife, Lolicia, had paid his part of it using money that he had given her.

In early April 1995, Aitken was on holiday in the Swiss Alps with his family. He was aware of an upcoming *World in Action* documentary titled 'Jonathan of Arabia' with allegations of involvement in secret Middle East arms deals that breached government restrictions, and that *The Guardian* would be pursuing new stories on his stay at the Ritz in Paris. But he was shocked when an aide rang on Sunday evening to warn of a *Guardian* story headlined 'Aitken "tried to arrange girls" for Saudi friends'.[5]

The report prompted Aitken to return to his home in Lord North Street, Westminster, where he was joined by Alan Duncan, the MP for Rutland; Patrick Robertson, his media adviser; and Bercow. After issuing writs to *The Guardian* and two of its journalists, he was ready to make a statement. The words were signed off by John Major, and Aitken had sought legal advice from the Attorney General, Sir Nicholas Lyell. Bercow accompanied Aitken to and from Conservative Central Office at

Smith Square, where Lolicia and his daughter, Victoria, were present for the speech.

Addressing TV cameras, Aitken denounced as 'wicked lies' claims in *The Guardian* that he had tried to arrange girls for a Saudi prince and his entourage during a business meeting at a health hydro. 'If it falls to me to start a fight to cut out the cancer of bent and twisted journalism in our country with the simple sword of truth and the trusty shield of British fair play, so be it,' he said. 'I am ready for the fight.' Later in April, Bercow issued a writ for defamation against Granada Television for its *World in Action* documentary on Aitken's behalf.[6]

Aitken was under considerable pressure and now had lawsuits pending against the press concerning his private and public conduct. On 5 July, after John Major defeated John Redwood in what he termed a 'Put up or shut up' leadership contest, Aitken resigned from the government before the Prime Minister could carry out a reshuffle of his top team.

In June 1997, when Aitken's libel case against *The Guardian* and Granada reached the High Court, he continued to insist that his wife had paid his bill at the Ritz. *The Guardian* produced evidence that his wife had been in Switzerland, not Paris, at the time in question. His friend Said Ayas, godfather to his daughter and an associate of Prince Mohammed of Saudi Arabia, had in fact paid the bill on his behalf. Aitken would later be jailed for perjury and perverting the course of justice.

Aitken maintains that Bercow knew nothing of the details surrounding what took place in Paris, and insists his adviser had only a very minor involvement in the 'sword of truth' speech: 'He may have helped with the punctuation … He wasn't responsible really for any of the content.'

Bercow wrote letters to Aitken during the latter's prison stay, and one of the first invitations he received after coming out was an invite to the wedding of Bercow and Sally Illman in December 2002. 'Kind is not an adjective that is always applied to John Bercow. Quite a lot of people who are close to him know he can be very kind, very considerate and he was with me,' Aitken says. In 2003, Aitken would repay the favour, not only by inviting him to his own wedding to his second wife, Elizabeth Harris, but by planting the idea of Bercow one day running for the Speakership.

Bercow's employment by Aitken was raised by Tony Blair in the House of Commons in November 1997, shortly after Aitken's libel case collapsed. Deflecting Bercow's question about party donations from Formula 1 mogul Bernie Ecclestone, the new Prime Minister said: 'I am intrigued that the hon. Gentleman should ask such a question as I understand that his last employment was as special adviser to Jonathan Aitken,' he said (incorrectly, as Bercow had held two further posts before joining the Commons in May that year. Tory MPs cried out 'Wrong!' in light of this error).[7]

If the picture of Bercow painted so far is of a careerist, then keeping in touch with Aitken, a disgraced former Cabinet minister, surely bucks that trend. Nor has Bercow dropped Aitken from his list of acquaintances as his own fame has increased. Aitken, who is now an Anglican priest, has held several charity events in Speaker's House with Bercow's sanction. 'Over the years I've asked at least half a dozen times "Would you put this charity on the list?"', and he's done it, turned up, been a good host and said OTT words of kindness about me,' he says. Julian Lewis, Bercow's close friend, explains: 'He won't drop people if they fall on hard times. Jonathan Aitken was a very good example of that.' He adds: 'He regards him highly and doesn't turn his back on people if they suffer a reversal.'

Back in 1995, with Aitken having resigned, Bercow was looking for work. Virginia Bottomley had been moved from the Department of Health to become National Heritage Secretary in Major's July reshuffle. Her previous special adviser, Tony Hockley, was not going with her. 'Major had offered her Transport and she declined. She wanted to go to Heritage, which was called the "Ministry of Fun". I really didn't want to go,' recalls Hockley. 'She then had to find a new special adviser and got stuck with Bercow, who was the only choice, really.'

Hockley and Bercow had encountered each other on the political circuit. They even lived in the same building: Marsham Court in

Westminster. 'In those days, the way politics worked was lunches at think tanks and drinks at think tanks. He was always good company,' Hockley recalls.

> He's a very different person with people he considers inferior to how he behaves with peers. He was always good company, charming, friendly if we passed in the street. All the reports I hear of people who've worked with him or for him is very different … Where we lived in Marsham Court, the porters hated him. It is a friendly 1930s building and you get to know the porters quite well. I think he just had no time for them. It was quite a gossipy building.

Peter Ainsworth, MP for East Surrey, had served as PPS to Aitken before he stood down, and subsequently moved to work with Bottomley. It was Ainsworth who suggested she consider Bercow for the job.

Bercow and Bottomley were far from political kindred spirits: he was an enthusiastic right-wing Thatcherite, while she hailed from the left of the party. 'She was a very old-style small "c", very left-wing Conservative,' says Hockley. 'Bercow was the opposite to that. Also, he was aggressively hunting a seat. So, he wouldn't have given her much time, and she is a very demanding person. It was a 24-hour job working with Virginia.'

The disparity in Bercow and Bottomley's political hinterlands provoked interest from the written press. In covering the appointment, *The Guardian* argued that 'no one at Westminster can imagine why the soaking-wet Mrs Bumley would appoint a bumptious, abrasive libertarian free-marketeer like Mr Bercow, who is said to have both the far-right politics and physical stature of Alan Duncan, but without the attendant personal charm'.[8]

A Conservative MP who became friendly with Bottomley says she asked Bercow for reassurances that he was not planning to stand at the next election. 'I'm perfectly happy to have you, but I want you for a full parliament,' she is alleged to have told Bercow. 'He gave that undertaking at the very time that he was actually looking for other seats. He gave her a bare-faced lie,' claims the MP.

On all accounts, Bottomley, now a Conservative peer, has few good things to say about Bercow. According to a former colleague, Bottomley felt that Bercow 'really got up the nose of the civil servants' and other members of her staff.

Her suspicions about his hopes of entering Parliament were undoubtedly true. With the help of his old mate Julian Lewis, he was about to pull off a political stunt for the ages.

CHAPTER TEN

JULIAN

'This is the best £1,000 I have ever spent.'

John Bercow rang Julian Lewis from a payphone at the University of Essex. It was October 1983, and Bercow was seeking advice on how to take on the Campaign for Nuclear Disarmament.

Along with fellow Tories Edward Leigh and Tony Kerpel, Lewis had founded a small pressure group, the Coalition for Peace Through Security, which was dedicated to countering CND propaganda. Word had reached Bercow of their work on briefing party activists. The Conservative Association at Essex had recently tabled a motion for their student union general meeting calling for a policy of multilateral disarmament, and he wanted Lewis's guidance. 'He seemed very quick on the uptake,' recalls Lewis, who is twelve years Bercow's senior. 'We had some feedback that John had done a very effective performance.'

Their paths crossed again five years later, when Bercow and Lewis attended a Conservative Party training weekend at the University of Nottingham. Bercow had been invited to talk about how to make effective political speeches, while Lewis spoke about how to rebut left-wing propaganda campaigns. This was the first time they had met in person.

The pair got the train back to London together at the end of the conference. For Lewis, a penny had dropped. He turned to Bercow and said: 'Those two presentations went together rather well. How do you feel about us joining forces?' Lewis explains: 'He liked the idea and we discussed it in detail on the way back. After that, we started meeting to work out what the components of such a course would be.'

Lewis had already set up a new company, Policy Research Associates, through which he did much of his consultancy work. In 1989, Bercow and Lewis established the PRA Advanced Speaking and Campaigning Course, which ran one Sunday every month from 1.30 to 6.30 in the afternoon. Around half the courses were carried out in the Athenaeum Club, a members' club on Pall Mall, and the rest in Tory Party HQ at 32 Smith Square. The course cost around £15. Bercow would start with a presentation on speaking and take questions, while Lewis would do similarly about campaigning. Participants would then have to deliver a five-minute speech, prepared under time restrictions, before being critiqued. This would be followed by a press release writing exercise and, finally, there would be a mini-debate on subjects that included the restoration of capital punishment. Many past and present Conservative MPs took part in the course. A future minister says:

Julian talked about the way you make a party conference speech. I remember him describing how the trick was to speak through applause because it gave the impression that you were fighting against the applause to sound even more powerful and strong. He used to use the example of Benn and Scargill, who were very good at that.

After the course ended, a 'bonding session' would take place at the Thames Tandoori in Waterloo. Lewis says: 'Sometimes people would ask us: "Why are you teaching your potential rivals? One day, you might be up against these people for parliamentary seats." We always took the view that you all get further on if you build a network and help each other.'

By the time Lewis and Bercow entered the Commons in 1997, they had trained up nearly 600 Conservative activists. They continued to hold two-hour sessions in Parliament for new Conservative Members on how to be an MP following the 2001 and 2005 general elections. A former minister who took part says: 'It was on how to be effective in the Chamber; it started with basics, what is the difference between a statement and an Urgent Question, how Question Time worked and so on. It was quite good.' When Bercow became Speaker in 2009, Charles Walker, another close political ally, carried out the induction sessions with Lewis.

After their first meeting, Lewis was a regular fixture throughout Bercow's political endeavours. When Bercow stood to be the Tory candidate in Bristol South, Lewis threw tricky questions at him as part of his preparation. For some time, Lewis had put his own parliamentary aspirations on ice. He had contested Swansea West at the 1983 general election, during which the Labour Party had stood on a commitment to unilateral disarmament. An expert in all things defence, he was in his element campaigning on a pro-multilateralism stance. But as Labour changed its position on nuclear weapons, and the issue quietened down in the public consciousness, Lewis hesitated over whether being an MP was right for him. Bercow, however, was 'applying all over the place', he jokes.

The merging of Kensington and Chelsea proved an alluring mix for wannabe Tory MPs ahead of the 1997 election. The constituency was set to become one of the safest Tory seats in the country. Among those to put themselves forward in November 1995 were Theresa May, Philip Hammond and Bercow. Gary Mond, whom Bercow had met in Scotland at the 1987 election, was a member of the Kensington and Chelsea Conservative Association and was chair of its constituency party. As a result, he found himself on the fifteen-person strong selection committee that included David Cameron and Mark Field, both of whom would become MPs in 2001. Bercow was giving a consummate performance. 'His answers were brilliant on the economy, on tax, on the National Health Service, on education – anything you can imagine. He even gave a brilliant answer to a tricky question on what to do about the prison population,' Mond recalls.

There was time for one more question. The chair of the meeting had to choose between Cameron and a local councillor, both of whom had raised their hands. Mond says:

> I bet my bottom dollar that the future Prime Minister's question would have been political; it would have been something that John could have batted for six. He would have got through to the final round and he might have been the MP for Kensington and Chelsea. But no, the association chairman asked the local worthy.

The councillor collected his thoughts. 'Mr Bercow, I looked at your CV and I see you enjoy going to the cinema. Please could you tell us, what was the most recent film you went to see?' Bercow floundered. 'The future Speaker of the House of Commons fell apart. He couldn't answer the question,' remembers Mond. 'It shows how single-minded he was about politics because politics was his life. He couldn't relate to anything outside politics. It was hilarious.'

Bercow called Mond that evening and asked: 'What are my chances?' Mond replied: 'Well, you wrecked it on your last question.' Despite the gaffe, Cameron put Bercow down to go forward to the final six, according to Mond, who was sitting next to him. 'I got a glimpse of his ballot paper and I saw a cross against Bercow's name.' Despite the support of the future Prime Minister, Bercow did not make the cut.

Bercow, who had made the last twenty in North Wiltshire, missed out on selection there too. James Gray, whom he would go on to work with at lobbying agency Westminster Strategy months later,[1] was appointed the candidate in January 1986. Bercow also lost out in North East Bedfordshire in October 1995, having at one point looked set for a guaranteed spot in the Commons before Sir Nicholas Lyell, the Attorney General, joined the race after losing a selection in his neighbouring seat of Mid Bedfordshire.

Bercow even found himself in the final six for West Worthing alongside Virginia Bottomley's husband Peter, the MP for Eltham, who would go on to win the seat. This was all the more remarkable as Bercow was still working for Bottomley at the time. In his tribute to Bercow as he stepped down from the chair, Peter Bottomley noted: 'I explained to my constituents that had they chosen you rather than me in Worthing West in 1996, they could have been represented by the Speaker for the last ten years.'[2]

By February 1996, Bercow had made the semi-final of Surrey Heath and the final of Buckingham. Both constituencies were prized assets; being selected for either meant all-but-guaranteed entrance into the Palace of Westminster. He visited Michael Keegan to try out his pitch and test his opening line: 'I may be a little guy, but I've got a big ambition.'

There was just one major issue in his way: the selection meetings were taking place on the same night. 'He was absolutely furious that the candidates' department couldn't have avoided a clash,' Lewis says. Bercow needed a miracle, or a well-executed plan, to make both. Lewis posed an idea. 'You could always try to use a helicopter?'

Lewis brought in his assistant, Nina Karsov, to help devise a strategy. On his end, Bercow persuaded the party bosses to ensure that he would be first up to speak in Surrey Heath and last on in Buckingham.

A chauffeur from a luxury car firm was waiting while Bercow delivered his speech for the Surrey Heath event. At 7.35 p.m., Lewis, Bercow and his then girlfriend, Louise Cumber, jumped into the car. They drove fifteen minutes to Blackbushe Airfield, where a five-seater Twin Squirrel helicopter was waiting. The passengers put on earmuffs and strapped themselves in. It was pitch black and there was snow on the ground. Thankfully for Bercow, it had stopped snowing sometime earlier. During the journey, an enthralled Bercow turned to Lewis and exclaimed: 'Julian, this is the best £1,000 I have ever spent.'

Waiting on a farm in Finmere was Karsov, who had already scoped out the journey to the school where the Buckingham selection was being held. Two cars with indicators flashing and headlights on full beam, one belonging to Karsov and the other to the farmer, marked out a makeshift helicopter landing zone.

Bercow and co. exited the helicopter and jumped into Karsov's car. There was one problem: it had all gone too smoothly. They were pulling up to the selection meeting too early. 'We drove around the block a couple of times to add to the drama of John's entry. Otherwise, there was a danger that it would look as if he made it without any haste at all,' says Lewis.

As planned, Bercow began his speech by saying: 'Just because I am a little chap, it doesn't mean I haven't got a big ambition.' According to Lewis, Bercow decided to ham up the evening's events. Watching was Howard Flight, another contestant for the Buckingham seat and another destined for the Commons. Bercow said:

> Ladies and gentlemen, you can imagine how distraught I was to discover that I had to choose between being here or being in Surrey Heath, two such wonderful Conservative-held seats. How did I resolve it? Did I do it this way, did I do it that way, no I did it by the surname of one of the other candidates here tonight – by flight!

Flight, who is now a Conservative peer, says: 'Fair game. A lot of the old ladies thought that was wonderful. I didn't hold that against him in any way.' Bercow beat Flight to the nomination. His dream of becoming an MP was now about to become reality. Lewis, who was competing for New Forest East the following week, was not only thrilled for his close friend; he was also relieved.

> I knew that only a few days later, the process of selecting for New Forest East was going to begin, and we were both on the longlist. I thought: 'If I can't get this blighter selected, I'm not going to have a chance,' so it worked out as a win–win situation.[3]

The victory meant that Bercow's time working for Virginia Bottomley, which ran from August 1995 to February 1996, had to come to an end.

Bercow's selection in Buckingham showed how integral his close political relationship with Lewis had become. He was able to return the favour by helping to write the speech that secured Lewis the nomination in New Forest East. The best friends were finally on their way to Westminster.

'In the course of working together, we formed a political partnership. We firmly believed that, if you promote one another, you both get further than just by striving individually.'

CHAPTER ELEVEN

ROTTWEILER

'Personally, I'd rather have a sex life.'

John Bercow would sit with his arms poised on the seatback, his shoulders hunched forward and his foot resting on the bench in front. In the brief but vital moments after another MP would finish their speech, he would kick the back of the bench to catch the Speaker's attention, while springing himself upright. Occasionally, he would be too eager and move too early. He would retreat back into his brace position, ready to pounce at the opportune moment.

Bercow, a permanent fixture in the Commons, was an absolutely prolific backbencher. He positioned himself three rows back on the opposition benches, just behind the despatch box. Along with another of his 1997 intake, Graham Brady, they had decided that the position represented the best vantage point for heckling a minister without the Speaker being able to identify who the culprits were. 'Pathetic,' he would exclaim at a Labour minister. 'You're useless!' he once barked at Gordon Brown, the Chancellor. 'God, what is that supposed to mean?'

In his first parliament, Bercow would be referred to in the media as 'the new stormtrooper', the 'have-a-go Norman Wisdom of the Tory backbenches', the 'Tories' bouncing bomb', a 'semi-automatic right-winger', the Tories' 'jumping jack', John 'Howling Wolf' Bercow, the 'Doberman of the Tory benches', and the 'erstwhile Pitbull biter of the right'.

Labour MPs referred to him as 'boing' for the way he would shoot up and down.

This reputation was hard-won. Right from the get-go, Bercow was ready to ensure he used to the fullest the opportunity of his life. He was a key member of the late-night crew of Conservative MPs, led by Eric Forth, the MP for Bromley and Chislehurst, who would keep Labour ministers working into the early hours through filibuster and scrutiny. Also in this coterie of wind-up merchants were fellow newcomers Brady, James Gray, Julian Lewis and Desmond Swayne, and more battle-weary MPs such as Christopher Chope, David Maclean and Gerald Howarth.

'Eric was the kind of leader of the gang and a past master. Once, he was debating some benighted piece of local government legislation, he'd been going for an hour and a half when he uttered the famous phrase, "Now, Mr Deputy Speaker, turning to the bill itself,"' says a Tory MP.

When Forth, who had visited the internal Parliament post office, turned up with reams of paper to a debate, Labour whips pulled the business in expectation of more filibustering. 'They thought this was his speech, and they didn't move whatever they were going to move. So, you win the battle without ever having to fight,' a backbencher says.

The protagonists deployed long-winded speeches about the legislation or discussion at hand, and used a tactic known as 'in-flight refuelling', where one MP would intervene to push their colleague down another potential avenue of debate, prolonging their speech. 'Can I tempt my honourable friend to consider...' was a typical refrain. On one notorious occasion, a filibuster over the Disqualifications Bill lasted through the night, prompting Prime Minister's Questions to be cancelled the next day, sullying Labour's 1,000 days in power celebrations. Fed up with the tactic, Labour MPs pressured Tony Blair to curb parliamentary hours. A report by the modernisation committee called for strict timetabling of debates and a 10 p.m. finishing time. Bercow commented: 'I would be delighted if we sat for forty weeks instead of thirty. But there's a part-time tendency among Labour Members who can't wait to get home to the chianti and olives. Some have wandered into the Commons as one wanders into the wrong bus queue.'¹

Such was Bercow's love for the Commons that Labour MP Stephen Pound, during one of Bercow's speeches in a debate on sports, heckled: 'Personally, I'd rather have a sex life.'² One former Conservative whip says of Bercow: 'At that stage he didn't have much of a life. Before he got married and all the rest of it, he was one of those people you would keep an eye on because they're so obsessed with politics and everything else.'

One of Bercow's first tasks as an MP was to choose a horse to back in the race to become the next Tory leader. In one of the most transform-ative elections of modern times, Blair's Labour Party had romped to a landslide victory, winning 418 seats to the Conservatives' 165. The Tory majority in Bercow's Buckingham constituency reduced from 19,791 to 12,386. Several Cabinet ministers lost their seats, including Michael Por-tillo, whom Bercow had come to greatly admire. John Major resigned a day later.

Behind the scenes, the contenders for Tory leader were battling to win over the Portillistas. Ken Clarke, William Hague, Michael Howard, John Redwood and Peter Lilley had all put themselves forward. Bercow initial-ly supported Lilley, the former Social Security Secretary, who launched his campaign with a slogan of 'Reunite, Rebuild, Renew'. '[It] shows that his judgement has changed a lot,' reflects Lilley, who remembers Bercow as a 'great admirer' of Enoch Powell. 'As things were going on, he would do an imitation of Enoch Powell's inimitable voice of what Enoch would have said in the circumstances.'

After the first round of voting, both Howard and Lilley pulled out and backed Hague, urging their supporters to follow suit. But that evening Bercow appeared on *Newsnight* and revealed he was supporting Red-wood. 'I'm sorry that Peter wasn't more successful, but I think John … is upright, direct, capable, has leadership quality … He's got a grasp, he's got a grip, he can win,' he said. Asked about Lilley's support for Hague, Bercow set out his stall as his own man. 'A leadership contender, once he withdraws from the contest, has relatively little influence over the direction in which his former supporters choose to go.'[3]

Though Redwood had surprised in the first round, he finished a distant third at the second ballot. Not for the first time, and hardly for the last, Bercow had failed to back the winning candidate. In a bid to win over Eurosceptic MPs, Clarke agreed to form an alliance with Redwood. The agreement would see Redwood become shadow Chancellor if Clarke won the nomination. Hague dismissed the alliance as 'a deal, not a solution'.[4] Many supporters of Redwood were similarly unconvinced – Clarke was well-known for his Europhilia – and backed Hague. 'People simply didn't buy the idea of the alliance,' said Bercow on the day of the final result.[5] Hague won by eighteen votes in the third ballot on 19 June, and Bercow kept his counsel as to whom he had supported.

Bercow's backing for Redwood paid off, however, when the former minister was made shadow Secretary of State for Trade and Industry. Bercow was one of four new MPs to take an informal role for the team, including Oliver Letwin, Theresa May and Andrew Lansley. He took on his duties assiduously, becoming a thorn in the side of Redwood's opposite number, Margaret Beckett, and her successor, Peter Mandelson. During a point of order on 10 November 1997, Bercow asked Betty Boothroyd, the Speaker, how he could find out the number of hours Beckett had spent in her department during the summer recess. In a minor rebuke, Boothroyd told him: 'It is not for ministers to be accountable to the House for the hours they spend in their departments. They are accountable at the despatch box for policy decisions.' Boothroyd noted that Bercow had got the 'bit between his teeth' and was 'very interested in procedure'.[6]

Midway through one Departmental Questions, Bercow was heckled by Labour MPs as a 'poison dwarf' when he rose to attack Beckett. He branded her speech on the government's approach to trade 'downmarket drivel from a senior member of the Cabinet', adding: 'I very much hope over a period of time, after due practice and several rehearsals, she will be capable of producing something better for the consumption of this House.'[7]

During a more tempestuous interaction, Bercow was given a ticking-off by Boothroyd when he questioned the impartiality of Greg Dyke, who was being considered as a candidate to become Director General of the BBC. He asked Beckett, by now Leader of the Commons, whether Dyke 'would be a most unsuitable occupant of that high office in view of the substantial financial donations that he has made over a period to the Labour Party'.[8] Boothroyd intervened: 'When we use the names of people outside, who have very great difficulty in responding, we should be extremely careful and consider our responsibilities as well as the privileges we have here.'

Despite this inauspicious start, Beckett's relationship with Bercow would blossom. Amid rumours that she was due for the chop from the Cabinet, Bercow said he hoped she would remain as Commons Leader 'for a long time to come', adding: 'She has undoubtedly discharged her obligations with great charm, style and dexterity.'[9] On a slightly more embarrassing occasion in March 2001, Bercow tried to illustrate his knowledge of football to Beckett, a supporter of Derby County, by saying that the team played at the Baseball Ground. 'The honourable gentleman is out of date. We have a brand-new football stadium, Pride Park, at which we hope to hold an international later this year, so the honourable gentleman will be able to see it on television,' she said.[10] Beckett would go on to play a key role in Bercow's future when Speaker of the Commons.

Though Boothroyd would occasionally put Bercow in his place – such as when he heckled 'Where's Blair?' when the Prime Minister sent Foreign Secretary Robin Cook to field questions in his stead – relations generally appeared to be cordial. The same cannot be said of her successor, Michael Martin.

After Boothroyd announced she was standing down in the summer of 2000, Bercow, during a point of order, called for a secret ballot to elect the Speaker. The election should be a matter for the legislature and not the executive, he argued. However, by the time the changes were debated, Bercow had performed another volte-face. 'We do not have the right to protect ourselves in that way. I go for an open vote. We should explain our decisions and defend them, and then be prepared to be judged by them,' he told MPs.[11]

Bercow was one of eight Conservative MPs to oppose Martin's anointing as Speaker on 23 October 2000, while the vast majority of Tory backbenchers did not vote in the division. A number of Conservative MPs appeared to test Martin early on. When Bercow heckled Gordon Brown as a 'conman', Martin called on him to withdraw. 'Of course, Mr Speaker, I withdraw it immediately,' Bercow sarcastically responded.[12] Commentators suspected that Martin began to overlook the bouncing Bercow in the Chamber. During another skirmish, Bercow raised a point of order to say that it would be helpful if certain members did not distract Speaker Martin by standing by the chair and talking to him. He suggested that MPs needed the full attention of the Speaker 'and of your intellectual resources'.

In an interview with *Freedom Today* magazine in October 2001, Bercow said he did not think Martin 'was of a calibre to be elected Speaker of the House of Commons'.[13] Having contravened the tradition of not criticising a sitting Speaker, Bercow said there is 'a difference between respecting the office and esteeming its occupant'. Speaker Martin, who was offensively referred to as 'Gorbals Mick' by certain factions of the press, came from even more humble beginnings than Bercow. He grew up in post-war Glasgow and worked as a sheet metal worker.

Bercow's maiden speech, watched by his mother Brenda in the public gallery, came early on 4 July 1997. It was quintessential early-day Bercow. There was an Enoch Powell quotation, praise for Margaret Thatcher, and a stinging venom in his critique of the newly elected Labour government. Attacking Gordon Brown, who had revealed his first Budget, Bercow said:

> He may prove to be a better Chancellor than some of us anticipate, but to date, given a choice between advancing the British competitive interest and appeasing the Labour vested interest, the right hon. Gentleman

has rushed helter-skelter, with barely a pause for breath, in the direction of the latter.[14]

While some take time to bed in at Parliament, Bercow, well informed from his time working in and around Westminster, started as he meant to go on. He began using the parliamentary tools at his disposal, tabling an early day motion on 8 July over Lord Simon, a minister in Beckett's department, who had failed to declare £2 million shares in BP on the register of Lords' interests.

He also sought out advice. He visited David Davis, then chair of the Public Accounts Committee, to try out questions he was going to put to ministers. 'I taught him what I always called the German question,' Davis says. The German question is 'a tactic whereby you ask the question in such a way that the minister only knows what the question is in the last two or three words … He'd sit there, and we would rework his question to make it more difficult to answer.'

His early efforts saw him earn plaudits in the media, with *The Time*s referring to him as an 'effective political bruiser in the Commons and on television'.[15] He was an avid user of parliamentary written questions, regularly submitting dozens of probes every day to ministers. But his use of the tool came in for criticism over the number of questions he was asking. Bercow, who argued his questions had revealed 'damaging' facts for the government, vowed to continue holding ministers to account.[16]

Bercow's questions had indeed exposed several revealing statistics, such as the amount the Foreign Office spent on newspapers, magazines and periodicals, and the Home Office's use of private finance initiative consultants. But the sheer volume irritated the government and prompted the *Daily Mirror* to take the inflammatory decision to reach out to a psychology professor at the University of Manchester Institute of Science and Technology, who described Bercow as 'obsessional'.[17] Bercow refused to comment to the paper about the matter thereafter.

On 10 July 2002, the Press Association reported that Bercow had asked

4,382 written questions at a cost to the taxpayer of £565,278 since the previous June. David Maclean, the Tory Chief Whip, 'had a word' with Bercow about his endeavours. Tory MP Sir Nicholas Winterton, chair of the Procedure Committee, said:

> On one day he handed in something like 350 questions. He's probably the most articulate man in the Commons and has a huge ability with words but why he feels it necessary to table this number of questions, I do not know. I believe it is an abuse of the system and causes problems in dealing with MPs' questions promptly and thoroughly.[18]

Labour MP Kevin Brennan dubbed Bercow the 'half-million-pound man' and accused him of an 'obsessive compulsive exegesis'.[19]

Bercow tried to recruit a former Conservative special adviser part-time to write his written parliamentary questions. 'He was offering to pay me a retainer to write a certain number for him each month or each week,' says the source. The former spad, who insists the request was not 'morally dodgy', turned down the offer.

Notwithstanding the relentless nature of his work, Bercow proved one of the most potent forces in the new intake of Tory MPs. His first use of what has now become his patented phrase came on 4 November 1997 during a debate on student finance. Noticing that David Blunkett, the Education Secretary, was muttering as he spoke, Bercow chided: 'The Secretary of State may chunter from a sedentary position, as has become his wont.'[20] Bercow said later: 'I inhaled that expression pretty early.'[21]

Bercow also took it upon himself to be a thorn in the side of Tony Blair. After it emerged that Blair had spent the Christmas holidays in the Seychelles, Bercow challenged the Prime Minister to publish rules governing publicly funded travel by ministers' partners. Blair said Bercow reminded him of David Shaw, a former MP 'whose hallmark ... was to be nasty and ineffectual in equal quantities'.[22] When Blair claimed to have been the first European leader to be interviewed on the internet, Bercow listed the foreign leaders who had beaten him to the punch. This was the latest in a 'long line of bogus boasts', he added.[23]

Though his abrasiveness and omnipresence in the Chamber drew the ire of his opponents – a jibe went around the Commons about who put the 'ow' on his surname – Bercow was recognised for his talents. On 25 November 1998, he, along with Labour MP Dr Lynne Jones, won Backbencher to Watch at *The Spectator* awards. As for MPs' bafflement about his love of the Commons, he said: 'I find it extraordinary that members of this House spend years and decades seeking election to it and having secured election seem reluctant to spend any time in the Chamber.'[24]

Angela Eagle recalls Bercow as someone who would 'never say suitcase when portmanteau would do'. Chris Leslie, a Labour MP who would go on to quit the party in 2019, went on a parliamentary trip to Canada with Maria Eagle, his colleague, and Tory backbenchers Forth, Howarth and Bercow. 'We thought, "Oh my god, we're going away with some really right-wing Conservatives." But actually, they were quite fun at a personal level because they didn't suffer fools gladly and they were energetic and all the rest of it,' Leslie says.

Not everyone was taken with Bercow's approach on the Conservative benches. 'I found John mercurial. He had the most enormous mood swings from being charming to suddenly becoming really vicious,' says one MP at the time, who recently stood down. 'There's obviously a personality problem here. He and Shaun Woodward were the two Tory MPs from my intake who launched the most vicious personal attacks on government ministers and government MPs.'

Bercow was also on the receiving end of some unfortunate abuse in his early days in Parliament. Some MPs would shout 'Taxi!' when they passed Bercow in the corridors, in reference to his father's job.[25] Multiple sources say that Nicholas Soames, the grandson of Winston Churchill, would refer to Bercow as 'Berkoff' in evocation of his Jewish heritage. One MP says:

He kept calling him 'Berkovski, Berkoff, Berkowitch' and stuff, which I thought was not on. Bercow took it as antisemitism. I don't think Soames is antisemitic – I think he's anti anybody who's not like him. If you don't shoot down nice attractive animals, if you don't like creating total carnage, then you're not like him.

A whip at the time adds: '[Soames] used to call Bercow "Berkoff". In today's world, that is thought of as antisemitism.' When asked, Soames described the allegations of antisemitism as 'total absolute rubbish', adding: 'I have nothing else to say about such idiotic bullshit.' Bercow declined to comment on the claims.

In November 2002, the *Mail on Sunday* reported that Bercow grew angry after a Conservative MP repeatedly greeted him with 'Hello, Jew boy'. 'It's only a tease, Berkoff,' the MP said. 'No, it's not,' Bercow replied. 'You're an antisemitic ****.'[26]

Bercow later recalled:

In twenty-two years, I never experienced antisemitism from a member of the Labour Party. But I did experience antisemitism from members of the Conservative Party … I remember a member saying, 'If I had my way, Berkoff, people like you wouldn't be allowed in this place.' And I said, 'Sorry, when you say people like me, do you mean lower-class or Jewish?' To which he replied, 'Both.'[27]

Bercow, who possesses powers of recall few can only dream about, would memorise his speeches by heart. 'Sally thinks that I sometimes forget things that I ought to remember and that I remember things that I ought to forget, but for political things I've got quite a good memory,' he told an interviewer in 2012.[28] In his eyes, a decent memory is a prerequisite for the Speakership: 'You have to know who's who and what's what and to remember in what order to proceed.'[29] After an election, Bercow would set aside three days to learn the names and constituencies of those newly elected to the Houses of Parliament.

Though the words were effectively painted on the inside of his eyelids, Bercow would have the text of his speeches nearby in case his memory bucked the habit of a lifetime and failed him. In knowledge of this, Nicholas Soames once took it upon himself to sit on top of Bercow's papers while taking his seat in the Commons.[30]

In those days, Bercow's political views occupied vastly different territory to where he would end up. A vocal Eurosceptic and opponent of joining the euro, as we will discover in later chapters, Bercow also initially opposed the introduction of the minimum wage, arguing that it would destroy jobs. Bercow sat on the Commons committee examining the policy and took part in a marathon sixteen-and-a-half-hour sitting (the first all-nighter of the 1997 parliament) after Labour whips decided to pursue a war of attrition, keeping MPs in place to make progress. Less than two years later, Bercow was performing a mea culpa on the minimum wage. 'My mother always said it was quite a good idea, and I probably should have listened to her at an earlier stage,' he said.[31]

This was not his only change of heart. Bercow stunned the Commons on 10 February 2000 by announcing that he had been 'wrong' for previously voting against reducing the age of consent for gay sex to sixteen (first in June 1998 and subsequently in January, February and March 1999). He had agonised over the decision; a Tory backbencher who voted for the move at the first time of asking was approached by Bercow ahead of the 2000 vote. 'When you voted as you did, did you have an awful lot of problems with your association?' Bercow asked the backbencher. 'To be frank, John, I don't think any of them agreed with me, but no, it wasn't a big issue either,' they replied. 'I thought it was a little insight into the calculation that was going on at that point,' comments the MP.

Bernard Jenkin saw Bercow pacing outside the Chamber. 'Are you going to speak in the debate?' he asked. 'I don't know, I don't know what to do,' replied Bercow. 'I've always been opposed to the equalisation of the age of consent and I think I've changed my mind.' Jenkin told him: 'That's fine because that's what the Chamber's all about. You get in there and explain why you changed your mind. Make the speech of your life and people will respect you for it and you'll do it very well.'

Bercow obliged. 'I have changed my mind on this subject, and I owe it to myself, the House and my constituents to explain why,' he began. 'The words "I was wrong" do not readily trip off my tongue, but that is what I believe. I think I was mistaken to vote for the status quo last time, and I intend to vote for the bill, for reform and, I think, for progress.'

Insisting that he had not 'fallen prey' to political correctness, which he 'abhorred', Bercow told the House that he had 'reflected upon the issues' and, while he still backed Section 28 of the Local Government Act 1988, which prohibited schools from promoting homosexuality, he felt he was duty bound to take into account the interests of his constituents who were themselves gay. His reasons for changing his mind were threefold: one, the status quo provided discrimination without benefit; two, the lead taken in European counties such as Germany had shown no damaging consequences (though he added: 'I yield to no one in my Euroscepticism'); and thirdly, that experts in medical and children's charities and members of the medical profession supported the change.

Noting that he was 'almost certain to incur the wrath of many of the people whom I admire most in politics', and would be accompanied in the voting lobbies by some 'whom I respect least in politics', Bercow said he had a 'duty in this regard'. At this point, Labour MP Claire Ward intervened to say: 'Following what he has said so far, we shall look on him in an entirely new light. We only hope that he will not do this too often; if he does, we shall feel most uncomfortable in the future.'

The bashful Bercow thanked Ward for the warm words but added: 'No doubt I have already inflicted massive political damage on myself, and I do not want to add to it.'

Bercow had partially upset some of the MPs he had long been affiliated with, such as Teresa Gorman, the MP for Billericay whose London home had been open to Bercow more than a decade earlier. Desmond Swayne, the Tory backbencher, said: 'The longer we drag this out, the more danger there is of seeing other spectacular and awful conversions such as that of my hon. Friend the Member for Buckingham, so I do not intend to detain the House for long.' Bercow also enjoyed exchanges with Gerald Howarth, who along with Swayne was another of the late-night brigade.[32]

The night of 10 February 2000 is a key date in Bercow's political calendar. While he had been at pains over the decision to support equalising the age of consent, in making the widely praised speech, he drew in new supporters from unlikely corners. Matthew Parris, a former Conservative MP and columnist at *The Times*, wrote the next day: 'In disappointing easy assumptions about himself, [Bercow] rose as fast in what is rather grandly called "the opinion of the House" as, in a nine-minute speech, I have ever seen a backbencher do.' Labour MPs such as Ward and Angela Eagle, herself a lesbian, took note of Bercow's conversion.

As ever with Bercow, once he had made up his mind on a political viewpoint, he threw himself wholeheartedly behind the cause. It would set in train his journey towards becoming a socially liberal Conservative – one that seemed a far cry from his early days in the Commons Chamber.

CHAPTER TWELVE

BACK TO FRONT

'He became more Catholic than the Pope about politically correct issues.'

After two years as leader, William Hague wanted to blood some of the younger talent on the Tory benches. Many of the 1997 intake would play prominent roles in British politics – the likes of Philip Hammond and Oliver Letwin spring to mind – and perhaps none more so than John Bercow and Theresa May. On 16 June 1999, Hague appointed May shadow Education Secretary, and Bercow a spokesman on Education and Employment (with Tim Boswell and James Clappison making up the rest of the shadow Education team).

Bercow went about his work with typical enthusiasm, robustly attacking his opposite numbers on the Labour benches. When David Blunkett committed the government to a policy of full employment in the wake of positive unemployment figures, Bercow responded: 'David Blunkett is a traditional socialist and is using these figures to change the government's objective. It is dangerous in the extreme to use good news to raise expectations which are not likely to be achieved.'[1] Bercow also warned against the 'dumbing down' of GCSEs and led the Conservative fight to preserve the UK's grammar schools. 'Tony Blair's government are playing educational vandalism, and we will fight to stop them. Our children's education is far more important than Tony Blair's dogma.'[2]

A source close to the team says:

John was a very hard-working spokesman. He put a lot of energy into it. But he didn't put a lot of work into his research. Basically, he was handed stuff and he just went with it. He didn't go away and tried to create his own lines to take; he expected the lines to take to be given to him. When we were in opposition, we had to do our own thinking, and John never thought that was part of his job.

While Bercow was acclimatising to frontbench life, he was not happy with every decision his party leader was making. He was among the critical Conservative voices to express their disappointment after Hague sacked John Redwood as shadow Environment Secretary. At a dinner of the right-wing 92 Group, attended by Hague, Bercow used a question-and-answer session to voice his concern.[3]

His speaking out went unpunished, and on 28 July 2000, Bercow was appointed a shadow Home Affairs spokesman, No. 3 in Ann Widdecombe's team. The news prompted outrage from other parties, who noted his previous involvement with the Monday Club. When Robin Cook, the Leader of the Commons, cited Bercow's appointment as evidence that Hague was legitimising racism and failing to stand up to extremism in his party, Bercow went on the offensive: 'He is the most arrogant, pompous and unsuitable Foreign Secretary in living memory … These are views I held when I was a teenager and I don't hold now,' he raged.[4]

Bercow's willingness to go after the Labour Party was well known. For this reason, Michael Ancram, the chairman of the Tory Party, approached Bercow two weeks after his appointment to discuss launching an attack on Cherie Blair, barrister and wife of the Prime Minister, who had written an article in the *Daily Telegraph* about the incorporation of the European Convention on Human Rights into British law. Conservative Central Office had been keeping a dossier of Cherie's public pronouncements for some time. Bercow accused Cherie of breaking a 'long-standing convention' that Prime Ministers' spouses do not use their position to promote their own political agenda, saying: 'It is unclear whether Cherie's end goal is to be Lord Chancellor or whether she is happy to direct policy from behind the throne. People in Britain will not put up with anyone who thinks they can be an unaccountable cross between First Lady and Lady Macbeth.'[5]

The outrage was swift. Labour MP Fraser Kemp described the 'extreme and unpleasant' attack as 'unwarranted'.[6] Bercow confirmed that he had been asked to make the statement by Ancram. 'I was chosen to do this. I am very happy to do it,' he said.[7] Hague, the wife of the Tory leader, was also angry with the remarks. 'She may have cavilled, I suspect,' Bercow conceded.[8] He admitted the attack had landed badly. 'I don't think it struck a chord with the public,' he said. 'It backfired because the people who agreed with me were anti the Blairs to start with and it didn't convince many others – I agree it might even have alienated them.'[9]

The comments on Cherie were a far cry from the Bercow we know today. Firstly, his unfavourable reference to the First Lady, who at this point was Hillary Clinton, jars with his subsequent enthusiasm for the twice US presidential hopeful. His criticism of Cherie for having political views also cuts across his enduring defence of his wife Sally for airing her own opinions. Most striking is the way in which Bercow took on board the reaction to what he said. Frontbench life would not always agree with him, as we shall soon find out, and having enthusiastically volunteered his services to deliver the remarks, perhaps it was a key lesson about the pitfalls of collective responsibility. The pushback that followed must also have registered; Bercow subsequently became more outspoken about the party's record on women and diversity.

* * *

If you want to hear unvarnished views from MPs, head to the fringes at party conferences. The events, hosted by think tanks, pressure groups, charities and other organisations, offer a chance for politicians to speak more freely. At Bournemouth in October 2000, Bercow decided to show a bit more skin. He warned that the Tories had 'helped to confirm an impression that at best the Conservative Party was indifferent and at worst was hostile' to black and Asian people. While acknowledging that there was more diversity in the Tory candidates for the next election, he noted that the progress had been 'modest', adding: 'I'm fed up of hearing people on selection committees saying that they are all in favour of it, but that it won't happen here. I am fully accepting culpability on behalf of our party for an unsatisfactory record.'[10]

Bercow would continue the charge on matters relating to diversity. When Michael Portillo, the shadow Chancellor, got an earful over his support for inclusiveness at a meeting of the Thatcherite group No Turning Back, prompting him to walk out and later quit the group, Bercow came to his defence: 'A lot of people on the right are allergic to the word "inclusive". But we cannot go on talking in language that alienates minorities. Conservatives have a message to get across. We have to find ways to do it that don't make us look as if we're foaming at the mouth.'[11]

Bercow also showed early signs of realising that the Conservative Party was a long way from the electorate, noting: 'Perhaps we gave people too many reasons not to like us.'[12]

There were still strong traces of his former self, however: Bercow continued to attack pro-EU 'federasts' at the BBC[13] – a slur that was favoured by Jean-Marie Le Pen, president of the far-right National Front – and would target his Labour opponents in typically uncompromising fashion.

He was also ingratiating himself with Ann Widdecombe, his boss on the shadow Home Affairs team, which included David Lidington and Oliver Heald. 'He was a good colleague; I was always got on well with him,' says Widdecombe. 'I never knew him to brief against what I was saying or anything like that.' But Bercow's struggles with sticking to the script emerged on 10 November, when he said that a 'vast clampdown' on cannabis was unrealistic, in a rebuke to the more strident Widdecombe, who had declared a zero-tolerance policy on soft drugs a month earlier. 'The idea that the police should raid every home in the land looking for dope-smokers is transparently absurd,' Bercow told the *New Statesman*.[14] Despite the public disagreement, Bercow made it to the 2001 election unscathed.

*   *   *

Twenty years after becoming secretary of its immigration and repatriation committee, John Bercow was preparing to call for the Monday Club to be disassociated from the Conservative Party.

In the wake of another bruising election defeat, the summer of 2001 brought with it a Tory leadership contest. William Hague had resigned after the party performed poorly on 7 June, picking up just 166 seats, an improvement of one on its total in 1997. Bercow found himself successfully re-elected with an increased majority of 13,325. Michael Portillo, who had returned to Parliament in November 1999 after losing his seat two years earlier, was top choice for MPs during the first ballot on 10 July. Ahead of the third ballot, Bercow approached his close friend Julian Lewis, who was supporting Iain Duncan Smith, about lending his vote to Portillo. 'Iain is bound to get to the last two anyway,' he encouraged. Lewis replied: 'I'm sorry, John, but I can have no guarantee that that would be the outcome.'

In the event, Duncan Smith beat Portillo into second place by one vote, with Ken Clarke ahead by five on fifty-nine. Lewis still counts himself lucky that he did not heed Bercow's advice. Portillo would later support unilateral disarmament – a cause Lewis had spent the best part of his adult life campaigning against. 'I would have been responsible for installing as Leader of the Opposition a man who would have removed our adherence to the one thing I regarded as essential to our national security,' he says.

Bercow now went out to bat for Duncan Smith. Speaking on ITV's *GMTV*, he said that while Ken Clarke was a 'seriously heavy hitter', he could not be Conservative leader because he was a 'Europhile who seeks to lead a Eurosceptic party'.[15] At a party meeting in Aylesbury, Bercow said he was supporting Duncan Smith's campaign as he introduced Clarke.

'But to provide some balance, I should say that my mother's backing Ken,' he told the audience.[16]

Seen as the frontrunner among party members, Duncan Smith had been at pains to play down his right-wing credentials in order to placate the Conservative left. His efforts were undermined when the Monday Club came out in support for his campaign.[17] The problem was compounded when it emerged that several active supporters of Duncan Smith, including Bercow, were current or former members of the right-wing group. Responding to the Monday Club's endorsement of his rival, Clarke mused: 'I wasn't remotely surprised to see the Monday Club backing Iain Duncan Smith. He puts up a spokesman, John Bercow, on air who was an activist in the Monday Club. They can't disown the Monday Club when the Monday Club has supplied enthusiasts on their behalf.'[18]

Duncan Smith, who accused Clarke of orchestrating a smear campaign against him, was hit by another blow when he was forced to sack Edgar Griffin, the vice-president of his campaign, for publicly sympathising with the BNP, which was led by his son, Nick Griffin.

Within ten days of the Monday Club endorsement, Duncan Smith vowed to hold an audit in which Tory members would be asked about their past and present membership of political organisations. 'If anyone is a member of, or involved with, the BNP, then there is no room for them,' he said.[19] The names of MPs with links to right-wing groups were then removed from the list of supporters on Duncan Smith's website, including that of Andrew Hunter, the deputy chairman of the Monday Club.

Following his election on 13 September, the new Tory leader was under pressure to follow through on his threat to purge the Tory Party of activists affiliated with hard-right organisations. In the meantime, though, he had a shadow Cabinet to appoint, and Bercow was rewarded for his loyalty with his first frontbench role, as shadow Chief Secretary to the Treasury.

The former Portillista was well on his journey from the right of the party towards its centre. In an interview with *Freedom Today* magazine, a publication run by the libertarian pressure group the Freedom Association, Bercow seized the chance to speak out. 'The time may well be coming when it is judged that membership of the Monday Club and membership of the Conservative Party should be mutually exclusive,' he said.

> Club members could be made to choose between the club and the party. If they insist on staying in the club, despite its unacceptable position on immigration and race relations over many years, they could be kicked out of the party. Such a purge would be morally right and politically cathartic.[20]

Andrew Rosindell, the newly elected MP for Romford, had known Bercow for some time. He was one of three MPs who were active members of the Monday Club, along with Andrew Hunter and Angela Watkinson; all three were asked to resign from the organisation by the Chief Whip, David Maclean.

Rosindell insists the 21st-century Monday Club was a different beast to the entity that Bercow had joined in the 1980s. 'It had been restored as a mainstream, right-of-centre group within the party of traditional Conservative values,' he says. Though members of the group argued that the Monday Club had changed, its website still said the organisation 'actively encourages financial assistance for voluntary repatriation', until removing the reference following press backlash that summer.

At Conservative conference in October, Rosindell tried to lobby David Davis, the Tory Party chairman, against cutting ties with the Monday Club. But on 19 October, Duncan Smith suspended Conservative links with the organisation until it proved its non-racist credentials.[21]

The row left some residual ill feeling for Tory MPs associated with the Monday Club. Rosindell in particular took issue with the strength of Bercow's intervention. 'I felt that those of us who had got involved in it and supported it and helped to put it on a decent footing again were thrown overboard by those sorts of comments,' he says. Relations between the pair soured. Rosindell remembers: 'He started just to blank me; he would walk down a corridor and he would just look straight ahead.' Bercow and Rosindell did not speak for at least two years. 'I didn't confront him, but I did feel aggrieved by it,' Rosindell says. A reconciliation of sorts took place in Portcullis House some years later, however. Rosindell, a staunch royalist, picked up a discarded takeaway cup from Coffee Republic and quipped: 'Bloody hell! Republic, I wouldn't like that.' Bercow, who was in earshot, laughed and replied: 'No, you wouldn't.' The pair have been on good terms ever since.

It is curious that Bercow made his first intervention on the Monday Club saga in an interview with *Freedom Today*, the publication of the Freedom Association. He had joined the FA in the late 1980s, sat on its council and had spoken at many of the pressure group's events. (Though he didn't always make himself popular: he was once admonished by Sir Frederick Corfield, a former MP and minister, for arriving late at an FA event at Queen's Hotel in Cheltenham and demanding to speak ahead of him. Corfield told the assembled guests that Bercow should 'learn some manners'.[22]) Simon Richards, now chief executive of the Freedom Association, remembers Bercow initially as a determined right-winger. 'He was very much on the radical Thatcherite Tory right. Bercow was never one to go by halves,' he says.

After the 2001 election, however, Richards noticed a change in tone from Bercow. 'He seemed to go out of his way to be offensive to people he'd been on side with and suddenly wanted to be more Portillo than Portillo,' he says. Richards called for Bercow to be removed from the FA's council and suggested giving his name as 'Berk' in the magazine. Bercow's link with the FA ended by mutual agreement in the mid-'00s, by which point the one-time libertarian was espousing centrist One Nation Conservatism. Over the course of two decades, many of Bercow's relationships with his former friends and allies on the right had ended. Many still feel betrayed to this day, as though they had in some way been duped.

Cynics will argue that Bercow's journey corresponded with prevailing political trends. He supported libertarianism in his university days when it was the dominant force in Conservative student politics, backed Thatcherism when it was an electoral powerhouse and ventured towards the centre when Tony Blair's Labour Party had won back-to-back landslide elections. 'He just didn't have the patience that perhaps some others would have to stick things out and wait until his side was in the ascendency,' says Richards. 'The difference between him and others was that in his case his ambition trumped his principles.'

Others might contend that Bercow is to be applauded for listening to the mood of the country and adapting accordingly, rather than doggedly clinging to a rigid ideology that was clearly unpopular with the public. In this reading, Bercow's actions are those of a man who was open to listening to new ideas and admitting the possibility of being wrong.

* * *

As shadow Chief Secretary to the Treasury, Bercow was working as No. 2 to Michael Howard, the shadow Chancellor. As he fought fires surrounding his previous membership of the Monday Club, Bercow, emboldened by the Tories' poor showing at the polls, continued to campaign on diversity and LGBT rights. At the Tory conference in Blackpool in October, he said the party must end the 'cold war' with the gay and lesbian community. 'In the last parliament we were widely and justifiably regarded as shrill, homophobic and eerily detached from the reality of the lives of a great many of our fellow citizens,' he said.[23] In the first speech by a member of a Conservative shadow Cabinet to a gay rights fringe event, he argued that the Tories could produce Britain's first gay Prime Minister as long as the party embraced change.

In part because of his willingness to stray from matters pertaining to his brief, Bercow's relationship with Howard was strained. In response, Howard would employ the help of David Davis, the party chairman, who held cordial relations with Bercow, to bring him into line. 'Michael

Howard asked me to tell him off,' Davis recalls. A Tory MP who was involved in the shadow Treasury team says:

> It was quite fraught because I don't think John was prepared to take a subordinate role, basically. The other stuff he was doing as a shadow minister, he really wasn't chiming in with the boss. If you're going to be part of a team, that's what you need to do. That said, he was showing his individualistic, idiosyncratic approach.

The shadow Treasury team would gather in Howard's office once a week. 'John Bercow would often be quite verbose and use ten words where one would have done,' recalls a former member of the Conservative Research Department, who was seconded to the team. 'You could see Michael Howard sitting back and getting progressively more annoyed.' The ex-CRD researcher recalls Bercow winding up Howard about a loss suffered by his beloved Liverpool Football Club. 'You could see Michael's contempt for him,' says the source. 'You could tell that he didn't take him seriously as a football fan, never mind as a politician.'

Bercow did not seem 'particularly on top of the detail', according to one person involved with the Treasury team. 'I don't think there was a great grip on the job,' the source says. Bercow became known in CRD for announcing 'You are a great man!' to various people who assisted him. 'He would always be quite jovial but in a showy way,' a CRD source says.

If Bercow had won an admirer in Duncan Smith, his actions at the turn of the year would change the new leader's perception. In a New Year letter to members of his Tory association in Buckingham, leaked to *The Times*, Bercow said the party was seen as racist, sexist, homophobic and anti-youth. The party was in the 'worst shape than ever before in my lifetime or yours', he added. 'Even when we were right ... we must recognise that we sounded shrill, paranoid and even nasty. We are grotesquely unrepresentative of the public at large and many Conservative-minded women recoil from joining our ranks.'[24]

The letter was handed to the press the same day that Duncan Smith was due to give a speech in Birmingham. The Tory leader was furious, telling reporters: 'The party I lead is a decent party, it is a tolerant party. It is basically just like the British people – it wants to get on, it wants the best for its country.' In a warning about Bercow's position, he added: 'I am a great believer that people should be able to express their concerns. I will deal with what I believe to be the right ones and I will deal with people in my party in the way that I believe.'[25]

Bercow was clearly learning from the successful model built up by Tony Blair, who had obliterated the Tories at consecutive elections on a socially liberal centrist platform.

Looking back in 2019, Bercow remembered: 'We were smashed to smithereens. I thought: there's something wrong, here. The electorate cared about public services that we had under-resourced, and it cared about fairness. In our attitude to women and minorities, we came across as the nasty party, and I didn't think I was a nasty person.'[26]

The cumulative effect of his proclamations was that, on 13 July 2002, Duncan Smith moved Bercow to the shadow Work and Pensions team in an effective demotion. 'His sin was to have taken the modernisation agenda seriously. Instead of seeking symbols, Mr Bercow has occasionally dared to mention policies,' wrote Steve Richards in *The Independent*.

Ten days before his change of role, Bercow had got engaged to on-and-off girlfriend Sally Illman. Sally, an advertising executive and a former Tory activist, was a dyed-in-the-wool Blairite and advocate of progressive politics. We will go on to consider the influence that Sally came to have on her future husband in later chapters.

As autumn arrived, Duncan Smith was facing another headache in the shape of another vote on the right to let gay couples adopt. Earlier in the year, three members of his shadow Cabinet – Bercow, Tim Yeo and Peter Ainsworth – had abstained, while four backbenchers, including Ken Clarke and Andrew Lansley, had voted in favour, despite the party imposing a three-line whip to oppose it. At a meeting of the shadow Cabinet,

Bercow said he could not support the party's line on opposing the extension of adoption rights to non-married gay and straight couples. Despite the protestations, Duncan Smith once more put down a three-line whip to vote against the proposals, but said he was willing to turn a blind eye to frontbenchers who wished to abstain. One shadow Cabinet member told him: 'This is a terrible mistake; this should be an issue of conscience and a free vote.'

Bercow was in regular conversation with his friend Jonathan Isaby, a BBC journalist and future editor of the website Brexit Central. With the vote on gay adoption rights due on Monday 4 November, Bercow spoke to Isaby and said he was minded to resign in order to vote in favour. Isaby spent the rest of the weekend writing a profile of Bercow, and when the news was announced the next day, he published it on the BBC's news wires.

At 10.45 a.m. on Sunday, Bercow rang David Maclean, the party's Chief Whip, to inform him of his plans. Duncan Smith was being driven to Bedford for a live interview on Jonathan Dimbleby's programme on ITV when he was told of the news. Staff at Bedford High School, where the interview was taking place, said he looked nervous and flustered.[27] In a lengthy subsequent phone call, he pleaded with Bercow to stay, to no avail.

By the evening, Bercow had sent his resignation letter and agreed not to disclose that he had quit. The resignation letter was made available to the *Evening Standard* by midnight. Arguing that not 'going to the wall over it' would be a 'cop-out' for someone with views on the subject as strong as his own, he concluded that he 'was not prepared to convict myself of that abdication of responsibility'.[28] He also pledged to support his party and its leader 'in the lobbies and on these benches in the weeks and months and years ahead'.[29]

However, Bercow had failed to tell his boss David Willetts, the shadow Work and Pensions Secretary. A former aide says: 'To come in the office and find out someone in your team has resigned and hasn't told you was a bit odd. He was on the right side of history and it was a brave decision. But he's not a team player.'

A shadow Cabinet member who abstained on the vote says: 'Under Iain Duncan Smith, he had become more Catholic than the Pope about politically correct issues.' The source adds:

> I ran into Bercow in the lobby and I said: 'I'm very sorry you resigned.' He said: 'I thought you were a radical like me on this sort of thing'. He was absolutely furious. I thought it was so unreasonable but, of course, what he was doing was redefining himself against people like me who were fairly moderate, and being just as strident and just as rude as he was when he was a right-winger.

The Commons supported the move by 344 to 145, with Clarke and Portillo joining Bercow in voting for the proposals.

New MPs George Osborne, David Cameron and Boris Johnson had also voted against the party whip. Osborne and Bercow got the train from Euston to Manchester together later in the week, as some months earlier the Tatton MP had invited Bercow to speak to his constituency patrons club. The journey up was Osborne's first in-depth conversation with Bercow, and he was surprised to find the overlap in their political beliefs and views on the state of the Tory Party. Local party members, however, were unimpressed by their recent antics in the Commons. 'I can remember it being quite a difficult dinner and, essentially, John and I had to defend the decision we had both taken,' recalls Osborne.

Bercow's intransigence had also upset some of his former allies, none more so than Norman Tebbit, his one-time mentor. The former minister took issue with the modernising agenda being put forward by some quarters of the party, prompting Bercow to tell a fringe meeting at Tory conference: 'Norman has been a mentor to me over the years. But ... it's simply not true that if only we said and did everything that Mrs Thatcher and he did, all would be well with the world.'[30]

Tebbit and his wife were due to attend Bercow's forthcoming wedding, but in a letter to Illman's mother soon after Bercow resigned from his Work and Pensions role, Tebbit wrote:

> You will not be surprised to know that I believe it would now be quite wrong for my wife and I to be guests at the marriage of your daughter and Mr Bercow. I hope you understand that we both regret any hurt or offence to you or your daughter, to whom we extend our very best wishes.

Bercow responded: 'It is sad. I had hoped that he could preserve a friendship irrespective of political differences.'[31] The pair would appear to patch up relations in March 2003, when they teamed up to produce a pamphlet called 'Common Ground', highlighting the areas they agreed on.

Despite committing to support Duncan Smith and his party, Bercow only became more critical following his resignation. He warned that, on the basis of current trends, the Tories' chances of winning the next election were 'about as great as that of finding an Eskimo in the desert'.[32] Allies of the Tory leader named Bercow as one of twelve potential signatories to a motion of no confidence against him, after Bercow said a challenge could happen 'sooner rather than later'.[33] Bercow and Clarke were among the Tory MPs to snub an away-day bonding session at the Latimer House Conference Centre in Chesham, with Bercow insisting he had prior commitments.

Bercow's embroilment with possible moves against Duncan Smith, whose leadership was under heavy strain, brought him some resistance at local level. His constituency chairman, Michael Edmonds, wrote to him: 'I need to know you are not involved in this disgraceful behaviour, because I will not tolerate such actions, and there is only one alternative left open to me.'[34]

Duncan Smith was under severe pressure. Tory MPs dismissed him as weak and lamented his communication skills. Despite his now infamous 'quiet man' speech to Tory conference, in which he warned his party critics to get on board or get out of the way, by 28 October 2003 the threshold of twenty-five letters of no confidence to hold a vote had been reached. Duncan Smith was ousted by ninety votes to seventy-five, and his beleaguered reign at the top of the Tory Party was over.

Michael Howard took on the leadership without challenge. Portillo, for so long Bercow's idol, had announced he would step down at the next election. Bercow was brought back into the shadow Cabinet as shadow International Development Secretary in November, despite previously having expressed reservations about Howard's candidacy. 'Sometimes there is considerable doubt as to whether he has signed up to the agenda of the modernisation of the Conservative Party,' he had told an interviewer only a year earlier.[35]

The role suited Bercow's new style of compassionate politics. He took particular interest in Zimbabwe and clamping down on Robert Mugabe, the country's President, and on Sudan, where thousands were dying of starvation and a million were homeless as a result of actions against Darfurians by the Janjaweed militia, which was supported by the government of Sudan. Bercow argued there was a 'good case' for considering military action. 'Foreign policy has not been robust enough,' he insisted.[36]

Bercow was also involved in a public row over spending commitments after Oliver Letwin, who had taken over from Howard as shadow Chancellor, said only education and health would receive spending boosts if the Tories got into power. In response, Bercow argued:

> If we are to be taken seriously as a party of government that cares about the most vulnerable people on the planet, there has to be a public spending commitment, but we also have to offer value for money, and we have to recognise above all the need for trade as aid.[37]

By July 2004, Bercow was calling for the Tories to match Labour's spending target on development.

His public and private pronouncements on Tony Blair, whom he had once sought to take apart in the Commons Chamber, were also turning heads in Conservative quarters. After a speech by Blair on Iraq, Bercow sent him a letter: 'Congratulations on your superb speech in the Iraq debate on Tuesday. On this subject, as on many other foreign affairs issues, you have provided outstanding statesmanship.'[38]

He sealed his fate in an interview in which he rehashed attacks over spending on aid, called on his party to embrace modernity, refused to rule out defecting (he later released a statement clarifying that he would not) and publicly praised Blair's 'enormous courage and statesmanship'.[39]

On 8 September, Bercow left the shadow Cabinet, having turned down a more junior role of shadow Secretary of State for Constitutional Affairs. Howard had hoped that Bercow would have taken on the role, as it would have meant him working alongside his best friend, Julian Lewis, who had just been moved from the shadow Defence team.

In an extraordinary confrontation in Howard's Commons office, Bercow told the party leader that Ann Widdecombe was right to say there was 'something of the night about him' (she had made the jibe in 1997). 'The party needs to be seen as attractive, but you are not seen as being attractive or as being able to empathise with people,' he said.[40] After Howard told Bercow he was not 'collegiate', he revealed that his letter to Blair over the summer had triggered the decision to sack him. 'It was not at all helpful because I believe that the Prime Minister lied about Iraq,' Howard told Bercow.

Though the row had been brewing for some time, the sacking brought home just how poor relations had become between Bercow and his party. Cast to the backbenches with no return in sight, the ambitious Bercow had to ponder his next move. His mind turned back to a conversation he had with an old friend two years earlier.

CHAPTER THIRTEEN

THE CANDIDATE

*'You just hit a glass ceiling when you join the
Conservative parliamentary party.'*

Jonathan Aitken was catching up with his one-time special adviser. John Bercow had resigned from Iain Duncan Smith's front bench a few months earlier over the rights of gay couples to adopt. Bercow, who had celebrated his fortieth birthday in January 2003, had been an MP for almost six years. With his frontbench career on ice, he was mulling his next move.

'You know, John, there are always other ways you can make a success of a political career and make your contribution,' Aitken said, mentioning his godfather, Selwyn Lloyd, who served as Speaker from 1971 to 1976. 'That was the first time the thought was even communicated to me as a possibility,' Bercow told an interviewer shortly after winning the Speakership.[1]

Around this time, Bercow found himself sitting next to his former boss, Ann Widdecombe, in the House of Commons. They discussed the grim state of the Conservatives' fortunes. 'What are you going to do?' Widdecombe asked. 'What are you hoping for?' To which Bercow replied: 'I'd really like to be Speaker.' According to Widdecombe, the conversation took place between 2002 and 2004.

Notwithstanding the mysterious anonymous registration of the website 'Bercow for Speaker' in 2000, the idea of running for the chair seems to have originated six years before Bercow was elected in 2009. By the autumn of 2005, he was certain of his intentions. 'Towards the end of 2005 the idea did germinate in my mind,' Bercow later told an interviewer.[2]

It was clear to anyone that Bercow had run out of road within his own party.

*   *   *

Conservative MPs were meeting for the first time since the 2005 general election. It had been another disappointing showing at the polls, with the Tories winning 198 seats. The Labour Party returned with 355 MPs on the government benches, eight years into their time in government.

As ever in politics, the post-mortem began before the body was cold. On the sofa of ITV's *GMTV*, Bercow picked over the holes in the Conservatives' offer. 'The Conservative Party has to aspire to govern Britain as she is, not Britain as she was. I've always felt in recent years that we sound as though we are a Victor Meldrew or, at worst, even an Alf Garnett,' he said.[3] Arguing that Conservative activists were 'hugely unrepresentative of the party as a whole', Bercow said the Tories must look, sound and think 'more like the country that we want to lead'. 'The Conservative Party has to reform itself as effectively and thoroughly as Tony Blair has reformed the Labour Party,' he said.

By now on the left of the party, Bercow had fewer allies among his colleagues than at any stage before. One MP who is now a minister recalls: 'I used to have lunch with him an awful lot. Bill Cash and he were the two people [who] if you saw that they were in, you would do a lap and eat somewhere else. They were just too intense and would bore on a particular subject.'

His willingness to speak out had many people questioning whether Bercow was a team player. 'You don't have to be slavishly obedient to your party, but equally you shouldn't be needlessly provocative and gratuitously offensive,' says a former Tory MP who is now a peer. Some felt abandoned by him personally, while others took issue with being lectured about the merits of a political ideology they had believed in long before his own Damascene conversion. 'There is no principle he won't sacrifice on the altar of his own advancement,' says a senior Tory MP.

With Parliament reconvened, Howard was due to address his MPs in one of the committee rooms in Portcullis House on 12 May. The mood among the Conservatives was sombre. For Charles Walker, the newly elected MP for Broxbourne, it was to be his first experience of a meeting of the 1922 Committee. During Howard's address, Bercow and fellow Tory MP Ian Taylor were singled out for their post-election attacks on the party and its leadership. Though Taylor was present, Bercow had not shown up.

Campaign strategist Lynton Crosby was presenting polling on what the public thought about the Conservatives. 'I think it was fairly uncomplimentary,' says Walker. Talk then turned to second jobs. Like many newcomers to Parliament with a zest for reform, Walker was particularly vexed by the idea that MPs would hold down work outside of Westminster. He stood up and said: 'Well, I don't think people should have second jobs. We should focus on being Members of Parliament.' He was greeted by a wall of 'harrumphing'. 'See, this is exactly the type of behaviour that I'm talking about,' Walker responded.

Alan Duncan, the MP for Rutland and Melton, offered Walker some advice: 'Make your friends in this place before you make your enemies.' Walker, perhaps harbouring a penchant for the underdog, took an instant liking to Bercow. It would prove to be one of Bercow's most crucial and close political friendships.

If Bercow's future in the Conservative Party looked precarious, his remarks during the 2005 leadership election about David Cameron, which will be explored in detail later, sealed his fate. He had once more backed the wrong horse – in this case Ken Clarke, his latter-day political hero – and a return to the front bench was not on the cards. For a man of Bercow's undoubted talent and sky-high ambitions, it must have been a grim realisation.

A former Tory minister says Bercow's stalled career was an indictment of the Conservatives: 'We still have a large degree of snobbery in our party. The school tie still counts, the university tie still counts. For me, the Conservative parliamentary party is the least meritocratic organisation that I've come across. You just hit a glass ceiling when you join the parliamentary party.'

Another senior Conservative says of Bercow: 'I suspect inside there is a burning resentment against the Conservative Party [for] turning him from what he saw himself as a rising star of the party to an outsider. The Speakership became his way of achieving a position.'

Indeed, Bercow's political recalibration, illustrated by his propensity to publicly attack his own side and praise the opposition, made him, in some Tory MPs' eyes, Conservative in name only, and the hostility to his Speakership ambitions began early.

The new Speaker would be the first to be elected by secret ballot. Previously, MPs had voted publicly in a series of binary choices between candidates. While some feared that a Speaker could seek retribution for an MP voting against them, the move to a secret ballot changed the nature of the campaign. Now, candidates would have to campaign harder to win over MPs to ensure they voted in the division the same way they had pledged to in person. The expectations on candidates were raised, with many opting to produce manifestos.

A tradition, though not a convention, had been bucked by the Labour Party in 2000 when Michael Martin became Speaker. Between 1965 and 1992, successive Speakers came from the opposite side of the House to their predecessor. When Martin succeeded Betty Boothroyd, this emerging consensus ended. The Labour Party knew that the next Speaker would need to come from the Tory benches. A Labour MP at the time says: 'So, a group of backbenchers on the Labour side, said, "OK, let's give them a Tory then – let's give them one of us." Because we had a majority, it was easier for us to propose him.' They add: 'It was a complete stitch-up. A terrible thing happened. Awful.'

To get elected, Bercow would need to rely on the votes of opposition parties. What followed was one of the most effective campaigns in recent times, and one that still jars with many Tory MPs.

* * *

Members of the 2005 intake of Labour MPs would receive handwritten notes from Bercow after their first speech in the Commons. 'Everybody who did their maiden speech, he was there, listening. I don't know how he got the information of when people were doing their maiden speeches, but he did. He'd be sitting there, going: "Oh, yes, yes." And then he'd write personal, handwritten letters, saying how moved he was,' says a former Labour MP.

David Davis recalls: 'He basically laid siege to the Speakership over years, writing to people, encouraging them and so on. Who would have thought of the younger John Bercow as a would-be Speaker?'

Michael Keegan, a close friend, says Bercow told him he would find a 'kind word' to say to every MP.

He decided, instead of disagreeing with them and being ideological, he was going to try and find a way to be nice to people. He thought this might stand him in good stead. It's kind of become his philosophy in life, to find the point that connects you to somebody rather than concentrate on the point that disconnects you from them.

Bercow had also begun to moderate his discourse towards Michael Martin, whom he had not only once openly criticised but voted against when he was made Speaker. When Martin came under pressure over his travel expenses and those of his wife in February 2008, Bercow said: 'What a pleasure it is to see you in the chair and to know that we have as our Speaker somebody who is simply not prepared to be pushed around either by snobs or by bullies.'[4] The praise irked two of Bercow's most ardent critics in the watching press gallery, Simon Carr at *The Independent* and Quentin Letts at the *Daily Mail*. Letts, outraged at what he deemed to be hypocrisy, outed Bercow as one of several Tory backbenchers he had spoken to six years earlier who were dissatisfied with Martin's performance. 'The telephone almost melted in my earhole,' he wrote, describing the strength of Bercow's displeasure.[5] Letts, who previously had a benign fascination with Bercow's eccentricities, would turn sharply against the Tory MP.

Talk of Bercow's possible defection to Labour first emerged in February 2003, around the time of his conversation with Aitken. His denial was not helped when Tessa Jowell, the Culture Secretary, said in May of that year: 'I think you are making a long journey to cross the floor of the Chamber and will be welcome on this side whenever you choose.' This comment came after Bercow had dubbed himself a 'modern, socially liberal Tory'.[6]

Bercow himself fanned the flames during an interview in November 2004 with *The Independent*'s Steve Richards – his paper and journalist of choice – in which he refused to comment on the rumours, saying only: 'I am working for a modern, progressive Conservative Party'. Soon after, Bercow was forced to release a statement. 'I've been a proud member of the Conservative Party for more than twenty-four years and there's no way I would ever defect to another party,' he said.[7]

With Gordon Brown set to take over as Prime Minister on 27 June 2007, the Chancellor had prioritised securing Tory defections as an early boost to his premiership. On the eve of his move to No. 10, and after five meetings over two months in the Treasury, Brown convinced Quentin Davies, a former member of the shadow Cabinet, to defect to Labour.

Attempts were also being made behind the scenes to lure Bercow across the floor, with Labour MP Ann Keen, Brown's principal private secretary, making a particular effort. 'Ann Keen was Gordon's link to John,' says a source close to Brown. 'She was clearly trying to persuade Gordon that John was somebody who might defect over when Gordon became Prime

Minister … John was definitely around in the mix as somebody who was talked of.'

His wife, Sally, was also encouraging him to join. 'I did lobby him to do that. But he's a Tory through and through,' she said in 2009.[8] A Conservative whip says: 'He was on our watchlist. We were slightly surprised that he didn't.'

Michael Keegan, Bercow's close confidant from their time together on Lambeth Council, says a future Labour leader was also deployed to try to convince Bercow. 'Ed Miliband was the guy they sent along to try and get him to defect. He said, "No thank you. I'm a Conservative,"' Keegan recalls. The Guido Fawkes website reported that Bercow was on the verge of crossing the floor the day Brown entered No. 10. When the *Daily Telegraph*'s Brendan Carlin asked Bercow about the rumours two days later in Portcullis House, it sparked an angry exchange. Carlin reported:

> John Bercow bit my head off today when I collared him in Portcullis House. John is mighty miffed that his name ever got mentioned by the media as a possible New Labour convert. Eventually, he calmed down to give a statement that the idea that he was defecting was nonsense and that he was right behind David Cameron.[9]

Gisela Stuart, the Labour MP for Edgbaston, approached Bercow in the corridors of Westminster to offer some advice. 'The history of defectors is not a happy one,' she told him. 'You end up not being trusted by your old side and you won't be trusted on your new one.' Stuart says now: 'He just acknowledged it, he didn't try and counter it. But he was very close to defecting from what I gathered.'

Those close to Bercow insist that he was never planning on crossing the floor of the House. His critics would argue the interest paid to him by senior Labour figures illustrated Bercow's left-leaning bias. Whether or not he ever seriously considered defecting, the fact that the conversations even took place is a testament to just how far he had travelled politically.

In the summer of 2019, the *Mail on Sunday* reported that Bercow had been approached by Ed Balls, then Children's Secretary, and offered the job of Schools Minister.[10] Balls denies this, noting that he had other ideas up his sleeve: 'I never had a conversation with John about defecting and I never raised the issue with him. I think, to be honest, I was rather sceptical that this was such an important, big deal.'

Bercow had introduced a Private Member's Bill calling for speech and language therapy for young offenders, and the legislation pricked Balls's interest. Balls, who has a stammer but at that point had not spoken publicly about it, knew that Bercow had a particular interest in the subject of communication challenges.

Sally and Bercow's first child, Oliver, had been diagnosed with autism. At six months old, they realised that Oliver had quirks such as fixating on a particular object or not looking at people. As he grew older, they noticed he was also behind on developmental milestones such as walking and crawling. At two and a half, Oliver wasn't babbling. 'We knew that there was a problem,' Sally told the charity Ambitious About Autism, of which the Bercows are patrons. At the age of three, after the diagnosis, Oliver was given a statement of special educational needs, allowing him to secure additional help.[11] He attended a speech and language unit attached to his primary school, and at the age of three and a half he started talking.

Balls knew of Bercow's connection to the subject and felt that rather than ask him to defect, it would be more effective to sign the Tory MP up to conducting a review on the government's behalf. He approached Bercow in the Commons. 'Look, John, you have regularly taken up the issue of speech and language services in Parliament over the last eighteen months,' he said. 'Would you be interested in heading up a review of provision?' Bercow replied: 'Ed, I would be interested, but it is a relatively unusual thing to be asked to take up when you are in opposition. I must consult colleagues.'[12] Bercow spoke to Patrick McLoughlin, the Chief Whip, and Michael Gove, the shadow Education Secretary, before accepting the offer.

On 3 September 2007, Brown announced a series of reviews by Conservatives – including former treasurer Johan Eliasch and Tory MP Patrick Mercer – during an interview on the *Today* programme. Bercow was asked to head a review of speech therapy services for children. Bercow was on holiday in the West Country with Sally, Oliver and their second son, Freddie, when the news broke. 'I don't want to wave Oliver around like a teddy bear in all this,' said Bercow.

A provisional diagnosis of our son suggested he had verbal dyspraxia. Since then we have discovered he is on the autistic spectrum … Sally and I were perfectly prepared to battle as hard as necessary to get him the help he needs but to date we haven't had to: he is getting help and making great progress.

Bercow had begun to realise, however, that not every parent of autistic children had such swift access to the services they needed. 'I know of parents who have had to wage Kafkaesque battles to get help, some encounter obstacles at every turn, lots have a rough time,' he added.[13]

The news of Bercow's involvement sparked an expected backlash from some quarters. Most troubling for Bercow at the time was the reaction of Bill Chappell, deputy leader of the Buckinghamshire County Council, who said: 'I would feel happier if John was feeding his expert knowledge into the Conservative machine.'[14] Two constituents wrote to express concerns, and Bercow responded by setting out details of the review. 'I accept that if you shift your ground on issues, it does fuel suspicion and anxiety,' he told the *Sunday Times*. 'But I am proud to be a Tory MP and want to remain one.'[15]

Bercow and Balls attended the Michael Palin Centre for Stammering Children in November 2007 and the launch of the interim report on 20 March the following year. On 8 July, the Bercow Report was published. The document, which was launched at a primary school in Westminster, included forty recommendations and five key themes. It included calls for parents to spend more time talking to their children during family meals to help them learn vital communication skills, and urged early assessment for speech, language and communication problems. In 2018, a 'Bercow: Ten Years On' report was launched to assess progress. Balls says now:

> This was a good, serious piece of work to do, it helped me to do something in that space, and John cared about it. Having somebody who was a moderating Tory doing this work for us showed that we were broad-based and eclectic and cared about the output, rather than simply the ideology. For him, it was a way of getting his teeth into an area he cared about. It really helped him build a different kind of profile to the one he had ten years before.

A senior Tory MP notes: 'Anybody who calls a report after themselves has got something of an ego. It actually said on the front, the Bercow Report. It said all you need to know about him. All these policy changes were all about him.'

* * *

The first time Bercow's name was mentioned as a potential successor to Michael Martin in the popular press came from his friend Jonathan Isaby on 18 July 2007. 'He's an independent-minded backbencher who has impressed colleagues on all sides,' Isaby wrote in the *Daily Telegraph*. Kevin Maguire at the *New Statesman* heard of Bercow's interest in October of that year, writing: 'Bercow believes by positioning himself as a man about the House, he'll pick up Labour as well as Tory support.'

Bercow had already been ingratiating himself with progressives on the Labour benches. One former Tory whip recalls: 'He worked hard at that. I can see him sitting at the top of the escalator down below, talking mainly to Labour and Liberal MPs.'

In the continuation of his journey on equality matters, he lent his support to all-women shortlists – a tool used by the Labour Party for selections of candidates – in the House of Commons. 'Whether or not it is popular in our party, there is a compelling case for the adoption of all-women shortlists as the best, and indeed the only, proven method by which dramatically to increase representation,' he said.[16]

His position helped to cultivate an affiliation with Harriet Harman, the Leader of the Commons and women's rights campaigner who in June 2008 unveiled an Equality Bill. 'He has proved that not all Conservative Members are still stuck in the Stone Age. Given his comments, I would say – although I would have to reflect on the matter with my colleagues – that he ought to be regarded as an honorary member of the sisterhood,' she told the Commons.[17] 'He clearly started working particularly on the Labour women to lay the ground for the Speakership,' observes a former Labour minister.

Bercow had also served on the Chairman's Panel (now known as Panel of Chairs) since May 2005, where he had gained his first experience chairing Public Bill Committees, Westminster Hall debates and Delegated Legislation Committees. He had approached Sir Alan Haselhurst, the most senior of the Deputy Speakers, who oversees the panel, about joining at the start of the parliament. Bercow would later refer to the work as evidence to support his bid for the Speakership.

Despite criticism from colleagues, Bercow's courting of votes is exactly what is expected of a politician. To win an election, you have to go out and campaign and win over the electorate. 'Obviously, if you're developing ambitions to stand as Speaker, you have to get a significant number of votes from the opposite side,' says Angela Eagle. The trouble for Bercow was that he would be, by and large, reliant on the votes from parties other than his own.

By early 2009, Bercow was still considered an outsider, in small part due to his own position on the Conservative benches. But his standing in the left-wing press and support among opposition MPs was growing by the day. Martin, who had been in post for more than eight years, had yet to name a date for his departure. However, a looming scandal was about to see him become the first Speaker to be forced out of office since 1835.

CHAPTER FOURTEEN

ELECTION NIGHT

'I do not want to be someone; I want to do something.'

The *Daily Telegraph* had been trickling out stories about MPs' expenses for nearly two weeks. Michael Martin, under relentless pressure over his handling of the scandal, had announced that he would relinquish his post. On 20 May 2009, the same day Martin revealed his departure date, Bercow announced his candidacy for the Speakership.

Michael Crick was sitting at a table underneath the atrium in Portcullis House when he spotted Bercow walking towards him. 'John, I've been looking at the betting lists for the Speakership and your name isn't there. They haven't got odds for you. You're not going to do very well if you're not mentioned,' said the BBC *Newsnight* journalist. Crick was aware that shortening betting odds can gather momentum behind a political campaign. Bercow was concerned, if a little perplexed. Crick, tongue in cheek, instructed: 'If I was in your shoes, I'd go and get a friend to put a large sum of money on you!'

The next day, Bercow got on the phone to Michael Keegan, who was working at Fujitsu. 'Michael, really need your help. Could you go and put a bet on me in all the bookies?' he asked. 'At that point in time, the political establishment hadn't really figured out who he was,' Keegan says. His friend went to various bookies, placing £10, £20, £30 and £50 bets. The odds began to shorten. 'What a great bet that turned out to be,' Keegan says.

Keegan, now a few thousand quid better off, took Bercow and Sally to dinner at the Oxo Tower soon after he became Speaker. 'That was the best bet he ever gave me.'

* * *

Bercow was the first candidate to put themselves forward. In a letter to Martin Salter, Labour MP for Reading West, who would chair his campaign, Bercow said: 'We must make no mistake: Parliament is broken. Disengagement from politics and indifference to what we do have given way to outright public ridicule and contempt. This is not just sad, it is deeply dangerous, because it provides fertile ground on which extremists feed.'[1]

In his manifesto, Bercow said the Speaker should do more to invigorate and enliven the Commons and act as an ambassador for Parliament, and made clear from the off that he would rip up convention. 'For far too long the House of Commons has been run as little more than a private club by and for gentleman amateurs,' he wrote. 'It remains beset by antiquated practices which would not survive for a moment in any well-run organisation in the public, private or voluntary sectors.'

The atmosphere in Parliament was sour. The Tories had helped to bring down Martin over his handling of the biggest and most controversial story to hit the Commons in years. There were some suggestions that, in response, the Labour Party was prepared to aggravate their political opponents. 'The Tories have tried to stuff us by taking down one of ours,' a government whip said. 'So we're going to stuff them by voting for someone they hate. But they can't complain. John Bercow is a Conservative MP, if only nominally.'[2]

Angela Eagle was one of those who did not approve of Martin's ousting.

'The Speaker of the House of Commons shouldn't be subject to the passing whims of newspapers,' she says. 'Once you've knocked one off, you think you can knock the next one off … It's not fair really to subject them to the slings and arrows of normal politics.'

Bercow's courting of Labour votes had left him nowhere to turn on the Tory side. 'He was probably the victim of a lot of Freudian projection. People would have looked at him and his change of views and assumed it was a calculated change because if it was them, that's what it would have been,' a former Cabinet minister says.

Bercow did still attempt to attract Tory votes, albeit not always successfully. On one occasion, he approached an MP and asked if he had his backing. 'Look John, one thing I will tell you, stop being so unpleasant to your own side,' he replied. 'Ah yes, OK, but you'll vote for me, you're not one of those terrible public-school types,' Bercow answered. The MP revealed that he had gone to public school. 'Well, you don't look like one or sound like one,' said Bercow. 'It was quite telling. That's where it all emanates from,' the former frontbencher recalls. 'If you want to be mean, he had a lot of chips accumulating on his shoulders.'

According to Julian Lewis, when Bercow told a senior Conservative figure of his intention to run for the Speakership, they tried to talk him out of it. 'You should settle for being a deputy. I'm sure the party would support that sort of thing,' said the Tory grandee. Lewis says the advice 'significantly irritated' Bercow.

Gillian Keegan, a future Conservative MP and wife of Michael, says:

He's been kind of bullied, ostracised, many, many times in his life. I think he is just somebody that's learned to grow a pair, grow a shell and he's realised that in a world that he wanted to go into, that if he didn't shout about him, there was not a single other person that would.

Charles Walker, who had grown friendly with Bercow since entering the Commons in 2005, admired his parliamentary performances. 'John, you're really good at this,' he told him in 2006. 'Why aren't you on the front bench?' Bercow responded: 'Being shadow Minister for Transport is not something that holds much attraction to me. But one day I'd like to be Speaker.' Walker said: 'Well, when that day comes, I would be happy to support you.' Bercow took up that offer years later.

To stand for the Speakership, candidates required between twelve and fifteen nominations from backbench MPs, three of whom had to be from other parties. 'It's just as well for John it's that way around because he'd never find three people in his own party,' says a former Tory frontbencher.

Bercow's challenge was finding a Conservative to nominate him. Lewis had a 'cross word' with Tory Deputy Chief Whip Andrew Robathan after he was told that he would not be allowed to nominate Bercow for the Speakership on the basis that he was a shadow minister. 'Obviously you can canvass support for John,' Robathan said. Walker, meanwhile, was facing calls from Tory colleagues not to put Bercow's name forward. 'I was getting quite a lot of pressure to back out. I thought: "Once I've signed this, people will get off my back" and I would almost have signed it in blood. I signed it and the rest is history,' he says.

A member of the Public Bill Office at the time, who dealt with the nominations, recalls: 'It was quite striking that there was one Conservative name on Bercow's papers.' The other nominees included future London Mayor Sadiq Khan, Natascha Engel, the SNP's Pete Wishart and Lib Dem MP David Laws. Notable names to have canvassed support include Labour MPs Mary Creagh, Joan Ruddock and Keith Vaz and Liberal Democrat MPs Alistair Carmichael and Malcolm Bruce.

Though Bercow had got the required nominees, his campaign was hit by setbacks. As his profile increased, the media began to scrutinise his involvement in the Monday Club and the Federation of Conservative Students. The question of 60 Hopton Road – the home of Teresa Gorman – began to surface, as did claims about his previous views and behaviour in the Commons. The *Mail on Sunday* uncovered a submission Bercow made to the Senior Salaries Review Body in December 2006, in which he lamented the 'perverse' way MPs' pay had fallen behind over the years, and called for members to be paid the same as a GP or local council boss. The most dangerous threat to Bercow came over his expenses.

The day after he announced his candidature, Bercow stood accused of flipping the designation of his main and second home to avoid tax. Homeowners are required to pay capital gains tax on the profit on the sale of any property which is not their main residence. However, the *Daily Telegraph* revealed that Bercow had bought and sold properties in both his constituency and London in 2003 and paid capital gains tax on neither. In May 2003, Bercow sold his constituency home in Adstock for £162,000 and bought a detached house in Buckingham for £145,950. In September of that year, Bercow sold a flat in Victoria, London, for £335,000 and then bought a flat nearby for £540,000.[3]

The day after the charges were made, Bercow offered to pay £6,508.40 plus interest in capital gains tax to HMRC. 'From 1997 until early 2003, I designated my constituency home as my second home,' he said. 'I did make changes in the designation of my homes during the course of 2003 as a result of which CGT was not payable.' Bercow revealed he had taken the advice of an accountant and would repay the amount he would have owed at the time.[4]

The controversy was not over, however. It later emerged that Bercow had claimed £1,197.51 for a blocked toilet caused by a sanitary towel, and £933.14 to replace it. The day before the Speakership election, the *Sunday Telegraph* reported that Bercow had claimed more than £960 in two years for accountancy advice – an act that had landed Alistair Darling, the Chancellor, and other MPs into hot water. The claims had been approved by the fees office.[5]

The coverage did little to derail Bercow's chances. As the Speakership election campaign got under way, he was the odds-on favourite to win.

*   *   *

At just forty-six years old, Bercow was twenty years younger than many of his rivals, and some Conservatives wanted assurances that, were he to win, he would not remain in post for time immemorial. In a bid to assuage his colleagues, Bercow wrote a letter committing to serve 'no more than' nine years in total.

His outriders in the media, Jonathan Isaby and Steve Richards, backed him for the role, and Bercow used pieces in the *New Statesman* and *The Independent* to set out his platform. With support from the *Mirror*'s Kevin Maguire and a tacit endorsement from *The Guardian* on election day, Bercow had completed the left-wing set.

Sir George Young, a former Cabinet minister and long-serving member of the Conservative Party, was Bercow's closest opponent. Such was the Tory appetite to defeat Bercow that talk even did the rounds of backing Margaret Beckett, the Labour MP who had quit as a minister just over two weeks prior to the election.

On Monday 22 June, MPs packed out the Chamber to hear the pitches from the candidates. Bercow had Walker and Lewis sitting next to him, the latter holding his speech and following the words with his pen as a failsafe. After mimicking Sir Peter Tapsell, the senior Conservative MP, and listing the previous Speakers who were younger than him at the time of entering the chair, Bercow reiterated his pledge to serve 'no longer than nine years in total'.

Bercow's platform was threefold. Firstly, in light of the expenses scandal, he pledged to implement 'radical reforms to the system of allowances' while respecting Parliament itself. Secondly, to restore authority to Parliament, he committed to granting more Urgent Questions, enabling greater scrutiny of legislation and ensuring that ministers felt obliged to make key policy statements to the House. 'The Speaker should always be neutral within this Chamber, but he or she should not be neutral about this Chamber. If elected, I would be a tireless advocate for our political relevance,' he said. Lastly, Bercow said a reforming Speaker must reconnect Parliament with the society that it seeks to represent.

Declaring himself to be the 'clean break' candidate, Bercow concluded:

> We need change, we need change permanently and we need change now, but I can help to deliver it with you only if you give me the opportunity. I know that that it is a tall order and I am only a little chap, but I believe that I can rise to the occasion.[6]

Andrew Mitchell, the shadow Secretary of State for International Development, was no fan of John Bercow's at the time (though he would later become a great admirer of the Speaker). Mitchell, who was helping with Young's campaign, was determined to ensure that Bercow did not emerge victorious. He missed three flights to New York as he fought to get Young's bid over the line.

After the first round of voting, Bercow was top with 179 votes, Young coming in second with 112. Labour's Parmjit Dhanda and Tories Patrick Cormack and Richard Shepherd were eliminated, along with Michael Lord, a Deputy Speaker. After the second round, Bercow had increased his votes to 221, with Young on 174. Ann Widdecombe was eliminated, while the other three candidates – Beckett, Sir Alan Haselhurst and Sir Alan Beith – all pulled out. It was down to the final two.

A Labour MP was stood next to Conservative leader David Cameron in the toilet as the voting began. 'David, I'm about to vote Tory for the very first time in my life.' Cameron replied: 'John Bercow doesn't count!'[7]

After the third and final round of voting, Alan Williams, the Father of the House, who was overseeing the election, announced the results. Bercow, who let out a deep exhale, won by 322 to 271 votes. Bar a smattering of applause from some Tory MPs, including Young, few Conservatives joined in with the clapping that followed.

As is customary when a new Speaker is elected, he was dragged to the chair by two MPs – in his case, Charles Walker and Lib Dem MP Sandra

Gidley. 'He wasn't dragged, he ran,' says one Tory MP. A Conservative backbencher was heard shouting 'Not in my name' when the result was announced. 'This wall of noise and opprobrium was being heaped down on my head from our benches. I then dropped him and then I went back to my benches,' recalls Walker.

Bercow thanked the House for bestowing upon him the greatest honour of his professional life. 'A Speaker has a responsibility immediately and permanently to cast aside all his or her previous political views. I said it and I meant it. My commitment to this House is to be completely impartial ... That is what it's about,' he said.[8]

Prime Minister Gordon Brown, who shook hands with Bercow behind the Speaker's chair, acknowledged his commitment to impartiality. 'You said that you had now cast aside all your past political views; some of us thought you had done that some time ago,' he said. David Cameron followed Brown's lead in his tribute, joking: 'Let's hope that includes all of them.'[9]

Walker's phone rang as he left the Commons Chamber. 'Darling, I've just seen you drag the Speaker to the chair. How was it? Where are you now?' his wife asked. Walker replied: 'I'm getting the fuck out of here.'

Within two weeks of Bercow becoming Speaker, Walker was beckoned over to a group of his colleagues. 'We're hatching a plot to get rid of Speaker Bercow. Will you be interested?' they said. 'Guys, can I just remind you that I was the only Tory who signed his nomination form and dragged him to the chair two weeks ago. Probably best not to have this conversation with me,' he replied. Walker comments: 'That demonstrated how quickly things are forgotten in Parliament.'

Following his election, Bercow hosted a thank-you party in Speaker's House for all those who'd helped organise his campaign. Among the attendees were Salter and Diane Abbott. One witness recalls Labour MPs complaining that their party whips had encouraged them to vote for Beckett, who had quit as a frontbencher in order to run for the Speakership.

'We told our whips to fuck off, we're going to vote for John,' the source recalls a Labour MP saying.

After years of careful campaigning, Bercow had found the position of influence that he craved. 'I do not want to be someone; I want to do something. Working with colleagues, I want to implement an agenda for reform, for renewal, for revitalisation, and for the reassertion of the core values of this great institution in the context of the twenty-first century,' he told MPs.[10]

In being elected, he had become not only the 157th to enter the chair but the first Jewish person to do so. Little did he know at this juncture how much his life or that of his family's would change.

CHAPTER FIFTEEN

SALLY

---

*'The problem with John Bercow is that he discovered sex
and New Labour at the same time.'*

A House of Commons doorkeeper approached Sally Bercow and
tapped her shoulder. 'Mrs Bercow, would you like to see the Speaker's residence?' he asked.

As her husband was announced as the new Speaker, Sally was watching from the gallery above the House of Commons. She was with Bercow's mother, Brenda, and their close friends Michael and Gillian Keegan, the latter of whom would become an MP in 2017. Both are godparents to Sally and Bercow's boys, Oliver and Freddie.

Bercow's entourage were taken across Speaker's Court through to Speaker's House, in the north-east corner of the Palace of Westminster, and upstairs to the four-bedroom apartment. As they were shown around, notable antiques were pointed out by officials. 'Christ, I've got three kids that are really small, and this thing has got the artefacts of the nation in it,' said Sally.

'She was completely overawed by the whole thing,' recalls Gillian. 'She's gripping my hand and saying, "You've got to come with me, I have no idea what I'm doing."'

The Bercows spent £45,581 on refurbishments to their new home. They converted a study into a playroom and purchased a new sofa and window seat cushions for the drawing room, costing £7,524. Much of the renovation budget went towards safety features and upgrades for the children, such as £3,600 on new locks to the windows, and £3,880 on additional child safety on the terrace below, which looks out onto the Thames. The major expense came on overhauling the heavy red decor, which disturbed their eldest son, Oliver. 'It really did bother him a lot, otherwise we would not have asked for the change,' Sally explained.[1]

Though undoubtedly plush surroundings, the confines of the Speaker's apartment would prove a testing place for a young family. Sally had enjoyed a life bathed in relative obscurity, away from the limelight, in nearby Pimlico. With three young children in tow, she was beginning to come to terms with what her husband's new position would entail for her family, and herself.

*　*　*

It was Julian Lewis who spotted her first. They were attending a dinner at the Conservatives' student conference in Nottingham in 1989 when Lewis saw a tall blonde woman with 'long flowing hair' on the other side of the room. He poked Bercow in the ribs and pointed her out. 'That's the most beautiful girl at this conference,' he said.

At the disco that followed, Lewis and Bercow found themselves dancing with the woman, whose name was Sally Illman. 'It was fairly obvious to me, pretty quickly, that she was much more interested in John,' he says. When they broke away, Lewis returned to his room for an early night. 'I really don't think I ought to detail anything more about the remainder of that evening! It is fair to conclude that they got together on that first occasion in a significant way,' he adds.

The eldest of four children born to Roland and Eileen Illman, Sally lost her father, who ran a builder's merchant, when she was sixteen. She used the money he left her to send herself to Marlborough College, a private school in Wiltshire. 'I didn't really fit in with those girls in Alice bands and everyone coming from a house with a long drive,' she said.[2]

Sally, who was studying at Keble College, Oxford, was twenty at the time she met her future husband, six years her senior. Strikingly tall and elegant at 5ft 11in., she was a full four and a half inches taller than Bercow, a fact that bothered her at the time. She was a member of the Oxford University Conservative Association, and as forthright in her political views as the man she had just met. She made press-worthy interventions at Tory conferences in 1989 and 1993, the latter of which she urged ministers to resist statutory regulation of the press, after Transport Minister Steven Norris was facing accusations of having multiple mistresses. 'MPs are free to have affairs if they wish. After all, it seems to be the male ones that do it, and boys will be boys,' she said. 'But if those affairs conflict with their public image, carefully cultivated, of marital harmony, they really cannot complain when the press catch them in their boxer shorts.'[3]

Bercow was instantly charmed. 'I was very attracted to her, and I was completely amazed she had the remotest interest in me,' he says.[4] He returned to Lambeth and had a drink in the members' bar with Keegan. 'He told me that he'd met this amazing blonde … He was really taken with her,' Keegan recalls.

Bercow had not previously had much luck on the romance front. Former members of the FCS recall his struggles at speaking to women. 'He was absolutely hopeless,' says one. 'I don't think he had much success with girls, possibly because of his odd mannerisms and behaviour and so forth,' says another.

Such were his shortfalls that his comrades on the FCS decided to stitch him up. A handful of activists bought an unseemly book from a shop in Covent Garden and published an edited extract of it in the right-wing Conservative students' magazine *Armageddon*. The 'John Bercow guide to women' included suggestions such as 'blow your nose in her hair' and featured categories on 'How to pick up drunk girls', 'How to pick up virgins', 'How to pick up refined girls', 'How to get rid of a girl after sex' and 'How to get rid of a girl during sex'. Women, the guide advised its readers, would 'settle for anything that breathes and has a credit card'.

The guide first emerged in Bercow's life when he was on Lambeth Council, and he immediately suspected his political enemies. 'This is the sort of bullshit you get from the left. I can prove that article was not written by me but was lifted from a tasteless book – I was incensed to see it under my name,' he said.[5]

But when the website Guido Fawkes uncovered it in early December 2009, a serious miscommunication (or lack of communication) saw a statement go out from the Speaker's Office saying: 'This article appeared in a magazine that specialised in being both funny and provocative. It in no way reflects the Speaker's views today.' Despite its false provenance, the mere fact that FCS students decided to send up Bercow in this way and on this particular topic speaks to his woes with women.

Bercow and Sally dated for six months before Bercow called time on their relationship. 'He dumped me for being too argumentative,' she said. 'But you have to remember that he was a right-wing headbanger at the time. He's much more rounded and moderate now, and he's rethought a lot.'[6]

Though their initial fling came to an end, they remained friends. When Sally needed a place to live, Bercow reached out to Gary Mond, whom he had met in Scotland during the 1987 election. Mond had a couple of rooms spare in his four-bedroom flat, and Sally lived with him for around nine months. During that time, Margaret Thatcher was challenged by Michael Heseltine and later resigned as Prime Minister. While Sally welcomed the manoeuvre and a change in Conservative leadership, Alice Little, the third roommate, had been working as one of Thatcher's secretaries. 'I had the situation in the evening the day she resigned of Alice crying her eyes out and Sally celebrating,' recalls Mond. A few months after Sally moved out, Bercow got in touch with Mond to say that they were now seeing each other.

'It was clearly a stop-go, on-off, highs-and-lows relationship. She was obviously really special for John, although only time would tell whether she was the one who was meant to be,' says Lewis. Bercow had 'several other girlfriends' in between dating Sally. 'There were one or two ladies in Conservative circles who showed serious interest in him, which he reciprocated. But, in the end, it came down to where he started with Sally,' Lewis adds.

Sally was going through some challenges of her own. She dropped out of university after two years, during which she had enjoyed a hedonistic lifestyle. (She would later have to defend herself after it was alleged that she had claimed on her CV to have received a 2:1. She maintains that she did no such thing, including only her grade for the exams she had taken.) 'I started drinking at Oxford, being a party girl, and it got out of control,' she recalled.[7] An acquaintance says: 'I would say Sally had these aspirations and they were probably partially unfulfilled.'

Sally worked as an account manager at Countrywide Communications after leaving Oxford, taking on jobs across the PR industry through the late '90s. She reined in her drinking initially, but eventually relapsed. 'I got a grip for a while, but in the mid-'90s I was working in advertising and I would drink wine at lunch then go out and drink a bottle in the evening: most evenings really. I had no stop button.'[8]

Sally agreed to accompany Bercow to constituency association events when he was campaigning to become a candidate. In the early '90s, having a wife or partner was deemed an important element of a person's suitability for the role. By 1997, however, Sally had renounced her Conservative sympathies and come out as a fully-fledged Blairite.

When they met up, Bercow would be largely unaware that Sally was, as she puts it, 'an alkie'. 'We were apart for long periods and I just didn't know. Perhaps I should have done but I didn't. When we went to the pub, she drank more than I did,' he told an interviewer in 2010. 'I think with alcoholics, you think of people who have gin over breakfast. I wasn't like that. But I think formally I would be called an alcoholic,' Sally said.[9]

Sally stopped drinking in late 2001, after attending Alcoholics Anonymous. Meeting up at 'an old favourite haunt', Sally told Bercow she was 'quitting booze'.[10]

*   *   *

At the time of his election in 1997, Bercow was dating Louise Cumber, who accompanied him on his helicopter ride from Surrey Heath to Buckingham. But during his early years in the Commons, Bercow was still very much a bachelor, dedicating vast swathes of his time to his work.

He often went on holiday with the Keegans, who had begun dating in the late '90s. The three of them travelled to French ski resort Val d'Isère for a New Year break. On the plane over, a nervous Bercow said to Gillian: 'I'll be absolutely fine so long as I don't have to go on a chairlift.' Michael and Gillian thought to themselves: 'How on earth are we going to get him up the mountain?' Bercow and Michael were both early-stage skiers, while Gillian was more of a dab hand. 'She would just whizz off and we would make our own way down in very slow time. But he really enjoyed skiing,' Michael recalls.

The Bercows and Keegans would continue to holiday together, spending time in Spain and at the Keegans' place in Petworth, West Sussex. 'We play a sort of annual croquet match, where, normally, Mr Oliver Bercow and me thrash his father at croquet every year, religiously and take great delight in doing so,' Michael says.

Around the turn of the millennium, Bercow had asked Sally to move in with him. But, given his unfailing commitment to the House of Commons, she was reluctant. She didn't fancy being the 'consort of a man wedded to the Commons'. 'He hardly ever left the office,' she said.[11]

Meanwhile, Sarah Westcott was working in the press gallery as a reporter for the Press Association. Bercow was regularly spotted staring up in the direction of the 26-year-old. 'It was faintly embarrassing,' she says. Before the House broke up for Christmas in 2000, Bercow sent Westcott a bottle of champagne with a card saying that her 'cherubic face was a source of inspiration to him'. News of the gift was passed on by colleagues to the diary desk of the *Daily Telegraph*.[12] 'I was a bit pissed off about that,' says Westcott.

Westcott, who was in a relationship at the time, agreed to meet out of curiosity, and they went for a drink at the members' bar in the Houses of Parliament. 'I felt he was scouting around for a potential partner,' says Westcott.

> He was a bit awkward, quite charming and sweet. He was a bit older than me and just like something from another era. You could tell he didn't have a lot of experience with women. I did feel that he was quite class-conscious as well; maybe it's always like that on a first date with somebody.

When Westcott gave Bercow a polite goodbye kiss on his cheek, he looked 'terrified'. When they met up for a second time, over dinner in Westminster, Bercow told Westcott she looked like Labour MP Yvette Cooper. 'Maybe he was meaning it nicely, or he was just completely in this weird Westminster bubble where everything is referenced back to Westminster.'

After two dates, they did not meet up again. 'I didn't feel like he was remotely lecherous or sleazy. But there was this kind of gallantry which was sweet but quite embarrassing. Even back then, nobody was really like that,' Westcott says.

After Sally caught wind that Bercow had been dating someone else, they got back together in December 2001. 'She was tall, blonde, glamorous, very trendy, edgy at that time,' says Gillian Keegan. 'I think he probably always adored her. He stepped up a leap, let's just say, so was probably quite keen to marry her as soon as he possibly could.'

Sally's influence on Bercow's political views has been a source of debate. 'A lot of it clearly must be to do with Sally and her journey,' argues Lewis. 'John's political journey accelerated greatly after his marriage.' Lewis, who recalls Bercow being 'absolutely furious' about Maastricht, remembers his friend's devout Euroscepticism. In a December 1997 debate on the Amsterdam Treaty, Bercow teased Lewis that he had taken 'far too long' to convert to the cause. 'He was an ardent right-wing Eurosceptic at that point in time,' Lewis notes.

Bercow had been a vocal LGBT and equality campaigner ever since his vote on lowering the age of consent in February 2000, prior to getting back together with Sally. However, his enthusiasm for members of the Labour Party, such as Tony Blair, and the force with which he began to vocalise his concerns does seem to correlate with her coming back into his life. A shadow Cabinet minister said: 'The problem with John Bercow is that he discovered sex and New Labour at the same time.'[13]

Though Bercow likes to play down the extent to which Sally has played a hand in his political beliefs, it is not innately insulting to suggest that someone so close and dear to you might have had an influence. Undoubtedly, Bercow is someone who knows his own views and is not always ready to take advice. But there is an element, perhaps, of Sally invigorating a social liberalness that had already caught light.

In the last week of June 2002, Bercow proposed to Sally, sans ring, at the Cinnamon Club, an Indian restaurant near the Houses of Parliament. 'We know what it will be – diamonds and sapphires – but John has still to go out and buy it,' she told a reporter the following week.[14] While they said they disagreed on matters such as joining the euro (Sally pro, John anti), Bercow added: 'It is a very happy state of affairs, and I am thoroughly in love.'

So in love was Bercow that he sold his Buckinghamshire cottage, a home for four years, in light of its low ceilings and doorways. The stag night, organised by best man Julian Lewis, was held in Westminster, with the wedding taking place the next day, on Saturday 7 December. Among those in attendance was Conservative MP Alan Duncan. With the big day following immediately on from the night before, it was a low-key affair. 'We were all sharing jokes about John,' recalls Mond. Sally and Bercow married in the crypt at the House of Commons, and the reception was held in the Churchill Dining Room. 'It was a family affair and there were a few people from Parliament, not tons. They were super happy. It was a nice occasion,' recalls one attendee. Mond remembers: 'My wife is way to the right of me politically. She got into a very gentle argument with John about the death penalty. She couldn't understand how a Conservative MP couldn't support it. It was just small talk, really.' Another guest recalls Mark MacGregor, the former FCS chair who was chief executive of the Conservatives at the time, regularly darting in and out to field phone calls. 'There was some news breaking on the *Daily Mail*, and we were on this guy's table and he was up every two minutes, very self-important, trying to deal with that,' the guest remembers.

During his best man speech, Lewis couldn't help pointing out that 7 December was Pearl Harbor Day, 'which was a somewhat explosive occasion, but that I trusted – for all the ups-and-downs of married life – this would be a day of celebration rather than a day of combustion', he jokes.

A day before their first wedding anniversary, on 6 December 2003, Sally and Bercow's first child, Oliver, was born at the Royal Surrey Free Hospital, weighing 6lb 10oz. 'He's very handsome, a fact that is obviously down to Sally and certainly not me. I'm now taking some paternity leave and have already started changing his nappies,' boasted a proud father.[15] Parenting changed Bercow permanently. 'I now know what people mean when they say children put everything in perspective,' he said.[16] Freddie, two years younger than Oliver, would come next, and their youngest, Jemima, was born in April 2008. Sally would later get a tattoo of all three of her children's names on her arm.

To deal with mice in the Speaker's apartment, the Bercows decided to get a cat. In February 2010, Sally held a Twitter poll to find a name, with users choosing Order over Betty, Hansard, Harriet and Tweetie.[17] The feline stayed with them until Bercow stood down. 'It was a decent but not a particularly friendly cat. I gather a very happy home has been found,' he said in late 2019.[18] With the Bercows moving to Battersea, it was reported that the cat had been rehoused. According to parliamentary insiders, initially the cat had gone to Battersea Dogs and Cats Home.

*   *   *

'It's my first ever interview,' said Sally Bercow, sitting down with Anne McElvoy from the *Evening Standard*. Six months after Bercow was elected Speaker, and Sally, adjusting to her new life in the limelight, was beginning a new relationship with the British media, one that would prove an alluring and potent mix.

In the interview, Sally was typically unfiltered. She spoke about her younger days at university, her struggles with alcohol and her relationship with her husband. Such was her candidness that McElvoy brutally remarked: 'How on earth did he get together with a woman who makes Bridget Jones seem a paragon of restraint?'

Though the more salacious comments stirred into life some tabloid newspapers, including when she admitted to having one-night stands in her twenties, it was her attack on David Cameron that caught most attention in Westminster. Describing the Tory leader as an 'archetypal Tory' who 'favours the interests of the few over the mainstream majority', she referred to his party as standing for the 'privileged few', noting: 'He has his children at state school now, but let's see what happens at secondary level.'[19]

Sally had also been selected as a Labour council candidate for the St James's Ward in Westminster, prompting critical Tory MPs to suggest this brought Bercow's own impartiality into question. She was rebuked by Malcolm Jack, the Clerk of the House, for seeking to run her campaign out of Speaker's House, which is supposed to be a politically neutral residence. 'He said: "You'll have to operate from somewhere else,"' says a former colleague. Jack invited the Bercows to a dinner party soon after to 'make friends and make up', says the source. Sally, who missed out on becoming a councillor, would later be added to Labour's list of prospective candidates for Parliament.

In February 2011, she contributed to a piece in the *Evening Standard* in which she described how 'sexy' she found it living under Big Ben. 'Since John became Speaker, the number of women who hit on him has gone up dramatically. I don't get jealous because more men have hit on me, too. I think it's hilarious and extremely flattering that I've been referred to as the Carla Bruni of British politics,' she wrote.[20]

The article was accompanied by a picture of Sally wearing a bed sheet, looking out of their living quarters over the Thames. Sally had told Iain Dale of the article while in a taxi one evening after appearing together on Sky News. 'Well, what did John make of it?' the broadcaster asked. 'Oh, I haven't told him, do you think I ought to?' Sally responded.

Dale says: 'I think his reaction was pretty volcanic. She was treading on very thin ice on a number of things before that, and the papers obviously just lapped it all up. She just seemed to have no idea that this could be quite detrimental to him.'

At the top of the staircase in Speaker's House is a table on which magazines and a copy of the *Evening Standard* would be laid out each day. Rumour has it that the first time Bercow saw the article was when he left his study to pick up a newspaper. That evening, the Bercows were due to attend a charity event.

Sally later said: 'When I told my husband that I posed in a bedsheet, he kind of hit the roof. I really genuinely didn't expect the media furore that it caused, but because of who I'm married to it's not acceptable – apparently.'[21]

On the claim that he was now a sex symbol, Bercow told *The House*, Parliament's weekly magazine: 'I have not noticed any such thing, not as far as I am aware. I have not looked for it and wouldn't want it and I love my wife very much.'[22]

Though Sally's interventions must have upset Bercow, the announcement in early August 2011 that she would take part in Channel 5's *Celebrity Big Brother* pushed the envelope. Upon entering the show, Sally described her husband as 'the one who tries to keep MPs in control', adding: 'I don't like it when he tries to get me into order; the very fact I'm on here shows that he hasn't succeeded, I think.'

Sally revealed that she had not 'definitively' informed Bercow of her plans to go on the programme. 'I hope he doesn't divorce me over it,' she joked. 'Because I am married to the Speaker, I have to behave a certain way. Well, sorry, no, I'm an individual in my own right. I am not my husband.'

Sally said she was entering the show in part to raise money for Ambitious About Autism, a charity for which she was a parent patron, and to 'stick two fingers up to the establishment who think it's not the kind of thing I should do'. Sally was the first of eleven contestants, who included pop duo Jedward and singer Kerry Katona, to be voted out. She donated £100,000 of her fee to Ambitious About Autism, £20,000 to her publicist, Max Clifford, and £30,000 to herself.[23]

Bercow was, as he would later attest, not pleased about her decision to go on the show, and was likely exceptionally relieved that she was voted out early on, at the end of August. He told *The House* magazine: 'We had a candid exchange of views on the merits of her participating in that programme. But in the end it was her choice and I do respect the fact that it was her right to choose.'[24]

Sally's TV exploits were far from over. She took part in a show called *When Paddy Met Sally* alongside Paddy Doherty, who had also been a contestant on *Big Brother*. She was also signed up to take part in *The Jump*, in which celebrities tried to master various winter sports, before fracturing two ribs during training early in January 2015.

*   *   *

Sally had become a prolific user of Twitter, the social media site whose usage had skyrocketed. She was forced to apologise after incorrectly suggesting that Carpetright was going under, prompting the company's chairman to threaten legal action. Commenting on the Queen's diamond jubilee celebrations, Sally said she was underwhelmed by the flotilla and despaired at 'mindless, flag-waving loons'. In March 2012, she sparked outrage after tweeting that she was 'slightly tempted to try mexxy' (methoxetamine), an alternative to ketamine that the Home Office had announced would be banned as part of a crackdown on legal highs. Labour MP John Mann branded the comments 'highly irresponsible and inappropriate'.

The most egregious tweet came in November 2012. A BBC *Newsnight* investigation had accused a senior Tory politician of allegedly abusing young boys at a Welsh care home. When Thatcher ally Lord McAlpine's name started being mentioned on Twitter, Sally tweeted: 'Why is Lord McAlpine trending? *innocent face*'. She tweeted an apology soon after.

Lord McAlpine sued successfully several individuals and *Newsnight* for defamatory remarks. On the case against Sally, the High Court ruled in his favour on 24 May 2013. Justice Tugendhat said a 'reasonable reader' would understand the words 'innocent face' as being 'insincere and ironical'. 'The reader would reasonably infer that Mrs Bercow had provided "the last piece in the jigsaw",' he said. Sally, who apologised to Lord McAlpine, said in a statement: 'Today's ruling should be seen as a warning to all social media users. Things can be held to be seriously defamatory, even when you do not intend them to be defamatory and do not make any express accusation. On this, I have learned my own lesson the hard way.'[25]

A source on McAlpine's legal team says: 'Sally lacked any sense of judgement or appreciation of what was right and what was wrong in relation to Lord McAlpine.' In October 2013, Sally agreed to pay £15,000 in damages.

In May 2013, around the time of the High Court judgment, Sally set up a new Twitter account, though it has been inactive since September 2018. Journalists have sniffed around a couple of 'burner' Twitter profiles that sources have suspected have been linked to Sally, though none have been proven.

On 7 February 2020, an Amazon review by a user called 'Elizabeth Baxter' gave John Bercow's autobiography, *Unspeakable*, five stars. 'I've just finished this and hugely enjoyed it. Fascinating account of John Bercow's background and early life in particular,' the reviewer wrote. 'As

Speaker, he was clearly controversial but he comes across as a genuine reformer who faced much hostility from "the establishment". I will buy a copy as a gift for my parents too as they are big fans.' A review by 'Elizabeth Baxter' of the novel *Capital* by John Lanchester, dated 12 October 2013, was signed off 'Sally Bercow x'. It also included the hashtag '#hiDaily MailIamagoodpersonactually', after revealing that the owner purchased books legally as opposed to downloading them for free. A day before the review by Elizabeth Baxter, a 'Simon Baxter' also gave the book five stars. The review read: 'If you enjoy a fascinating life story brilliantly told, read Unspeakable. If Bercow brought Westminster to life for you, if you believe backbench MPs should be more than lobby fodder, if you want to peer behind the curtain of the most tumultuous period in recent history... you MUST read this book.' This was the first and only review by the profile.

In April 2013, Sally turned down an invitation to Margaret Thatcher's funeral. During a debate on BBC radio three years earlier, she had described herself as 'no fan' of the former Prime Minister, whom she accused of wrecking the country. 'To have a state funeral at a cost of three or four million funded by the taxpayer would not be the right thing to do,' she said.

A member of the House of Lords recalls Sally telling a Tory peer at a reception in Parliament that she 'hates' Tories. 'She was absolutely extreme in her left-wingness,' the source says. 'I find her quite treacherous. She has said things that are so inappropriate.'

It was also becoming increasingly clear that Sally's sobriety had ended. On 10 February 2014, she tweeted: 'I know AA lobby won't like this ... but for some (few) ppl is poss to resume drinking after prolonged period of abstinence.' A week earlier, *The Sun* had splashed with a picture of her kissing a 49-year-old man named Clinton Oliver, a dance instructor, at the nightclub No. 5 Cavendish Square in London's West End. Sally said the man was her friend and insisted the pictures, which were taken at a birthday party, had been taken out of context. 'I don't need to apologise to John, I've done nothing wrong. My marriage is my business. I couldn't give a damn what people think,' she said.[26]

A friend says:

When I first met Sally, she didn't drink at all but chain smoked with Diet Coke. Then she had the kids, so there was no drinking, smoking went, and it was pureeing broccoli, earth mother, the whole thing. As the kids got a bit older, then she went back to drinking ... Drink has been a thing for her in her life, either abstaining from it, enjoying it, or perhaps wanting or craving it more. It's definitely been a feature.

The confines of the Houses of Parliament were becoming too much for Sally. She resented that visitors would have to pass through security to visit her home, and felt neglected by her husband, as he would later reveal. She also felt claustrophobic with the number of staff around. However, a source says: 'It was a different story if she wanted an Ocado delivery taken up to the flat.'

Some staff felt Sally had her favourites. 'She had people she liked and people she didn't. If she didn't like you, she would make that clear to him and it would have an impact on the quality of your working life,' says an insider. Those in the room were shocked one morning when Sally allegedly entered a Speaker's conference, the daily briefings between the Speaker, Deputy Speakers and senior members of the House of Commons Service, with two of her children.

Sally was often pictured out with Farah Sassoon, a wealthy businesswoman and Labour Party donor who would later contribute £5,000 to Bercow's re-election fund in 2015. In 2012, Bercow approved a parliamentary pass for Sassoon, which sparked debate when Conservative MP Rob Wilson demanded to know what access Sassoon had been granted. The pass was countersigned by the Serjeant-at-Arms, Lawrence Ward, who was in charge of security. 'It was strictly limited to two ways into Speaker's House,' he says.

Ward stepped down from the role in 2015. His friendship with Sally was the source of gossip in the House of Commons Service, but he categorically denies any impropriety. On the issuing of the pass to Sassoon, Bercow said: 'My family is entitled to apply for security clearance for those who visit us regularly. A close personal friend of my wife holds such a pass. The security pass in question does not permit that person to access the wider Parliamentary Estate unless escorted by a full pass holder.'[27]

John and Sally's relationship was going through perhaps its most difficult phase. Sally had also been somewhat seduced by the lure of fame. 'It did go to her head a bit,' says Gillian Keegan. 'Becoming a public figure is a big deal if you haven't really thought it was going to happen ... You get pulled in all kinds of directions, and some of them were not the right direction for her.' A horrific skiing accident in February 2015, while Sally was on holiday with the three children in Lienz, Austria, left her temporarily wheelchair bound. Her leg had been broken in nine places, and it came just a month after she had broken two ribs while training for *The Jump*.

The degree to which things had soured between the couple was rammed home on 10 May 2015 when it emerged that Sally had been having an affair with Alan Bercow, the Speaker's cousin. Alan, a commercial litigation lawyer, is the son of Samson Bercow, a brother of Charlie. Sally had moved out of Parliament to a mews house in Battersea, and Alan had joined her while Bercow was campaigning in Buckinghamshire for the general election. The affair was said to have lasted for almost a year. They had bonded over 'a mutual appreciation of fine wine', according to the *Mail on Sunday*, which reported the story. Erica Scott-Young, Alan's wife, confirmed the affair but said that she was back with her husband. 'We are very much together and that's all I want to say,' she said.

In an impromptu press conference in Battersea, Sally, still in crutches from her skiing injury and without her wedding ring, said she was a 'terrible wife', and Alan had left her 'fucking heartbroken'. In an emotional and at times rambling statement, she revealed how unhappy she had been living in Parliament and vowed that she would not go back.

Gillian Keegan explains:

Their marriage had gone through some tough patches – most people do when they've got young children and busy jobs. They had this sort of spotlight – not only a spotlight – but a relatively negative public spotlight. That created other tensions. I don't know whether John saw it coming; we didn't see it coming.

The public nature of the revelations, which saw Sally and Erica trade blows in the media, only worsened an already exceptionally difficult set of circumstances. The saga also revealed that Samson and Charlie Bercow had fallen out years earlier after Charlie had failed to offer his brother a share of the family business, Bercow Motors. Bercow had worked to repair relations with Alan, leading to a rapprochement three years earlier.[28]

Charles Walker spoke to Bercow midway through the controversy. 'I don't know how you keep going. You must feel so embarrassed,' he said. 'I'm not embarrassed,' Bercow told his close ally. 'I haven't done anything wrong.' As for how he coped, Bercow said years later that he 'compartmentalised'.[29]

In June, the Bercows decided to try to save their marriage. By October, Sally had moved back to the Palace of Westminster. The Bercows have always felt their marriage is worth fighting for, and by all accounts, they are now in a good place. 'We've had periods of turbulence,' Bercow understatedly said in late 2019.[30] 'I didn't feel a great certainty, but I thought it was worth trying. I do [love her a lot], and I'm happier together than apart. It's easy for people to think the grass is greener. I like to stick with things.' More recently, Bercow said that Sally had felt 'down, miserable, rather neglected' prior to the affair. 'She thought I was enormously focused on what I was doing, but that the balance was wrong and I wasn't finding enough time for her, so I bear some responsibility for that,' he said.[31]

In many ways, Sally is the ideal match for Bercow: abrasive, forthright, uncompromising. Like Bercow, she divides opinion and can evoke vitriol from her critics. Also like her husband, she lost her father young, and that would have had a formative impact on her life. The drawbacks of fame, however, were perhaps never suited to her personality, and in recent years she has been markedly less vocal in public.

While his personal life would often prove a distraction, Bercow never truly lost focus from his stated ambition: to be a great reforming Speaker.

CHAPTER SIXTEEN

REFORMER

'He has been an amazing reformer, and reformers are not often popular.'

For traditionalists who championed the status quo, John Bercow posed a very real threat. The newly elected Speaker was determined to see through the mandate upon which he was elected, and he wasted no time in going about his work.

On his first day in office, he revealed that he would break with tradition by abandoning the traditional court dress worn by his predecessor. In its place, Bercow would wear a suit and tie with plain robes, often accompanied by what Conservative MPs describe as 'garish' ties. 'That is very much a personal choice for me. I think that is right for the spirit of the times,' Bercow said.[1]

Bercow did follow his predecessors, Michael Martin and Betty Boothroyd, in refusing to wear a wig, and in February 2017, he announced that the senior clerks in the Commons, who sit at a table in front of the Speaker's chair, would no longer have to wear wigs or court dress. The idea was proposed by David Natzler, the Clerk of the House, and endorsed by the House of Commons Commission, a parliamentary body chaired by the Speaker that deals with matters relating to the House. The group, which meets once a month, is responsible for the administration and services of the Commons, including issues relating to the pay and conditions of staff in the House. Its membership comprises MPs from across the political divide, including the Leader and shadow Leader of the Commons and senior House officials.

Overseeing his first debate, Bercow called for brevity in ministers' answers to ensure that MPs who were on the order paper could have their questions heard. This would be one of Bercow's leading areas of reform. Previous Speakers had been reticent to keep members of the government at the despatch box for long, and prioritised questioners based on seniority. 'Bercow has been very good at making everybody get in and varying the order in which he calls people,' says Tory MP Sir Desmond Swayne.

Jeremy Corbyn, the Labour MP for Islington North, watched on with interest. Writing in the *Morning Star*, Corbyn argued that Bercow's 'real test' would be his ability and the preparedness of MPs to challenge the 'overwhelming executive power over Parliament'.[2]

Bercow's first media round as Speaker was running smoothly until an encounter with ITV's political editor, Tom Bradby. In at times tense exchanges, Bercow took issue with Bradby's questioning over his lack of support from the Conservatives. 'Your reflections and thoughts on precisely how many people voted for me from my party are really of absolutely no consequence whatsoever,' he said. Bradby was midway through a question when an aide cut in to try to wrap things up. 'I certainly haven't had eight minutes,' said Bradby. Bercow said: 'Well, you have. You've had rather more.' After the aide said that Bradby had repeated the same question, Bercow added: 'Yeah, about four times.'

Bercow prompted Bradby to 'briefly' ask a question. 'Well, yes or no?' he asked, as Bradby took issue with his tone. 'Do you want to ask the question? Please, go ahead.' The incident gave an insight into Bercow's at times strained relationship with the UK media.

Nick Robinson, a former adversary on the Conservative student politics scene, reached out to Bercow after he became Speaker. The BBC political editor was mildly hesitant of how he should approach the meeting. Entering the 'amazingly ornate and gilded rooms' that comprise Speaker's House, Robinson was shown into Bercow's study. 'It has been a long time, lots has happened,' he told Bercow. The Speaker responded: 'Quite.'

The morning after his election victory, Bercow held his inaugural Speaker's conference. The daily meeting, which includes the three Deputy Speakers, the Speaker's secretary, the Clerk of the House and other senior staff members, involves discussion of the day's business and matters pertaining to the Commons. Alan Haselhurst, who had been defeated by Bercow the evening before, offered his congratulations. 'Could I just ask how you feel about your colleagues?' he asked, in reference to himself, Sylvia Heal and Michael Lord, the three Deputy Speakers. 'I need time to think about that,' Bercow responded. Deputies were appointed by the House on a motion moved, without notice, by a government minister. After becoming the first Speaker to have been elected by secret ballot, Bercow was keen to widen the use of this more democratic route.

Haselhurst visited Patrick McLoughlin, the Tory Chief Whip, and asked for his guidance. The three deputies had been approved by the House in 2005, and he feared Bercow was plotting the route to usurping them before the general election. In early July, Bercow's plans were passed on to the media. The leak infuriated Bercow, who suspected the whips of briefing the press.

In the autumn, the Procedure Committee endorsed Bercow's suggestion of electing Deputy Speakers by secret ballot. MPs supported the proposals in March 2010, alongside a bundle of reforms recommended by the Wright Committee. The committee, named after Labour MP Tony Wright, was tasked with restoring the Commons' authority over its own affairs and improving backbench MPs' ability to scrutinise legislation effectively. Among its fifty recommendations there were calls for select committee chairs to be elected and for the creation of a Backbench Business Committee, which took the scheduling of backbench business from government control. The committee also called for a House Business Committee, composed of members of the backbench business committee and frontbench representatives, which would take responsibility for the

House's weekly agenda. But, in a running sore for Bercow, successive governments failed to introduce the committee.

* * *

In the year before Bercow's election, two Urgent Questions were awarded in the Commons. In his first twelve months, this rose by twenty. Towards the end of his career, he was averaging over fifty a year and finished with a tally of more than 750. 'That is a well overdue reform,' says Swayne. The Commons was now the focal point for key developments in the news cycle, with Bercow granting UQs on topics that were often the story of the day. Labour MP Hilary Benn says: 'John's approach was first of all, if the nation is talking about it, then Parliament should be talking about it.'

The idea of using UQs as a means of emboldening the House of Commons actually came from two senior clerks, Robert Rogers and David Natzler, prior to the Speakership election. They had distributed a briefing note outlining seventy-five reforms the next chair could pursue. Among them were calls to empower select committees and discourage ministerial statements in the Chamber if they have already been aired in the media (another frustration shared by Bercow). They also recommended granting more UQs. A Commons source comments: 'I don't remember [Bercow] ever saying since that he owed any debt to them for coming up with that. It's as if he just dreamt it all up himself.' Nonetheless, it still fell to Bercow to implement change and champion the use of UQs as a means of holding the government to account.

His willingness to award UQs in part soured his relationship with the Cameron government, who felt he used the process in order to cause the administration further harm. 'He was an irritant,' says a former Cabinet minister. Such was Bercow's prolific awarding of UQs that aides in the Department of Health created an early morning rota to respond to requests from Speaker's Office. 'If it was the 8.10 on the *Today* programme, you probably had a 50 per cent chance of it being a UQ as well. If it was an emotive story, which health often is, it stood a good chance,' says a former special adviser.

UQs would be discussed at Speaker's conferences. An insider says the talks were often 'pretty farcical' and formulaic, with Bercow having already made up his mind. A parliamentary source claims Bercow would occasionally discuss UQs with clerks at the end of a Speaker's conference, rather than with his deputies.

The issuing of UQs is the number one reform that MPs most welcome, whether they are critical of Bercow or not. The measure enlivened a dormant House of Commons and ensured that ministers were scrutinised in a more public and pressurised way than otherwise was the case. Backbenchers too were given a more prominent role, and a platform upon which to influence. Though he could be profligate with UQs – they would often count as topical, rather than urgent – Bercow's greatest influence on modern-day British politics would come through his reawakening of the House of Commons as an institution.

*   *   *

During the 2009 Speakership contest, Labour MP Parmjit Dhanda had called for Parliament to set up a crèche. Bercow adopted the idea as a pet project months into his Speakership, when he announced that the House of Commons Commission had approved the creation of a nursery. But, as with many of his reforms, he encountered resistance from different quarters of Parliament.

It was decided that the crèche would replace Bellamy's bar, one of several taxpayer-subsidised watering holes on the parliamentary estate, situated in 1 Parliament Street. The bar, which had an enviable view of the Palace and Parliament Square, was popular with MPs and staffers, prompting Christopher Chope, the backbench Tory MP, to start a petition opposing the move. With Bellamy's having recently undergone a £480,000 refurbishment, and the nursery costing more than £550,000 to create, opponents cried foul at the cost of the project. Some felt that Bercow had provocatively chosen the preferred haunt of Conservative MPs as the landing post for his coveted crèche. 'There were objections,' Bercow recalls. He notes that the *Daily Mail* was among the papers to be critical of the move, adding: 'You have to think: 'Well, if the *Daily Mail* is that angry about it, you're probably onto a good course.'[3]

A former official says: 'He had made promises to Martin Salter and the Labour side about the things he would do, not least the nursery, which was a classic example of that. Also, of various other things which he obviously had to deliver on and had been his secret manifesto.'

To Bercow's chagrin, the crèche was beset by delays. This made him suspicious of the House authorities, particularly Malcolm Jack, the Clerk of the Commons, who he felt could have been seeking to resist his reforms. Due to the nature of a nursery, there were various health and safety hurdles to climb over, while there were also setbacks with the tendering of contracts. 'The result of all this was a delay, and he got very annoyed about this. He thought this was a ruse to stop the whole thing,' says a former official. 'He was sure that it was us blocking it. It was the only occasion I recall him being annoyed with Malcolm personally.'

The crèche opened in September 2010. Among its users were David and Samantha Cameron, who signed up their daughter Florence. There was an initial preoccupation with its finances – an important consideration given it was funded and subsidised by the taxpayer – and it failed to meet its break-even targets in successive years, before making £7,000 in the year 2015/16. As questions over money were addressed, however, the crèche became emblematic of the direction Parliament needed to move in to become a modern place of work, and, despite some residual hostility, it is now regarded as one of Bercow's finest reforms outside of the House of Commons Chamber. Bercow would often note in his public speeches that when he became Speaker, Parliament had a shooting gallery but no nursery. While the bar may well have been popular, few can argue successfully that taxpayers were better served subsidising alcohol for those who work on the estate than providing care for minors.

Bercow also came up against stern resistance on the introduction of a multi-million-pound education centre, designed to more than double the number of schoolchildren who visit the Commons from 45,000 to 100,000 a year. The plan, dubbed 'Bercow's Folly' in the *Mail on Sunday*, was for a cutting-edge £7 million building to be constructed alongside the Palace in Victoria Tower Gardens. Baroness D'Souza, the Speaker of the Lords, was one of those to oppose the plan. 'We didn't think that building it in a royal park had a snowball's chance in hell because you would have to get permission, you would have to move the bus stop, you'd have to move the crossing. It seemed insurmountable,' she says. At a joint meeting with Bercow, attended by architects who were designing the proposals, D'Souza outlined her concerns and set out some alternatives.

> He got really, really cross and he was about to explode. But he didn't; we were all very heated about that. But you know what, he was right. And I told him, 'John, I was wrong.' It's a really fantastic asset. I don't think there are many people who would have got that through.

On 15 July 2015, the education centre, which cost £7.5 million, was opened. 'That centre is oversubscribed week after week after week as schoolchildren come to see what goes on. That to me is a source of pride. We want to bring people into our democracy, not repel them from it,' Bercow said in 2019.[4]

* * *

Bercow was a reforming Speaker capable of achieving great things, often in uncompromising and aggressive ways. That is the common thread across many of his endeavours during his time as Speaker. 'He has been an amazing reformer, and reformers are not often popular. He hasn't got there by being nice to everyone. I think he's got there in spite of being particularly not nice to most people and actually fiendishly rude,' says D'Souza, who counts herself as a fan of Bercow.

Take his use of Westminster Hall, often a source of contention for Bercow and those advising him. From his time as shadow International Development Secretary, Bercow took a particular interest in the country of Burma, which was decades into a civil war. Benedict Rogers, a human rights campaigner and senior figure at Christian Solidarity Worldwide, took Bercow to refugee camps on the Thailand/Burma border in April 2004. They also went into conflict zones in eastern Burma. 'He was very easy to get on with, very down to earth, no airs, very willing to rough it a bit and traipse through the jungle,' says Rogers. Bercow met children whose parents had been killed by the Burmese Army and parents whose children had similarly perished. In one encounter, Bercow asked a person how they felt about a soldier who had tortured him. The victim responded: 'I love him; he is my brother as a fellow citizen of Burma.' Rogers explains: 'The absence of bitterness had a real impact on him.' Bercow said the trip had changed his life and vowed to speak out on Burma throughout his political career. 'He's been more than as good as his word,' says Rogers.

As co-chair of the All-Party Parliamentary Group for Democracy in Burma, Bercow was a vocal opponent of the Burmese government, which acted as a military dictatorship. In October 2007, at a protest in Trafalgar Square, he said: 'The government of Burma is one of the most sadistic dictatorships on the face of the earth.'[5] During the protest, he met Rogers's mother and proceeded to do an impression of her son.

After Andrew Mitchell, his successor as shadow International Development Secretary, visited Burma in 2008 despite an embargo being in place, Bercow was said to be 'furious'. 'He shouted at Andrew in the lobby and was very obstreperous and cross,' says a witness. Mitchell had travelled to the country to confront officials face to face about their treatment of the

Burmese people. Despite this incident, their relationship would improve greatly over time.

Bercow was naturally very keen for Aung San Suu Kyi, the leader of the National League for Democracy party in Burma, to address Parliament in Westminster Hall. Suu Kyi had been awarded the Nobel Peace Prize in 1991 for her efforts to bring democracy to Myanmar, during which time she faced fifteen years of house arrest and was unable to see her husband, who died of cancer in 1999, or her sons. She was released in November 2010 and elected to the Burmese Parliament in April 2012, becoming the official leader of the opposition in the process.

Though William Hague, the Foreign Secretary, was very much on board, there were some who expressed caution about Suu Kyi speaking in Westminster Hall. An address in Westminster Hall is traditionally reserved for heads of state. Barack Obama, the US President, had spoken in the venue a year earlier. Lt-Gen David Leakey, who as Black Rod was the Queen's official representative in Parliament, was cautious about setting a precedent, as was Baroness D'Souza. Despite his reservations and those of Lord Strathclyde, the Leader of the Lords, Bercow announced to MPs that the event would take place in Westminster Hall on 21 June 2012.

D'Souza says: 'When Black Rod went down the corridor with the instructions from my office that we didn't think it was entirely appropriate at the time ... Bercow went absolutely berserk.'

According to multiple accounts of this exchange, the issue centred on the seating of the Burmese diaspora. Westminster Hall addresses require meticulous planning in which all possible contingencies are considered. The organisers have to take into account the various stakeholders at play and deal often with the sensitive issues around where people are positioned. A lot of egos are, inevitably, involved.

Bercow and Leakey enjoyed decent relations, but they had had one previous clash, again over an event in Westminster Hall. Bercow took issue with the seating arrangement for Sally Bercow at Obama's address in May 2011. 'Without any warning at all, he just leapt up from behind the chair and thumped the table. He just went into a torrent of rage about it,' says a source who is familiar with what took place.

For Suu Kyi, Bercow was keen that the representatives of the Burmese community were given prominence in the seating arrangement. Lawrence Ward, the Serjeant-at-Arms, who was responsible for security in the Commons, took this message to Ted Lloyd-Jukes, the Yeoman Usher, who acts as Black Rod's deputy. Lloyd-Jukes, according to Ward, refused to change the seating plan. When Ward told Lloyd-Jukes the news would not go down well with Bercow, he is alleged to have replied: 'Well, you can go and tell him, sunshine, that this is the way it's going to be.' When Ward informed Bercow of the exchange, the Speaker cried out 'No!' in disbelief. 'He was absolutely slack jawed. If there's one thing about Bercow, he hates pomposity. He will take it on at any opportunity. It was a bit of a red flag,' says Ward.

Leakey and Lloyd-Jukes had concerns that if the Burmese diaspora were moved further forward there would be questions from MPs and peers, who would in turn be moved back, and whom Suu Kyi was due to address. Ward proposed a compromise of giving more prominence to certain Burmese representatives.

With just days to go, a resolution still had not been agreed. Leakey went to Bercow's office to discuss the matter with his private secretary, Peter Barratt. Bercow came in during the conversation and said he wanted the Burmese diaspora 'right in the very front'. Leakey said he had been discussing options with Barratt about a possible solution. 'No, you're not listening, I want them at the front,' Bercow replied. The Speaker broke out into what sources describe as a 'furious rage', which culminated in him saying: 'You're a typical product of your background and an antisemite to boot.' Leakey responded: 'Antisemitic, me? You don't know anything about me.' Bercow left the office and apologised on his return, according to a parliamentary source.

D'Souza explains: 'There were tremendous set-tos, which for some unknown and wonderful reason I managed to avoid most of. Black Rod, David Leakey, took most of the flak for me, whether that was intentionally or whether John actually refused to throw his demented tantrums at me, I don't know.'

During the event, Bercow praised Suu Kyi as 'the conscience of a country and a heroine for humanity'. Rogers, who was recruited to help identify members of the Burmese diaspora, says of the event: 'I had never really expected to see Aung San Suu Kyi in Westminster Hall, and to see her with someone that I had recruited to the Burma cause as Speaker alongside her, it was very, very special.' Suu Kyi also attended a Speaker's conference, the daily meeting of Bercow, clerks and Deputy Speakers.

Though it should be noted that there was not much public resistance to her address at the time, subsequent events have brought the decision into question. Suu Kyi was elected State Counsellor in 2015 – the de facto head of government – and has since overseen a profound refugee crisis, as 700,000 Rohingya refugees fled Myanmar after a brutal military-led campaign of ethnic cleansing. 'As things have turned out, perhaps it wasn't such a good idea. We gave a huge amount of privilege to someone without a huge moral compass,' says D'Souza.

Rogers says both he and Bercow initially resisted joining the 'growing bandwagon of criticism' of Suu Kyi. 'It has become more and more difficult to do that. I can't now really defend the position she has ended up in,' he says.

At Bercow's insistence, a tribute was held to Nelson Mandela in Westminster Hall on 12 December 2013. 'He was a man who became a mission and then a message. A giant. A hero. A friend. We are honoured this afternoon to honour him,' said Bercow. Some found Bercow's praise for the South African President somewhat jarring, given his previous membership of the Federation of Conservative Students.

*　　*　　*

Lawrence Ward was having a drink at St Stephen's Tavern in Westminster when he was approached by a politician. 'Do you mind if I sit with you?'

John Bercow asked. Six months into his Speakership, Bercow took an interest in Ward. 'He wanted to know about my background, how the House worked, the frustrations, what were the good things, who were the good people, who were the people that can deliver change,' says Ward. 'We ended up leaving the pub – we'd had a few beers – then we ended up in the Serjeant's office, where we had a case of old beer.'

Ward was then working as assistant to Jill Pay, the Serjeant-at-Arms, who is responsible for keeping order in the Commons, committee rooms and public areas. Ward told Bercow that 'people like me' would never be given the role. Three years later, Bercow reminded Ward of this story when he told him he had been selected as Pay's replacement after she stood down.

Bercow's reforming zeal carried over to appointments within the House. As with so many of his reforms, these did not always come without controversy. His most notable appointment was that of Rose Hudson-Wilkin, who became the first female Speaker's chaplain and the first from a minority background when she joined the House in the summer of 2010. 'I've made a particular point of appointing more women and more BME citizens of the United Kingdom to prominent positions,' Bercow said in 2019.[6]

The Speaker's chaplain provides pastoral and spiritual support for Members and staff of both Houses, alongside taking prayers in the Chamber every sitting day. The Commons previously had an arrangement with the Church of England whereby the Speaker's chaplain also acted as the Rector of St Margaret's Church, which is situated in Parliament Square next to Westminster Abbey. For a new chaplain, Rev. John Hall, the Dean of Westminster, nominated a list of candidates. His top pick was Andrew Tremlett, the Canon of Bristol Cathedral. But Bercow did not want 'another white middle-aged man' to take on the post, and instead preferred 'a priest with the personal and popular touch', said a source.[7] He decided to go 'below the line', says an ex-Commons staff member, and picked out Hudson-Wilkin. In response, the Church of England pulled out of the St Margaret's arrangement, and Hudson-Wilkin continued to serve her parish in Dalston, east London.

By the time of her departure in late 2019, MPs were lining up to pay tribute to Hudson-Wilkin's service in the House. On announcing her next move, Bercow broke down in tears as he told MPs that Hudson-Wilkin was to become the first black Bishop of Dover. 'I am so proud to say this.' (Indeed, she would be not only the first black Bishop of Dover but the first black female bishop in the Church of England.) In October 2016, Saira Salimi became the first female and first BAME Speaker's Counsel. House of Commons staff are full of praise for her performance.

Other appointments would not prove as successful. In 2016, Kamal El-Hajji succeeded Ward as Serjeant-at-Arms. El-Hajji had served as front of house and VIP relations at the Ministry of Justice and had been awarded the British Empire Medal in 2015. But colleagues say others would have to pick up the pieces around him to ensure his tasks were carried out. A parliamentary official says: 'He was completely and utterly out of his depth … I do not know how the House of Commons allowed Bercow to even have him on the shortlist, frankly.' Another official adds: 'It is just such a bizarre appointment. He was a million miles away from having the ability to do the job.' However, Tasmina Ahmed-Sheikh, the former SNP MP who sat on the committee to select the new Serjeant-at-Arms and Speaker's Counsel, insists both candidates were the right people for the job. '[Saira] was the best of all the candidates as Kamal was the best of all the candidates.'

In a move that faced widespread criticism, El-Hajji, writing in *The House* magazine in June 2018, said Bercow was a victim of a 'witch-hunt' over claims of bullying against him. This was further compounded the following February when an independent investigation found that El-Hajji had bullied one of his deputies.[8] In an appearance on BBC 4's *Woman's Hour*, Hudson-Wilkin also defended Bercow as a 'decent, generous human being'.[9]

Bercow's approach to appointments irritated some members of the House of Commons Service, who felt he had a 'crude' notion of diversity and how to improve it. They argue that tackling the issue goes beyond simply appointing people of colour to senior positions, and contend that Bercow was less concerned with addressing the systemic challenge. 'It's like everything else with that man: it's all about him. He made those appointments so he could say he made the appointment, boast about the appointment, and posture as a doughty champion of underrepresented groups,' a former official says. Others accuse Bercow of circumventing normal processes in order to select a candidate of his choice. It can be noted that in taking such a risk, Bercow earned their enduring loyalty of those he appointed, which may in part explain why El-Hajji and Hudson-Wilkin took the unusual decision to speak out in his defence. Lawrence Ward, too, is a staunch proponent of Bercow and his Speakership.

Improving diversity among senior positions is an important component towards progress, however. To that end, Bercow has earned praise from MPs across the House for his determination in this area. MPs also speak of Bercow's welcoming approach when they joined the Commons. The Speaker had already learned details of their lives which he recounted to them as they swore in or met him for the first time. 'He knew my children's names; he knew how old they were. That will immediately endear you to a person, wouldn't it, when they've bothered to find out stuff about you,' says Labour MP Jess Phillips. 'It immediately brings a sense of trust between you and him.' Bercow would also be 'incredibly patient and protective' of new joiners as they acclimatised to Westminster life. When Phillips approached the Speaker in March 2016 to let him know that she planned to read out the names and ages of women murdered by men in the past year, he promised he would let it go ahead without interruption. 'He has done that every single year,' she notes.

Bercow opened up Speaker's House to numerous charities, regularly granting the space to MPs who wanted to hold gatherings for their various causes. At the events, he would lavish praise on those present. 'If you're in the room, he will find some way of mentioning the parliamentarian and their efforts about that subject when he speaks. He very much tries to promote Members of Parliament, even ones I know have tried to sign letters of no confidence,' says Phillips. In March 2010, Bercow gave permission for Labour MP Chris Bryant to marry his partner Jared Cranney in the first civil partnership ever held in the Houses of Parliament. (The Speaker had obtained a licence from Westminster City Council to hold civil partnerships within the parliamentary estate.) After the ceremony, Bercow hosted drinks in Speaker's House. 'Parliament is special because it has made it possible. We are delighted that everyone in the UK can now share in a privilege that used to be available just to straight MPs,' said Cranney and Bryant.[10]

Bercow was happy for some practices to go unreformed. Sources say that he ran Speaker's Office like a 'court'. He continued the tradition of having attendees announced as they entered the room at the start of every Speaker's conference. Ian Davis, the Trainbearer, would read out the names; Members of Parliament would enter first, followed by the clerks. 'For all his frank man-of-the-people stuff, he kind of liked that bit of hierarchy and deference,' says a Commons source. Attendees were expected to stand until he entered the room. Bercow would also try to guess which minister would respond to the day's upcoming adjournment debate, though insiders suspect that he would often have been tipped off by his office as to the answer.

Bercow declined to follow suit after David Cameron announced a change in the law to end the special pension arrangements for the Prime Minister and Lord Chancellor. He announced that he would not take the £37,000 a year pension until he reaches sixty-five. 'At current prices this will mean, along with the pay cut he took in 2010, a total minimum saving of approximately £430,000 to the exchequer. The Speaker believes it would be wrong, especially in the current economic conditions, not to depart from the status quo in his particular circumstances,' a spokesperson said.[11] He did, however, accept a pay rise in 2015 that took his salary to £150,236 – nearly £800 more than that earned by David Cameron.

Bercow made good on his pledge to be a bastion for the Commons. He seized every possible opportunity to speak at universities and across the world to promote the work of Parliament and convey the reforms he was pursuing. He was instrumental in the creation of a parliamentary studies module that was rolled out across universities. In 2014, he allowed cameras into Parliament for a fly-on-the-wall BBC Two series, *Inside the Commons*. He relaxed the dress code so that men no longer had to wear ties in the Chamber. Babies and young children came into the Chamber during votes. During his tenure, proxy voting was also introduced, granting MPs who are pregnant or new mothers to cast their vote from home. In October 2010, members of the UK Youth Parliament became the first group other than MPs in 300 years to have debated in the Commons and sat on the green benches. Bercow has presided over every annual sitting of the caucus.

'One thing you can say is much people know much more about Parliament under the reign of John Bercow,' says Jess Phillips. 'People say words to me that they would never have said ten years ago. People understand about amendments, bill committees and things. In that, you could say he's had some success. But the reputation of the place is in tatters.'

Bercow's unrelenting desire for change would incur a lot of collateral damage along the way. If a wall was put up in front of him, he would shout at it before knocking it down.

CHAPTER SEVENTEEN

WHIPS

'I had a relationship with my whips characterised by trust and under-standing. I didn't trust them, and they didn't understand me.'

There are few groups that John Bercow holds more in contempt than whips, the collection of MPs who operate behind the scenes. Whips work to ensure the mechanics of their parliamentary party run smoothly and their MPs enter the correct division lobby. If an MP is refusing to co-operate, they can deploy various means to try to ensure that they do. The *House of Cards* trilogy has only added to the air of mystique and intrigue that surrounds the shadowy cabal. While the use of blackmail and threats are said to be a thing of the past, whips can deploy a combination of carrot and stick in their pursuit of party unity.

In retrospect, John Bercow would have been a whip's worst nightmare. 'They've always been very sceptical about Bercow, and they basically don't like anybody who is on manoeuvres or moving around,' says a former whip.

A story that lives in infamy within the Conservative whips' office took place in the summer of 2000. Tory MP Shaun Woodward had defected to Labour the previous December, and Bercow had been asked to appear on a live BBC radio chat show alongside him over the weekend. Bercow, believing there was a briefing paper compiled by the Conservative Re-search Department on Woodward lying in the whips' office, turned up to

Parliament on a Saturday. However, the door was locked. According to the first account of the story, Bercow asked security officers to open the door, but they did not have a key. In order to gain access, the security officers shouldered the door open, causing almost £1,000 worth of damage, the *Sunday People* reported. To make matters worse, the papers were not there. 'It was unfortunate and accidental, and I was terribly sorry… I'm happy to pay the bill for repair,' Bercow said.[1]

However, multiple sources, including those who served in the whips' office at the time, describe this version of events as 'complete bollocks'. One says: 'There's no way a security guard would do that. The security guard, if he was there, would have had the key.' Instead, sources allege that Bercow 'rammed' the door open to gain access. A spokesperson for Bercow says: 'He opened it, damaging it in the process, and subsequently paid the repair cost.' A Conservative source says: 'Betty Boothroyd was incandescent. I don't think that's ever endeared him to her. We hushed it up. We were a bit surprised to say the least.'

Bercow's travails would not end there. A week later, he burst through a Commons door and sent a painter flying. 'I do seem to have a problem with doors. I just didn't see him. I immediately said sorry and he wasn't hurt,' Bercow said.[2] Eye-witness Lindsay Hoyle, the Labour MP who would go on to succeed Bercow as Speaker, recounted: 'He knocked the man clean over. He then had to apologise and pick the guy up. The poor bloke was not hurt – just shocked that an MP had shoved the door straight at him.'

Keith Simpson was the whip assigned to the shadow Home Affairs team when Bercow worked under Ann Widdecombe. He remembers the MP being particularly difficult to handle. 'You never knew with John when you turned up what mood he was going to be in. Some days he sulked and said nothing. Other days he was very animated, amusing and everything else,' Simpson says. 'He was always having rows with people. Whether it was little man syndrome, I don't know.' Widdecombe, however, does not recall Bercow having such mood swings. 'With me he was a) perfectly affable, b) perfectly stable about things. I don't really remember that,' she says.

By 2005, he was beginning his campaign for the Speakership. 'This was rather a tricky period as he was on his journey by then. He could blow up at the drop of a hat,' says a whip during this period. Whips practically stopped trying to get Bercow to follow the party line. One recalls: 'I didn't try and persuade him because, to be quite frank, it was impossible once he made his mind up.'

One of Bercow's most noted critics was Simon Burns, Tory MP for Chelmsford, who was first elected in 1987. Their relationship deteriorated in early May 2009. In the Commons, Julian Lewis denounced his Lib Dem opponent in his constituency of New Forest East, Terry Scriven, as 'manic and malevolent'. Bercow, according to Hansard and eyewitnesses at the time, remarked: 'He's a nutter.' Burns, who was Bercow's whip, confronted him in the division lobbies. 'I understand that at Business Questions you shouted out language about someone being a "nutter",' said Burns. 'No, I didn't,' Bercow replied. 'That's what I was told.' 'Well, get your facts right. You're pathetic, what's wrong with you. You can't even get your facts right.'

An insider says: 'Bercow ranted and raved about how pathetic he was, how inadequate he was, how misinformed he was, and off he stormed.' Whether there had been some confusion and Bercow was denying calling another MP a nutter, as was originally alleged to me by my source, is unclear. What is clear is that he did use the term. Bercow and Burns's relationship would sour greatly after this incident. 'That broke it for me,' he told friends.

Patrick McLoughlin, the Chief Whip, did not have a good relationship with Bercow. The two men, who both came from working-class backgrounds, had never seen eye-to-eye. Late on in proceedings on Monday 6 December 2010, Bercow asked a question of the House to which a Labour MP had objected. But the MP had done so prematurely, so Bercow asked the question again and then gestured for the MP to make known their objection. Believing the Speaker was assisting the opposition, McLough-lin took issue and heckled Bercow as he walked out of the Chamber.

In an angry exchange, Bercow barked 'Order' at the Chief Whip eight times. 'The government Chief Whip has absolutely no business what-soever shouting from a sedentary position. He – Order! The right hon. Gentleman will remain in the Chamber. He has absolutely no business scurrying out of the Chamber,' said Bercow. 'We all saw you,' McLoughlin replied.

McLoughlin's team were watching events unfold on a monitor. He slammed his office door as he returned from the Commons. John Ran-dall, the Deputy Chief Whip, looked at McLoughlin's adviser and said: 'Leave it.' He then went down and spoke to McLoughlin. 'It was one of those examples of Bercow publicly humiliating Tories. To go back to a Cabinet minister in public was a sign of what was going on behind the scenes as well,' says an aide.

A Tory minister, who was a whip at the time of the incident, says: '[Bercow] would try to bully [McLoughlin]. It sounds silly with a small man and a big guy, but that was the dynamics of a bully. I never forgave him for that.' Another former whip says: 'Patrick is very mild-mannered. He had had enough. He was being treated pretty poorly by Bercow; [Bercow] always regarded us as the enemy.'

Over time, rumours about Bercow's private treatment of staff began to circulate in the whips' office. 'The bullying was appalling,' says an ex-whip. 'The doorkeepers used to tell us about the shouting, especially in the evenings,' they add, in relation to the Speaker's apartment.

Several sources also speak of an incident involving Sir George Young while he was working as Leader of the House, prior to becoming Chief Whip in 2012. A source with knowledge of the exchange says:

He had his weekly meeting with Bercow, and they had a disagreement. George is the most mild-mannered person you'll ever come across, the most courteous, polite person. It ended up with Bercow effectively screaming, shouting and swearing at him, jabbing his finger in his face, spittle flying from him. Effectively, George said, 'I don't think there's any point in my continuing this conversation,' and just walked out. He felt how on earth was he supposed to deal with that.

Another source recalls: '[George] said there was one memorable incident. The point is, you only need to have one memorable incident with him and then you avoid setting the conditions for another one.'

During a tempestuous evening in the Commons on 25 March 2019, in which MPs voted to take control of the order paper to allow for a series of indicative votes on Brexit, Greg Hands, a former deputy whip, was heckling from the backbenches. Bercow sought to bring Hands into line. 'He was once a whip; he wasn't a very good whip. It would be better if he could keep quiet,' Bercow said. Amid a swathe of backlash from irate Tory MPs, Bercow later apologised. 'He is normally a most genial character, and most of our exchanges are in that vein. I am very happy to tender that apology,' he said.

When approached about the put-down, Hands said: 'He was entirely right to silence me. I am known for having pretty much the loudest voice in Parliament, and I was being very, very loud, vocal... He then went too far... Bercow had figured that I must be unpopular for whatever reason, and he just misjudged it.'

Bercow maintained decent relationships with the Chief Whips of opposition parties, most notably Labour's Rosie Winterton, who helped marshal the resistance to the attempt to unseat him, and her successor, Nick Brown (who had also served in the position under Gordon Brown). In a rare appearance at the despatch box at the end of October 2019, Brown branded Bercow an 'outstanding Speaker' who deserves 'the gratitude of us all'. 'I can truthfully say, Mr Speaker, that nobody is going to miss you more than I am,' he said.[3]

According to a Commons source, there was an effective 'direct line' from Speaker's House to the Labour whips' office. 'Rosie was the one I heard about and was best placed to do it. I'm absolutely confident that was the case,' they say. Former Labour MP John Mann says: 'He's claimed to be the champion of Parliament; he's actually been the champion of the opposition whips. He's allowed individuals to do things, but it's entirely at his say.'

Not every Conservative Chief Whip would have difficulties with Bercow. Mark Harper, who served under David Cameron before the Prime Minister stood down, would visit Bercow every week and keep him abreast of what was coming down the tracks from the government. This amicable relationship is all the more noteworthy given the ill feeling between the Prime Minister and the Speaker. 'Sometimes, as Chief Whip, you ended up being the one that tried to make it all work properly,' Harper says.

The job of a Chief Whip is to ensure the government to treat Parliament in the correct manner, he continues.

> Sometimes, if you think the Speaker's been reasonable, you try to persuade ministerial colleagues that he's been reasonable and that they ought to do this. When he's not, your job is to try and push back and go, 'Actually, we don't think that's reasonable.' If he thinks you take Parliament seriously, you're more able to push back and you're trying to make it work properly.

Bercow could not hide his disdain for whips. 'When I was a Conservative backbencher, I had a relationship with my whips characterised by trust and understanding. I didn't trust them and they didn't understand me,' he told a university audience in 2015.[4] He argued that too much power is concentrated in ministerial and whip hands. 'But I do feel very strongly that whips have got their role; there's an important role for whips to play in a parliamentary system just as you need sewers in any civilised society. It would be very unhealthy for public purposes if we didn't have sewers,' he said, in an echo of a joke used by his former hero, Enoch Powell.

A former whip says: 'I think we handled him as well as we could have done. The thing that upset most people was his conversion from ultra-right-wing. In '97, '98, he would have been the ERG with knobs on.'

Bercow's relationship with whips would reflect continuing friction in his political life: at first, between his personal views and his loyalty to his party, and, latterly, in his commitment to ensure the Commons was heard and government overreach was reined in. Against this backdrop, with a Speaker of Bercow's reforming disposition and a government seeking to push its agenda, fireworks were always likely.

CHAPTER EIGHTEEN

BOLLOCKED BY BERCOW

'Stupid, sanctimonious little dwarf.'

After the 2015 election, Charles Walker decided it would be wise to meet John Bercow on a regular basis. Walker had proved to be not only one of Bercow's staunchest defenders but also one of his most reliable sounding boards. Given he was intimate with many of the Speaker's failings, he would counsel him on keeping his cool. Walker would often say to Bercow: 'Mr Speaker, the more relaxed you are, the better humour the House is in. The more irascible you are, the more it has a negative effect on the Chamber.'

Even Bercow has admitted that, particularly in his early days, he had a propensity to be aggressive from the chair. 'I tended, particularly early on, sometimes to react to displays of bad temper or anger rather officiously. But I think on the whole it works better in calming people down and defusing difficult situations if you can deploy humour,' he told an audience in 2017.[1]

To outsiders, his eccentricities and unique use of the English language have made him a figure of intrigue. But those on the receiving end of his reprimands lament the trivialisation of his behaviour, which they believe speaks to an underlying character failing. Some go further than that and argue that his actions are tantamount to bullying.

As the number of MPs told off by the Speaker grew, a new group in the Commons began to take shape: the Bollocked By Bercow Club.

* * *

Anna Soubry first came across Bercow on the student politics scene as a former member of the Federation of Conservative Students. When she was sworn in as an MP in 2010, Bercow reminded her of their past affiliation.

Soubry proved to be one of the more vocal backbenchers in what was dubbed the 'naughty corner', a section where Tory MPs sat to the right of the Speaker's eye. But her approach, she tells me, was sanctioned by certain members of the front bench. 'We were all hugely encouraged to be as loud as possible. It came quite naturally to me,' she says.

Soubry had bedded in well and was appointed as PPS to Simon Burns, the Health Minister and Bercow enemy no. 1. This, she feels, did not ingratiate her to Bercow. 'I think that was a big problem. One of the dangers in this place, people assume that you're like them in the way that you think and operate,' she explains. 'So, if they have been ambitious and have been prepared to hitch their career to somebody else's tailcoat, then they project on other people.'

A former Tory MP who stepped down in 2019 says they used to 'fantasise' about Soubry walking over to Bercow in the chair, giving him a 'smack across the face' and saying: 'Don't you ever speak to me like that again.'

In September 2012, Soubry was made a minister in the Department of Health. Two months later, in the space of ninety minutes, she received three reprimands from Bercow. The first time, during Prime Minister's Questions, Bercow called her out for making excessive noise. '[She] thinks her views are relevant, but we are not interested,' he said. In a subsequent debate on regional pay, Bercow rebuked Soubry twice more. 'I do not want the sedentary chuntering, the finger-wagging and all the rest of it. The hon. Lady can say "pooh" if she wants, but she will accept the ruling of the chair and either behave or get out of the Chamber. I do not mind which it is.' After a further interruption, Bercow said: 'It is totally unacceptable to behave in this way and it will stop straight away. I hope the whip has noticed it, and I will be speaking to others about the matter.'

Soubry comments:

> When I became a government minister, I'm afraid there were a number of occasions when he publicly humiliated me. It was awful. A certain absolute criticism of John that I have is that he can't help himself. There have been a number of instances when he would pick somebody and deliberately humiliate them in a way that is profoundly... not just unfair, but it is profoundly unseemly in somebody who holds such an incredibly powerful and important office. It's a complete contradiction with the other things that he clearly believes in and he stands for.

Notwithstanding these remarks, Soubry was in danger of being named and chucked out of the Chamber over her behaviour. Sir George Young, the Chief Whip, told her she would have to go and see the Speaker, who was threatening to take a minister's scalp.

Soubry spoke to Bercow's office and asked to see him. She pre-empted a telling off by saying: 'Mr Speaker, I am so sorry – it's inexcusable and it's not good enough and I know that I'm in the wrong and this is not acceptable behaviour. I know it's got to stop.' Soubry says: 'You could see him thinking, "I was going to give her a bollocking."'

Claire Perry, another Tory MP who started in 2010, was so incandescent that she had not been called during a debate that she stormed into a tearoom and asked: 'What have I got to do to be called by the Speaker? Give him a blow job?'[2] At the Tory Party conference later that year, Perry reflected: 'I suppose it was a lesson in that you can't be too careful about what you say.'[3]

Six years later, after Bercow called Perry out for 'dilation', the then

Business Minister commented: 'The last time I talked about dilation, I was in labour.' In a condescending tone, Bercow shot back: 'What is required is a brief answer and a brief question – no dilation.' Perry wrote to the Speaker the next day and accused him publicly of sexism.[4] Bercow wrote back: 'While, respectfully, I do not accept the points made, perhaps it would be nice to meet for a "clear the air" cup of tea as soon as possible?'

Bercow and Burns's feud would peak in June 2010. Bercow twice encouraged Burns to face forward during Health Questions when speaking at the despatch box rather than turning to face questioners who were sat behind him, so the House could hear his responses. 'It's a very simple point; I have made it to others, and they have understood it,' he said. Unamused, Burns mouthed to himself 'Stupid, sanctimonious little dwarf'. Burns told friends: 'With hindsight, little was probably superfluous.'

Simon Carr, sketchwriter at *The Independent*, called Burns when he returned to his office. 'Did you really mouth "Stupid, sanctimonious little dwarf"?' he asked. Burns said yes. The news sparked outrage from dwarfism charities, including Walking with Giants, who demanded a meeting. His press secretary had typed out an apology to Bercow the next day, but Burns changed it to say he was sorry if he offended 'any group of people'. No formal reprimand came through from No. 10, and no meeting with Walking with Giants took place. British politics was denied the most unlikely of duos when Burns's 2013 bid to become Deputy Speaker, after Tory MP Nigel Evans stood down, fell short.

The tickings-off were upsetting many on the Conservative side, some of whom remembered Bercow's own choice behaviour as a backbencher. It also further entrenched perceptions among Bercow sceptics that he was biased against them. One MP, Rob Wilson, went to extraordinary lengths to prove the Speaker's partiality. In a study, produced on 18 July 2011, Wilson found that since the general election in May 2010, Tories had been admonished 257 times compared to 109 for Labour MPs, based on the number of times he had barked 'Order' at an MP. For a comparison, Wilson found that Bercow interrupted Labour MPs 162 times when they were in power during his first year, twenty more times than their Tory counterparts.[5] At the time, there were 349 Labour MPs and only 210 Tories. 'Those MPs who have suggested bias in the Speaker's handling of the Commons would feel vindicated by these figures,' said Wilson.[6] The following year, Wilson produced another report that claimed the number of Urgent Questions granted by the Speaker was 'massively in Labour's favour', with Bercow twice as likely to force coalition ministers into appearing before the House than their Labour predecessors.[7]

By way of response, Bercow told an audience some years later:

> Being fair and impartial isn't about having a statistical quota, it's about dealing with the issue that arises. Now, if at a particular time, on a given day or over a period, one side is particularly aggressively criticising the chair, or particularly aggressively shouting, then it is that side with which you have to deal. You can't make up miscreants on the other side of the House where they don't exist.[8]

The person who received the most Bercow rebukes was Michael Gove with eighteen (Burns had ten). Bercow once famously told the Education Secretary: 'Mr Gove, you really are a very over-excitable individual. You need to write out 1,000 times "I will behave myself at Prime Minister's Questions."' In a more recent encounter, Bercow would highlight that his and Gove's children attended the same school:

> When he turns up at our children's school as a parent, he is a very well-behaved fellow. He would not dare to behave like that in front of Colin Hall, and neither would I. Do not gesticulate. Do not rant. Spare us the theatrics. Behave yourself. Be a good boy, young man. Be a good boy.[9]

Sarah Vine, a *Daily Mail* columnist who is married to Gove, tweeted: 'Insult me, insult my husband – but don't bring the kids into it. Please. And thank you.'

* * *

Mark Pritchard was sitting in the Chamber waiting to ask a question during Business Questions on Thursday 13 January 2011. He had been in his place at the start of the session, as Bercow expected of all would-be questioners. To him, it amounted to a basic courtesy to the House. However, he had left the Chamber briefly for a toilet break, leading to confusion, and Bercow did not call him on his return.

Pritchard wrote a note to Bercow about the mix-up and dropped it in Speaker's Office. He was walking along the corridor behind the Speaker's chair when he saw Bercow and his parliamentary entourage coming back the other way.

After he walked past, Pritchard heard Bercow mutter: 'The courtesy of the House is that Honourable Members should stand aside when the Speaker passes by.' Pritchard responded: 'Mr Speaker, don't point at me. I am not here to be abused by you'. Bercow countered: 'You will obey the courtesies of the House!' Pritchard exclaimed: 'Who do you think you are, you're not fucking royalty!'

Allies of Pritchard note that he is not prone to using such language – indeed, he had been known to say 'schmidt' instead of 'shit'. As the outburst became known, Pritchard received texts of appreciation from fellow MPs, journalists and other Speakers in the Commonwealth, a friend reports. Some enterprising soul even printed off a batch of T-shirts carrying the remark.

So when Keith Simpson became the latest Tory MP to receive a slap-down from the Speaker, Pritchard tapped him on the shoulder and commented: 'Welcome to the BBB Club.' The Bollocked By Bercow Club was in its relative infancy. Tory whips had joked about creating badges inscribed with the letters, and two years later, Sheryll Murray, who had the required equipment, was approached to produce them. Joining Burns, Soubry, Pritchard and co. in the BBB Club was Ian Liddell-Grainger, who on 1 July 2013 was falsely accused by Bercow of 'rude, stupid and pompous' behaviour for appearing to interrupt Labour MP Stella Creasy (it was in fact his colleague Alan Duncan who had interjected).

Some backbenchers took issue with the way Bercow would announce MPs' names when calling them to speak. Famously, he would bellow 'Mr Kenneth Claaaaarke' when calling the former Chancellor (Clarke says he was never bothered by this). Conservative backbenchers Andrew Selous and Peter Bone would also have their own monikers. Friends say it speaks to Bercow's sense of humour.

Though he was accumulating detractors, Bercow was a dab hand at rapprochements. His relationship with Soubry, who left the Conservative Party in February 2019, has vastly improved over the years. 'After I did what I did, I like to think that there was respect there. That was the impression I got,' she says.

Bercow would similarly extend olive branches to Pritchard, Perry and former arch-opponent Nadine Dorries, who had previously campaigned against his Speakership bid in 2009. In Pritchard's case, there was a reconciliation which culminated in him receiving an invite to a New Year's Eve party at the Bercows' a year later. He, like Dorries, would be invited to join the Chairman's Panel, which carries an extra £15,000 in salary.

'The thing is he's clever. The people he fears or feared, he would try and neutralise them,' says a source in the Conservative Party.

Few argue that Bercow would prevent any of his opponents from having the opportunity to speak in the Chamber. 'He's pretty good at making certain that all views in the House are called,' says a member of the BBB Club.

A former Cabinet minister argues: 'You've got to control the House of Commons. In general terms, we have to have broad shoulders and we have to accept to some extent that sticks and stones may break my bones but words will never hurt me. Being given a bollocking by the Speaker falls within that bracket.'

Charles Walker explains:

In most cases, when he snaps at a colleague, it's a bit like a normally
well-behaved dog: when they snap, they suddenly get frighteningly
worried afterwards. John doesn't like it and he's very good at making it
up with colleagues if they allow him to and he allows himself to, which
in most cases he does.

*　*　*

Despite some people's best efforts to prove otherwise, Bercow did take
action against opposition MPs. During his tenure, Bercow expelled
from the Commons five MPs, not one of whom was a Conservative. His
first expulsion was Paul Flynn, who accused Philip Hammond, the Defence Secretary, of lying to Parliament over the conflict in Afghanistan.
Next up was Nigel Dodds, the deputy leader of the Democratic Unionist Party, who accused Northern Ireland Secretary Theresa Villiers
of 'deliberate deception'. Labour's Dennis Skinner, the long-serving
backbencher, was despatched for referring to David Cameron as 'dodgy
Dave' (though Bercow had previously let the remark go unchecked on
four occasions). In June 2018, SNP leader Ian Blackford was named for
disregarding Bercow's ruling during PMQs and was followed out of the
Chamber by the rest of his party. And Labour MP Lloyd Russell-Moyle
was asked to leave after he grabbed the mace in protest at Theresa May's decision to pull the vote on her Brexit deal on 10 December
2018. According to Hansard, Bercow has instructed MPs of all sides
to take a 'medicament' – often a 'soothing' one – twenty times. He has
encouraged MPs to calm themselves on 100 occasions, while he has ex-
tolled the virtues of yoga for keeping calm in the Chamber on fourteen
separate instances. SNP MP Angus MacNeil, whom Bercow referred to
as a 'cheeky chappy', would also be called out for heckling on multiple
occasions. 'I loved it,' he says. 'I can't complain about any of the times

that he reprimanded me. I've contributed my fair share of decibels to the Commons Chamber.'

MPs from smaller parties in the Commons are broadly positive about Bercow's Speakership. 'He was greatly admired and loved by an awful lot on our side. There was another lot who were not so sure of him. He was a mercurial figure,' says MacNeil. Tasmina Ahmed-Sheikh, the former SNP MP, adds: 'For me, Bercow definitely championed the opportunity for backbenchers to speak in Parliament. As a result of that and along with Brexit, there are more and more people watching Parliament.' During the coalition years, some Lib Dems did feel that Bercow should have allowed them more opportunity to express their own independent voice when it diverged with that of the Conservatives. 'I felt there could have been more accommodation to allow that to help us increase the profile of the Lib Dems as opposed to the coalition,' says Tom Brake. After the 2015 election, when the Lib Dems were left with just eight MPs, some felt that Bercow was not playing fair. 'He treated the Liberal Democrats poorly in the 2015–17 parliament,' says former Lib Dem MP Greg Mulholland. 'Not because they had lost their third-party status, which we had, but by not giving the same parity and time to the leader and MPs that had been afforded to previous smaller parties.'

Bercow was often by no means in the wrong. In October 2015, he accused Sajid Javid, the Business Secretary, of behaving in a 'discourteous and incompetent' way for the length of his response to an Urgent Question, which curtailed time allotted for backbenchers. Boris Johnson, then Foreign Secretary, was firmly rebuked for referring to his opposite number, Emily Thornberry, as Lady Nugee, in reference to her husband, Sir Christopher Nugee, a High Court judge. 'We do not address people by the titles of their spouses. It is inappropriate and frankly sexist to speak in those terms, and I am not having it in this Chamber,' he said.

Ed Balls recalls an incident in which a Conservative MP mocked his stammer. 'The Speaker jumped up and really went for her. The next day, she wrote me a letter apologising,' he says.

There's a fighting for fairness and the underdog and against bullies. When the executive is bullying, he gets very angry. When people bully him, as he sees it from the top right-hand corner, he gets very angry. That all, in my mind, goes back to the review he did for us and his kids, and a personal sense of the right way to treat people.

Though Wilson's numbers point to a willingness to tell off Tory MPs, to conclude that Bercow is biased on that basis seems a stretch. As Bercow put it: 'Yes, I periodically excoriate a colleague for bad behaviour. But I do so on the basis of who's behaving badly, not on the basis of a party allegiance.'[10]

Bercow is far from being the first Speaker to be accused of bias. The election of Selwyn Lloyd in 1971 was controversial, not least because he had served as Foreign Secretary and Chancellor for Conservative governments. However, as Vernon Bogdanor, professor at King's College London, notes, Lloyd 'proved a successful and impartial Speaker'. Margaret Thatcher took issue with Jack Weatherill, claiming that he was biased against her administration, while many Tories felt Speaker Martin was in hock to the Labour government.

Critics of Bercow say that his temperament would not allow calmer heads to prevail in the Chamber. As politics became more contentious, this shortfall would become more pronounced. 'I don't think he has helped what would have been a charged atmosphere anyway,' says a former aide to Theresa May.

Sir Malcolm Rifkind, the former Conservative Cabinet minister, says while it is right for the Speaker to keep backbenchers in check, Bercow went out of his way 'to try and humiliate them'. Bercow, he argues, 'makes long, very sarcastic remarks, and you're left with the view that he's more interested in the sound of his own voice and how smart he's being. I don't think that's the Speaker's job.'

Rifkind concludes: 'He'll be one of the most interesting, fascinating, perhaps one of the most successful, but he won't [go down as] a great Speaker. Why not? Because of his personality. He's a bully.'

CHAPTER NINETEEN

CAMERON

'He thinks people like him are born to rule.'

John Bercow and his former boss at Rowland Salingbury Cascy, Leighton Andrews, walked into a restaurant after a long day at Tory Party conference in October 1996. They had a lot of catching up to do; Andrews was now working at the BBC and Bercow had been selected as the Conservative candidate for Buckingham in February.

David Cameron, who was sitting with a large group of people, had spotted them enter the restaurant. As they were in earshot, Cameron said in a loud voice: 'Even fuckwits like Bercow have got safe seats now!' Turning to face his acquaintance, he said: 'Oh, hello John!'

Seven years on from their first encounter in Vauxhall, Bercow and Cameron were at similar points in their career. After working for the Conservative Research Department, his first job after graduating from Oxford University, Cameron was seconded to Downing Street, where he would brief John Major ahead of Prime Minister's Questions. Like Bercow, he would work as a special adviser, first for Norman Lamont and later for Michael Howard. At the time of the encounter, he was working as director of corporate affairs at Carlton Communications and had been chosen as the Tory candidate in Stafford.

The colourful remark across a restaurant in Bournemouth was said to have been good-natured joshing. 'I would say it was banter. But who knows whether there was a bit of steel in that banter,' says Andrews. It is an early insight into a professional and personal relationship that, on paper, should have been a harmonious one but in fact proved to be anything but.

* * *

By the time Cameron entered Parliament in 2001, both men had been on something of a journey, though Bercow believes his own liberal awakening came before that of the future Prime Minister. 'I was in favour of more modernisation earlier and I was of that view, with all due respect, considerably before David Cameron was. But he was the facilitator of change,' Bercow told an audience in 2017.[1] 'He was John the Baptist to David Cameron's Jesus Christ,' says Michael Keegan. Along with Bercow, Cameron would rebel on the matter of gay adoption late in November 2002. Both had initially supported Michael Portillo for the party leadership a year earlier.

David Davis, who was recently criticised by Cameron in his memoirs, says: 'Someone like Cameron dressed up his views, in as much as he had any ... I wouldn't say that of Bercow. I think Bercow is sincere about his change of view.'

Both Bercow and Cameron fostered deep-rooted and lofty ambitions. With Michael Howard stepping down as leader in 2005, Cameron had been preparing to put himself forward after only four years as an MP. George Osborne, who was running his campaign, stopped Bercow in the voting lobby to ask if he would be supporting his candidate. 'Let me tell you, I don't like David, I don't like anything that he stands for and I won't be supporting him,' Bercow told Osborne.

On the face of it, Bercow should have been the first name on the list of supporters for Cameron's modernisation agenda. It chimed with what he had been promoting over the course of the previous five years. But innate reservations over Cameron's hinterland would preclude him from coming on board. Instead, Ken Clarke, the grammar school boy from more humble beginnings, had become his political doyen. Osborne says: 'I guess I never really understood why David Cameron didn't like him and why he didn't like David Cameron. And I still don't, actually, because they agreed on a lot about what was wrong with the Conservative Party.'

Bercow, who four years previously had said Clarke was too Europhiliac to win an election, now firmly backed the former Chancellor. 'Polls have consistently shown that Ken Clarke is the most popular Tory in the country … Many MPs would surely welcome the chance to vote for the most impressive beast in the Tory jungle,' he said.[2]

Bercow would unceremoniously put his foot in it, however, when he said publicly what he told Osborne in private. 'I think there are serious problems with [Cameron's] candidature,' he told GMTV's Sunday programme. 'In the modern world, the combination of Eton, hunting, shooting and lunch at Whites is not the most helpful when you are trying to appeal to millions of ordinary people who simply don't identify with any of those institutions or pastimes.' David's wife Samantha saw the interview and alerted her husband to what had been said. 'That was the fork in the road,' says Keegan.

When Clarke pulled out of the race, Bercow lent his support to Cameron. Relations between the two had been altogether solid until this point. They played together as first pair in the House of Commons and House of Lords tennis team, during which time Bercow says he 'used to get on well' with his colleague. 'In fairness to Cameron he was a very good partner; McEnroe like intolerance of his own mistakes but pretty tolerant of mine. But after we ceased to play together for the House of Commons and House of Lords tennis team our relationship seemed permanently to deteriorate,' he said in 2017.[3]

After his remarks on Cameron's background, any hopes of a frontbench return had been squandered, and Bercow's mind turned to the Speakership. After he had undertaken a review for Gordon Brown's government, while still launching periodic calls for his party to change its approach on immigration and other matters, Cameron was already against the concept of Speaker Bercow. There was nothing he could do to stem the tide, however.

At the 2010 election, Cameron found himself under pressure to stand a candidate against Bercow in Buckingham. While there was a convention that major parties would not contest seats occupied by the Speaker, there was some precedent for a challenge. In 1974, Selwyn Lloyd was opposed by Labour and the Liberals. Labour and the SDP stood against Jack Weatherill in 1987, and the SNP ran candidates against Michael Martin in 2001 and 2005. Nigel Farage, the UKIP leader, had put himself forward against Bercow, as had a number of independent candidates. After some deliberation, Cameron announced the Tories would not contest the Buckingham constituency.

Without the power of the party behind him, Bercow's re-election in Buckingham posed a real headache. He no longer had an election agent, a ready-made group of local activists to go out campaigning, or the might of the Tory fundraising machine. 'I've got an election to fight and I've got nothing. Can you please help me?' Bercow asked Michael Keegan. Keegan established a campaign group called the 'Friends of Speaker Bercow', which he chaired, and set up a bank account for donations under the same name. Keegan would donate to all of Bercow's re-election campaigns from 2010 onwards.

Bercow's inner circle were concerned by Farage. 'We thought, "That's really cute politics because he's going to try and come in and take all the disaffected Tories,"' says Keegan.

On 10 December 2009, a meeting on Bercow's campaign strategy was held at a pub in central London. Among those present were Martin Salter, who ran Bercow's bid for the Speakership, and Tom Watson, the Labour MP for West Bromwich East. Also in attendance were Sadie Smith, Bercow's future spokesperson, who worked for Salter; Keegan; Frank Donlon, a constituent who played a key role in shaping the campaign; and Bercow's election agent, Gordon Bell. 'Quite a motley crew, when you look at it,' says Donlon. According to the minutes of the meeting, the Friends of Speaker Bercow account contained just £225.

Salter, who had investigated Farage's expenses record as an MEP and also had access to information on the BNP candidate, urged Bercow to run a positive campaign and to 'rise above' attacks from UKIP and the BNP. It was agreed that Bercow would package the two parties together as 'extremists'. Salter outlined a three-pronged approach to the campaign message: that voters are not disenfranchised as a result of electing a Speaker; that, while Bercow was no longer a Conservative, 'he voted with the Conservative Party 99 per cent of the time'; and that UKIP's candidate went against tradition and was 'un-British'.

On polling day, Farage had one final trick up his sleeve. He hired a two-seater light aircraft to fly over the constituency carrying a banner that read: 'Vote for your country – Vote UKIP'. The banner became entangled, causing the aircraft to nosedive and crash-land at Hinton-in-the-Hedges Airfield near Brackley. Both people on board, Farage and Justin Adams, the pilot, were taken to the John Radcliffe Hospital in Banbury.

Donlon and Bell were watching the television coverage of the crash when Bercow walked into campaign HQ. 'Have you heard the news?' they asked. Bell was frantically checking electoral law. If Farage died from his injuries, polling in Buckingham would be stopped immediately and a by-election would be held later, as per the rules of the Representation of the People Act 1983. If Parliament resumed without Bercow, he would lose the Speakership. Donlon recalls: 'We were standing there looking at each other, saying, "Bloody hell, what do we do?"'

Bercow spoke to Keegan, who says: 'I can remember John being really concerned because Farage was quite badly hurt during the plane crash. John said: "You do realise, if he dies before the polls close, we have to re-run the whole thing?"' Bercow telephoned Farage in hospital to offer his best wishes for a speedy recovery.

Farage and Adams survived the plane crash. Bercow was elected with a majority of 12,529, with independent candidate John Stevens, who had run an abrasive campaign targeting Bercow's record on expenses, beating Farage into second.

For future election campaigns, Bercow ran a much more slimmed-down operation. Tom Tweddle, a senior member of his constituency staff, was one of the leading members of the campaign team. Donlon continued to leaflet for Bercow. 'I've got a lot of respect for John as our constituency MP. People outside the constituency don't realise how well thought of he is,' he says.

With the House reconvened on 18 May 2010, the first task was to deal with the appointment of the Speaker. The Father of the House, Sir Peter Tapsell, whom Bercow had mimicked during his speech for the Speaker-ship, would oversee proceedings. If objections were heard when Tapsell asked the House if they wished to re-elect Bercow as Speaker, a vote would take place.

Bercow had asked Sir Malcolm Rifkind to propose him. Though the former minister had voted for a rival candidate in June 2009, Rifkind had taken issue with the response of his colleagues on the evening of Bercow's first election, and made a point of congratulating the new Speaker when he left the Chamber. Proposing Bercow, Rifkind said: 'We have had in the past eleven months a modern Speaker for a modern age ... The House can be reassured that if it chooses him today, we will have some experience and gravitas in the Speaker's chair. I commend him to the House.' When Tapsell put the matter to a vote, opposing voices were drowned out by the majority of MPs who gave their support. Tapsell did not force a division, and Bercow was re-elected without challenge.

* * *

True to his word, Bercow enlivened the Commons by granting more Urgent Questions and encouraging more statements be made to the House. The result was that ministers were being made to come before

Parliament more than had previously been the case. To Cameron, Bercow was becoming irksome. 'I used to have a rule: when I got out of bed every morning, I always used to think, "Whatever John Bercow can do to make my day utterly miserable, he will." And on the whole, it was a very good guide to life,' he told *The Times* in 2019.[4]

In April 2012, Cameron became the first Prime Minister since Tony Blair ten years earlier to answer an Urgent Question, as concerns grew about Jeremy Hunt, the Culture Secretary, and his connections to Rupert Murdoch's News Corporation when he was considering its takeover of BSkyB. Cameron, who was campaigning in the forthcoming local elections, had to cancel a planned event in Milton Keynes. One Downing Street source complained: 'If John Bercow has any opportunity to be self-important or the centre of attention, he'll take it.'[5]

Likewise, Prime Minister's Questions, which is supposed to run for thirty minutes, routinely went beyond the expected 12.30 finish. An ex-Cabinet minister recalls Cameron confronting Bercow after he allowed PMQs to run until 12.37. 'The Speaker looked regretful and thanked the Prime Minister for his comments. The next week, he let it go on until 12.45,' they say.

The source adds:

> That was a wonderful example of Bercow making very clear he was not going to be bullied or dictated to by the executive. That's what you want from a Speaker. You want a Speaker who stands up for Parliament, for the rights of Members of Parliament, and remembers that the executive is accountable to Parliament and not the other way around.

More personal animosity between Cameron and Bercow surfaced in late 2010. In an unusual move for a sitting Prime Minister, Cameron addressed journalists in Parliament at an event known as a lobby lunch, where politicians deliver a speech and answer questions. The previous evening, Cameron had heard a gag from one of his senior whips riffing on Simon Burns's 'sanctimonious little dwarf' comment, and he decided to recount the joke a day later. Cameron described Burns persuading his driver to reverse his vehicle into the Speaker's car. An angry Bercow, the joke continued, came rushing out of Speaker's House and confronted the minister, saying: 'I'm not happy.' To which Burns replied: 'Well, which one are you, then?'

Their most public confrontations came in the Chamber. After being cut off twice by Bercow during the previous PMQs, Cameron decided to soldier on and ignore Bercow's call for order until he had completed his answer to Ed Miliband's question. Tory MPs roared with delight. Bercow reprimanded Tim Loughton, the Children's Minister, only to intervene on him again. 'No, it's not funny; only in your mind, Mr Loughton, is it funny. It's not funny at all; it's disgraceful,' said Bercow.

Bercow also clamped down on Cameron after he described Ed Balls, the shadow Chancellor, as a 'muttering idiot'. 'The Prime Minister will please withdraw the word "idiot". It is unparliamentary. A simple withdrawal will suffice. We are grateful,' said Bercow. In perhaps their most famous exchange, Bercow stopped Cameron mid-flow during an attack on Miliband over his new economic adviser, David Axelrod. 'But I haven't finished,' cried Cameron. 'In response to that question, the Prime Minister has finished, and he can take it from me that he has finished,' Bercow shot back.

Walker, a senior member of the 1922 Committee, recalls Cameron ventilating about Bercow during a meeting in No. 10: 'I was sitting at the far end of the Cabinet table. David Cameron was going, "Bloody Speaker! God, he's impossible. And it's all your fault, Charles!" he said, swinging around. He was joking, with a big wolfish smile.'

The great and the good gathered in Westminster Hall on 20 March 2012 to honour the Queen on her diamond jubilee. Baroness D'Souza, the Lord Speaker, spoke first, and Bercow followed. The previous September, Bercow had been made honorary president of the newly established Kaleidoscope Trust, which supports LGBT people suffering persecution around the world. During his speech, Bercow said: 'This is a nation of many races, faiths and customs, now beginning to be reflected in Parliament. All this progress has occurred during your reign. You have become, to many of us, a kaleidoscope Queen of a kaleidoscope country in a kaleidoscope Commonwealth.'

Cameron, sat on the front row, furrowed his brow. Soon after his address, Kaleidoscope put out a statement. 'John Bercow has once again demonstrated his commitment to upholding the human rights of lesbian and gay people,' it said. A spokesman for Bercow said that the reference was not 'necessarily about the Kaleidoscope Trust', adding: 'It refers to the fact Her Majesty is Queen of many different faiths, colours, creeds, ethnicities and, yes, sexualities.'

Baroness D'Souza comments: 'It's an LGBT lobby organisation, which again is admirable, absolutely admirable and good for him. In different circumstances, I would have done the same. But it was inappropriate; he got a lot of flak for that. He used it to campaign for one of his favourite organisations.' At PMQs a week later, Cameron teased: 'I am not going to prejudge what is in the Chancellor's Budget. However, I think that we can say that it is – if you like, Mr Speaker – a kaleidoscope Budget.' Bercow responded: 'I am so encouraged that the Prime Minister is using my language. Good on him!'

* * *

Like successive Tory leaders before him, Cameron was under pressure from Eurosceptic backbenchers who wanted a vote on the UK's relationship with Europe. In October 2011, they were granted an opportunity to express their desire in the Commons. A non-binding backbench motion on a referendum was politically sensitive – many frontbenchers were said to be angling to vote in favour. A series of amendments to the motion were being considered by some MPs, but Cameron feared that Bercow would not select them – to do so could have undercut the main motion. He was proved correct.

The House voted overwhelmingly against a referendum, but eighty-one Tory MPs voted in favour, with a further fifteen abstaining. At the time, it amounted to the largest post-war rebellion on Europe ever suffered by a Prime Minister. Just over a year later, Cameron was preparing to do battle over the vexed issue of the EU budget, which member states were due to agree for the next seven years. Cameron said he would wield the UK's veto on any increase above inflation, but Tory MPs put forward an amendment to the government motion calling for a real-terms cut. The amendment was selected by Bercow. In Cameron's first major Commons defeat, Labour sided with Tory rebels in voting for the amendment by 307 to 294. Though non-binding, it put Cameron in a tricky position. A former minister says there was 'hard feeling' in the government about Bercow's role, and a perception that he had deliberately called opposing voices to question the Prime Minister in the preceding debate, adding: 'There was a feeling that Bercow was becoming more actively partisan.'

Bercow's most controversial move to date came in March 2013 after he accepted an additional amendment to the Queen's Speech by backbench MP John Baron, which criticised the lack of legislation to hold an in/out referendum on the EU. Amendments to the Queen's Speech, which sets out the government's legislative agenda, are usually only offered to opposition parties. The amendment was defeated by 277 votes to 130, after Cameron moved to quell the rebellion by pledging to produce a draft referendum bill. 'That was just something that had never happened. It came out of the blue,' Cameron said.[6] An ex-whip says: 'Bercow was regarded in the whips' office as being somebody who was rarely helpful, virtually always unhelpful, and often actively conspiring against the government.'

George Osborne disagrees, saying:

I didn't really understand where all this animosity came from. Did he cause trouble for the government? Yes, by picking rebels, but in those days it was the Brexiteer, Eurosceptic bloc. Selecting an amendment to the Queen's Speech was really unhelpful to us. But, in a way, he was giving a voice to whoever the minority was and especially exposing when the government itself didn't have a majority on an issue. I thought that was his proper role.

In 2017, Bercow also selected a third amendment to the Queen's Speech, this time by Labour MP Stella Creasy, who called for women from Northern Ireland to get free access to abortions on the NHS in England. Creasy withdrew the amendment after the government conceded.

On the evening of 10 November 2014, years of tension between the executive and the legislature resulted in Parliament's ugliest night for decades. Britain had opted out of more than 100 EU-wide police and justice directives, but wanted to re-join thirty-five, including the European Arrest Warrant. Around thirty Conservatives were against the re-adoption of the EAW and demanded a vote on the matter.

In an incendiary move, Theresa May, the Home Secretary, introduced a statutory instrument – a secondary piece of legislation – which covered only ten of the thirty-five measures, and, crucially, not the EAW. She argued that a vote on the measures would be interpreted as a tacit vote on the EAW, and any loss would be considered as such. Backbenchers were furious and unconvinced. Meanwhile, the whips scrambled to get Tory MPs to return to the Commons as Labour tried procedural manoeuvres to delay the vote. Cameron, dressed in white tie, was called back to the House after giving a speech at the Lord Mayor's banquet. The government won the final vote by 464 to 38, but at the cost of bad blood across the House.

Bercow was furious. 'Some people think it is very clever, but people outside of the House expect straightforward dealing and they are, frankly, contemptuous ... of what is not straight dealing,' he said. The strength of Bercow's words would force many to conclude that he would have to be taken on. The following March, the Tories tried to oust him from the chair.

* * *

As Speaker, part of Bercow's role was to safeguard and promote the role of the Commons. Throughout his Speakership, he showed an antenna for the mood of the House. Holding an EU referendum was far from the majority view of the Commons during the coalition government, but Bercow wanted to ensure that minority voices were heard.

'David is relentlessly tactical rather than strategic. Let's face it, he chose to call the referendum. Was there a clamour for it? There was not,' Bercow said in late 2019. 'There was chuntering in his own party, but the public wasn't demanding one. He just thought it would work for him.'[7]

When defending himself against charges of bias on Brexit, Bercow would point to some of his earlier rulings in which he sought to facilitate Eurosceptic backbenchers. The same is true of how he approached Remainers in the 2017–19 parliament, as we shall explore.

The perception among Cameron and others was that Bercow was determined to do everything within his power to be a nuisance. A former Cabinet minister argues: 'The honest truth is ever since John became Speaker he has appeared to lean towards the other side of the House. He will say he's defending the rights of backbenchers, but it's been more than that.' However, Ken Clarke says: 'Half the Conservative Party thinks if you have a Conservative Speaker, he should support a Conservative government.'

Power in the coalition government lay largely in the hands of four people: Cameron, Osborne and the two senior Lib Dems, Nick Clegg and Danny Alexander. MPs from both parties at times felt marginalised from the decision-making process and relied on Bercow to ensure that their voices were heard.

It is not the Speaker's job to make ministers' lives easy. Bercow was under no obligation to make choices based on what would be the most convenient for the executive. However, his poor relations with Cameron undermined his role, as it allowed his detractors to cast aspersions about his motivations. '[Cameron] thinks people like him are born to rule, that the natural order is that people like him run things, and that he is in a superior position,' he maintained in 2019.[8]

It is clear that Bercow saw his role in part as standing up for the rights of MPs against the bully boys in government. Having experienced Michael Martin, who was ultimately far more impotent in the chair than his successor, Cameron's expectations of the way a Speaker should act were a far cry from how Bercow would carry out the role.

'Before Bercow, there were lots of difficulties, lots of difficult votes, but the Speaker wouldn't always pick the most out-there motion,' Cameron said.[9] 'On the one hand, you want a Speaker that supports backbenchers and stands up for Parliament. But you've got to try and follow some sort of rules and precedents to have a sense of fair play.'

On a personal level, Bercow self-evidently was no fan of Cameron. To him, the Old Etonian Oxbridge graduate had everything handed to him. Cameron was part of an establishment that Bercow would come to despise and crave acceptance from in equal measure.

In different circumstances, their ideological rapport could have seen a fruitful political relationship. Instead, their contrasting dispositions, rooted deeply in their respective upbringings, put paid to that.

CHAPTER TWENTY

CLERKS

'The guy has mercurial mood swings within a sentence.'

Libby Bradshaw worked in the House of Commons Service for twelve years. For six of those, from 2002 to 2008, she was based in the Members' Library. She quickly worked out the different types of MPs: some were collegiate and patient; others were not. John Bercow fell into the latter category. 'He was one of the ones that when he came to the door, people's heart sank and said: "Oh God." You just never knew what mood he was going to be in. He would flip,' says Bradshaw.

When Bradshaw was on night duty, Bercow phoned in an inquiry. Bercow sent along his researcher to collect the information, which Bradshaw had placed in a tray. However, the researcher returned empty-handed after failing to locate the envelope. Bercow came down half an hour later. 'Are you Elizabeth?' he asked, before launching into a tirade. 'He went on and on and on, proper loud shouting. I just literally picked it up and gave it to him, because it was there. He just stormed out: no apology, nothing. It felt like for ever, but it probably went on for three or four minutes, this tirade of abuse.'

During his ventilation, Bercow referred to Bradshaw as a 'little girl'. 'I don't think he swore. It was just very pompous. He definitely called me "little girl". At the time I was about thirty and I'd been working there for years – not that it's an appropriate thing to call anybody.' A spokesman for Bercow said he had no recollection of this event.

These angry tirades and supercilious attitudes are an ugly side of Bercow, and one that would come out in clear detail through his relationship with members of the House of Commons Service.

*   *   *

When Bercow was a member of the Panel of Chairs, the group of MPs who chaired events such as Westminster Hall debates and Public Bill Committees, he enjoyed a fruitful relationship with Commons staff. 'He was extremely good. He was very procedurally aware. He knew his onions from a very early stage,' says Eliot Wilson, who worked in the Public Bill Office. 'In personality terms, he was completely different [to what he is now]. He was very warm, polite and sympathetic to officials.'

Another staff member who worked in the Public Bill Office says Bercow would always take advice and sought guidance where necessary. 'He wanted to do it well, which is not something that all MPs exhibit and isn't necessarily I guess quite so much where he is now,' the source says.

The tide appeared to turn soon after his election as Speaker, when Bercow's desire to implement reforms came up against what he perceived to be resistance from the establishment.

Despite a clash over the creation of a nursery, and over Sally Bercow's attempts to run a political campaign out of Speaker's House, Bercow enjoyed a decent working relationship with Malcolm Jack, his first Clerk of the House, who had been in post since 2006. 'He may have thought that I was in some way trying to hold him up on one or two of his projects,' says Jack. 'Of course, I wasn't. All I was trying to do was just to make sure that he understood the pitfalls of going down this particular route. But in the end, if the Speaker wants to do that, that's up to him.'

The Clerk of the House acts as the principal adviser to both the Speaker and the House. To handle Bercow's more mercurial side, Jack would let some issues go if he deemed them to be a low priority. On one occasion, Bercow was taken aback when Jack did not resist a proposed change at the first time of asking. 'What? I thought we were going to discuss this?' Bercow asked. 'It appears you have made your mind up,' replied Jack.

Senior members of the House administration would meet with Bercow about the day's agenda. One ex-clerk says Bercow would often turn for support in the Chamber 'however unpleasant he had been to you in private'. 'He would then be effusively thankful and grateful afterward. Our professional code was strong about turning the other cheek and keeping the show on the road,' the source says.

On 1 October 2011, Robert Rogers succeeded Jack as Clerk of the Commons. Initially, Rogers enjoyed decent relations with Bercow. 'He had a fantastic relationship with Bercow and [Robert] totally had him in the palm of his hand, essentially because he wanted to be Clerk. They got on really well. Then as soon as he became Clerk it started to go downhill,' says an insider.

By comparison with Bercow, Rogers was something of an establishment figure. He is a privately educated Oxbridge graduate who had entered the House of Commons Service in 1972. Rogers, whose wife was High Sheriff of Herefordshire, plays the organ, is a member of the Skinners' Company and knows members of the royal family. 'All that made it quite hard for them to get on. Instead of being in a supplicant role, he was in a rival role. That just put [Bercow's] back up and made it much harder for the relationship to work,' says a former staff member.

Another source says: 'Because Bercow's constantly pushing against the system and not listening to advice, and doing radical things for which he thought he had a mandate, he was probably running up against the Clerk on quite a lot of things.'

From January 2011 to April 2012, Eliot Wilson worked as private secretary to Lindsay Hoyle, the most senior Deputy Speaker as Chairman of Ways and Means, who was elected to the post in 2010. Early on in Rogers's time as clerk, Wilson accompanied Hoyle to Speaker's Office for a meeting, which was delayed. Bercow was inside talking to Rogers. 'You could hear the tone if not the words that were being used. It was pretty hectoring on the Speaker's behalf. It was him dressing Robert down in a way that frankly I thought a Clerk of the House who had served for forty years deserved better than,' recalls Wilson.

Bercow's relationship with Hoyle is also much discussed in Westminster. A source in the room recalls Bercow's 'bellicose anger' at Hoyle during a Speaker's conference early on during his time as Deputy Speaker. 'The guy has mercurial mood swings within a sentence,' the observer says.

> I can't remember what Lindsay told him, but he shouted at him and Lindsay wouldn't let it go, which is quite right too. Lindsay was actually quite calm, but [Bercow] absolutely bellowed at him. There was total silence, and to this day I regret that I did not stand up and say: 'Do not talk to another human being like that.' We should have all walked out.

A parliamentary insider says Hoyle and Bercow were 'at war' for many years. '[Lindsay] loathed him. They loathed each other.' Wilson says he had the impression that relationship was already 'stiff' and 'strained' by the time he joined Hoyle's office in 2011. An ex-Deputy Speaker says of Bercow: 'His instincts are confrontational. I wouldn't say I've ever seen him build a consensus. That's not in his nature. But it's not a crime.' Bercow is also said to have had difficult relations with Eleanor Laing, who became Deputy Speaker in 2013. Sources say that Bercow felt the only Deputy Speaker he could trust was Rosie Winterton, who was elected after the 2017 election.

Friction between Hoyle and Bercow came from suspicions that the Deputy Speaker had eyes on Bercow's position. 'Like all Speakers, they always think that their deputies are after their job,' says a parliamentary source. '[Bercow's] very robust and bruising. Sparks can fly if he meets someone coming the other way.'

The breakdown in Bercow's relationship with Rogers was a known secret in Westminster. A former Cabinet minister claims Bercow often 'berated' Rogers in front of other people: 'The fact is, John behaved towards Robert in a way that in normal circumstances would be regarded as unacceptable. He spoke to him in ways that, in my view, showed no sufficient respect for either his character or his position or his authority.'

A member of the House of Lords recalls Rogers expressing his dismay with Bercow to them at a dinner party. 'They really, really, really loathed one another. It was a very unhappy place,' the peer says.

> One of the things I suppose that really drives John to a complete and utter frenzy is being thwarted. And I think that characteristic of going berserk is an indication of a real lack of confidence in yourself. That's quite sad, that he has to bully his way through because otherwise he might get bullied.

The most explosive clash between the pair emerged after Rogers announced on 30 April 2014 that he was stepping down as Clerk. A source from outside the Commons met Bercow at three o'clock one afternoon in Speaker's Office, which boasts a large desk and a magnificent view of the river Thames. 'You can't sit in that room without running the risk of becoming pompous. It's very imperial,' says the source.

Rogers knocked on the door at 3.25 to let them know they had five more minutes before the next engagement. At 3.30, he knocked again. 'Why don't you fuck off? Don't you know that we're in a meeting? Fuck off,' Bercow said, according to the source in the room. 'I was shocked,' they add. 'This is the most distinguished man, and there was considerable animus between him and Robert Rogers because Rogers was more keen to do things straight down the line and he wasn't prepared to veer off.'

The witness kept things under wraps until they had dinner with Michael Fabricant, the MP for Lichfield and arch-Bercow protagonist, whom they would occasionally meet to sound out the mood of Parliament. 'The first and only time I made a mistake was I told him that story.

He hated the Speaker,' says the source. During a tribute to Rogers in the Chamber, Fabricant referenced the tale. 'Despite Sir Robert having studied Anglo-Saxon at Oxford and being told at least once in front of others to F. U. C. K. off by you, Mr Speaker, I think that would not have encouraged him to stay.' Bercow responded: 'I will ignore that last observation, which suffered from the disadvantage of being wrong.' Sources close to the Speaker denied Bercow had used the f-word.

Rogers was awarded a peerage in October 2014. A former Cabinet minister says: 'David Cameron put him in the Lords simply to spite John, because he knew that [Bercow] had behaved very badly towards him and he wanted to demonstrate that fact.' A former senior official says: 'Bercow was unbelievably rude to Robert. Not just discourteous, but abusively, insultingly rude.'

As we will explore in later chapters, Rogers, now Lord Lisvane, lodged a formal bullying complaint to the Parliamentary Commissioner for Standards against Bercow in January 2020, shortly after it emerged that Jeremy Corbyn had nominated Bercow for a peerage.

Chris Leslie, the former Labour MP, says:

A bit of challenge to the orthodoxy view of the clerks is a really important thing to have. That's what happens; conventions evolve and change. Now, my suspicion is that a lot of the animus towards [Bercow] is partly because the civil service as it were doesn't really like too much of an activist Speaker because it means they're not necessarily in the driving seat. That can be frustrating for the clerks and others. I think he's managed to move things on in a very good way.

Many staff members often refer to the grandiose surroundings of Speaker's House, and its relative isolation, as being partly behind Bercow's tendency to overlook advice. 'It's quite easy to get a bit isolated and cut off from reality,' says an ex-official. An ex-clerk argues: 'Power went to his head, essentially. He got grander. The Speaker's Office is a weird place in that everyone is employed by the House but serves the Speaker in a way that everyone serves the House more generally.' A source adds: 'That office operates like a Royal Court with the Speaker at the centre. It's not healthy or good for any of the people who work in it, from either a deference point of view or getting work done.'

Sir Ian Kennedy, a leading QC, served as head of the Independent Parliamentary Standards Authority from 2009 to 2016. He had several meetings with Bercow over the course of his tenure. 'I was fascinated about the way he spoke to me, which was always in performance mode, as if I was some ten or fifteen yards away. He never broke into what I would describe as conversation mode,' he says.

IPSA, a public body, had been formed following the expenses scandal to make decisions on MPs' pay and implement a new system on expenses. The nature of its work often brought the watchdog into confrontation with MPs and therefore Bercow, who also oversaw the Speaker's Committee on IPSA, known as SCIPSA. 'He could be very vituperative, and you'd just have to sit there,' he says. 'The bottom line was, he had this capacity to bully and to be overbearing while at the same time there was this other side which was helpful and sensitive.'

During a conversation with Andrew McDonald, the chief executive of IPSA, Bercow is said to have sounded off about Kennedy, to a point where McDonald had to ask the Speaker to stop 'swearing at him' or he would leave the meeting (the exchange was reported back to Kennedy). In early 2011, Bercow had a frosty encounter with Kennedy and Ken Olisa, a board member of IPSA who had been critical of MPs and their complaints of the new system in an interview with *Total Politics* magazine.[1]

That was an example of the Speaker seeing his role as dressing us down. He was a defender of a view of Parliament and a view of the world which didn't brook criticism or comment about the ways MPs led their lives. We weren't really interested in that; we were interested in how they spent their money and how they justified it.

In April 2012, Bercow told Kennedy that members of IPSA's board would have to reapply when their four-year terms expired. He also established a selection panel to vet prospective members. Rather than be vetted, four board members, including Olisa, a businessman, quit their posts. Bercow argued that he had been acting under the advice of independent lawyers to ensure the selection process was fair and lawful. Members of IPSA interpreted it as a form of revenge for the controversies surrounding its work on MPs' pay and expenses. Kennedy argues: 'That was an example of the ruthlessness of the Speaker.'

Kennedy and Bercow had a workable professional relationship, but there were tensions. Bercow would often say to Kennedy: 'The problem with you is you're a bit too clever.' 'What do you say to that?' asks Kennedy. 'It was him wanting to put me in my place, coupled with a degree of insecurity.'

As ministers often experience with civil servants, reforming politicians can face challenges in delivering their respective agendas. Malcolm Jack argues:

> Don't forget they've come up the greasy pole ... It's very important that people deal decently with each other and are respectful and so on, but you have to take that into account that sometimes people have come up through this path and they really want to get something or other done. If they feel that something is blocking that, then they will become aggressive, particularly if that's their personality.

That said, there are examples, many of which we will examine, of Bercow behaving in a way that is simply unacceptable towards members of the House of Commons staff. 'He is someone who fills everyone else with fear in the institution,' says an active staff member.

Bercow says:

> I've sought to be a progressive change-maker and some people don't

like change. And so in very simple terms, it's reform versus reaction. When you insist on reform, and you say, 'Well, I've got a mandate for reform and I want to deliver reform and I want to do it my way,' there are sometimes forces of resistance who say, 'Well, no, it's not appropriate or it shouldn't be done like this.' In the end, somebody has to prevail, and I think that the Speaker, in this case, who's got a mandate, is entitled to proceed as he set out to do.[2]

With Rogers stepping down, thoughts quickly turned to his successor. David Natzler, who had served in the House of Commons Service since 1976, was Rogers's preferred choice. Bercow, however, was keen to look elsewhere. It was here that the Speaker would later admit he got slightly above his station. 'Have I sometimes mishandled something or over-reached myself? Yes.'

CHAPTER TWENTY-ONE

CAROL

'It was the worst time in my career.'

When London-based recruiters Saxton Bampfylde reached out to Carol Mills, she wondered how on earth they had tracked her down. Little did the Australian know how her life would change from that moment forward.

Mills was born and raised in the Northern Beaches area of Sydney, a series of coastal neighbourhoods that includes a number of popular surfing beaches and villages, such as Manly, Newport and Palm Beach. In 1990, after graduating from the University of Sydney, Mills became a civil servant. Her first role was in the Department of Housing in the New South Wales government. By 2012, Mills had risen to the position of Director General responsible for Communities.

The Australian Parliament in Canberra is split into two elected Houses, the Senate and the House of Representatives, led respectively by the President of the Senate and the Speaker. The Speaker and the President of the Senate were looking for reformers to change the way Parliament House was perceived by the wider public. They wanted to ensure better access to the building, more transparency, better tools for communicating with constituents, and a stronger focus on a modern civil service-type management. Mills was approached by a recruiter about the position of Secretary of Parliamentary Services. 'I have a background of doing a lot of change management, so that's what interested me in it,' she says, speaking from Australia. In mid-2012, Mills started her new job. 'That's how I got to be in Canberra.'

Mills first saw John Bercow speak at the World e-Parliament Conference in Seoul, South Korea, in May 2014. The Speaker was delivering a talk about his newly created Digital Democracy Commission, which had been tasked to consider the way Parliament utilises technology to connect with the modern world. Mills had presented a paper on developing IT strategy in Australia. 'He talked about the same sorts of things that had attracted me to go into Canberra, particularly about better engagement with the community, rebuilding trust in the Parliament,' Mills says.

Later that month, head-hunters from Saxton Bampfylde informed her of a new role in the House of Commons. They were recruiting for the position of Clerk of the House of Commons, which came with a salary just shy of £200,000. For the first time since its creation in 1363, the role was being opened up to outsiders. Previously, outgoing Clerks had put forward a list of names, with the Speaker making the pick. The job called for 'the ability to represent the House of Commons, at both national and international level' and 'experience in policy decision-making at high levels and under pressure'.

Bercow believed that while the Clerk role had traditionally been filled by a procedural specialist, the candidates with the necessary immersion in parliamentary procedure were unlikely to have the experience to be able to act as chief executive of the House of Commons Service, as the role entailed. 'The skillsets are just different. The idea that a person who's Clerk of the House should also be in charge of the management of the House as a service provider, and as a deliverer of fairness to employees … struck me as bizarre,' he argued.[1]

Bercow, however, had failed to convince Rogers and Andrew Lansley, the Commons Leader, that the role of Clerk should be split. 'Therefore, I decided I would try to bring about a change by having a wider variety of applicants invited, and I remember saying: "Well, just as the Clerk can be a chief executive" – wrongly in my view – "somebody with a chief executive background can be the Clerk,'" he said.[2]

Over the course of three conversations, Mills conveyed that she was not a procedural expert. 'I was really clear about what I did do and what I didn't do,' she says. The recruiters said they had been tasked with looking beyond the 'traditional narrow scope', with Westminster facing challenges surrounding the building, security and community access. 'What they talked about was very similar to what I had been asked to do in Australia,' Mills adds.

Mills submitted a formal application and was called for an interview in front of a panel, which consisted of Bercow, Lansley, Labour MPs Angela Eagle and Margaret Hodge, Lib Dem MP John Thurso and the parliamentary and health service ombudsman, Dame Julie Mellor. Arrangements had been made for Bercow to meet Mills privately a day before the interview, as other applicants had already met the Speaker. Of the thirty-minute meeting, Mills says: 'He asked me if I had any particular questions and gave me a bit of view about what he wanted to achieve as Speaker. So, that was quite useful context.'

Mills completed the interview and flew back to Australia. Soon after she returned to Sydney, she received a call to say that she was shortlisted. Also under consideration were David Natzler and a 'female Whitehall official'.[3] On 29 June 2014, the *Mail on Sunday* reported her candidacy. 'I wasn't thrilled that it had leaked out,' she says.[4]

Returning for a second interview, Mills sensed some pushback from the Commons human resources department over her candidacy. 'I had to ring from Dubai on my stopover because they still hadn't confirmed a hotel room for me. It was stuff like that which just made me think: "People are not here to make it easy,"' she says. Appearing before the panel in late July, Mills reiterated that she did not have a background as a clerk but was capable of learning on the job. 'It was a question for them as to whether they wanted to bring somebody else who could hit the ground running in certain areas and had to build their capacity in others,' she explains.

During an interval of *Great Britain*, a play on phone hacking at the

National Theatre on London's South Bank, Mills received a call from Bercow. She was the preferred candidate of the panel. 'I was aware that the formal offer would only be subject to royal approval and there would be a parliamentary process for that,' she says. Mills returned to the Hilton Hotel by Westminster Bridge for a glass of wine. 'I was fully aware through the whole process that appointing anyone from outside the Parliament would be a significant step and would likely attract attention, as change always does. However, I did not anticipate the full extent of the backlash.'

Bercow sent a letter to David Cameron with the recommendation, which was due to be given royal assent. In early August, the media caught wind of the appointment. Tory MPs, including Bercow opponents Simon Burns and Rob Wilson, urged the Prime Minister to pause proceedings. Reports emerged that Natzler was considering taking legal action, after he asked for all the documents from the selection process.

A source claims that Bercow had behaved in a way that was 'prejudicial' against Natzler by seeking to 'denigrate' and pick apart his answers in front of other members of the panel once he had left the room: 'That would not be acceptable in any normal recruitment process. No self-respecting chair of recruitment processes would be tempted to say such things.'

The media furore grew exponentially on 17 August after an email from Dr Rosemary Laing, the Clerk of the Australian Senate, was leaked to the *Mail on Sunday*. Laing expressed her 'disbelief and dismay' at the 'bizarre' decision to appoint Mills, which she argued was an 'affront'. 'It seemed to us impossible that someone without parliamentary knowledge and experience could be under consideration for such a role,' she wrote. Laing said Mills's role in Australia was 'essentially the role of an administrator and bears no resemblance to the role of a professional parliamentary officer'.

In an incendiary move, Laing also said that Mills was subject to an investigation over claims that her department used CCTV to spy on the office of an Australian senator. The email was seized upon by MPs opposed to the appointment. 'It would be wrong for the Queen to approve this appointment before MPs have been fully consulted,' said Jacob Rees-Mogg.[5]

A former government aide says:

Essentially, we played a very quiet game of ringing up a few people in Australia and finding out about this. Effectively, she wasn't a clerk, she was an administrative person. She had no understanding or grounding in procedure. We just played a very long game of dribbling it out and making Bercow's life as uncomfortable as possible.

Mills says:

I think [Lansley] didn't like me. You look at a panel, who asks you the questions, who's engaged, who's not engaged, who uses the opportunity to test you out, he was pretty disengaged of all the people on the panel. So, I thought that was quite possible that it was that side.

Laing's email proved crucial. Robert Rogers called for Sir Jeremy Heywood, the head of the civil service, to intervene. Betty Boothroyd, the former Speaker, said it would be an 'embarrassment to the crown, to government and to Parliament to put this name before the Queen'.[6] In Australia, Senate President Stephen Parry had words with Laing over her intervention. 'I'm disappointed with some of the content of that email,' he said. 'Since becoming aware of that email, I have spoken to the Clerk of the Senate and I have spoken to the Speaker of the House of Commons, John Bercow.' Mills says: 'The initial reaction in Canberra was very supportive of me.'

Mills was subject to attack in both hemispheres.

Clearly it was the worst time in my career. I had a very successful career up until that point. It was highly personalised, I sort of expected it in the UK, I wasn't that surprised. I was surprised how vindictive certain people in Australia chose to be, particularly the Clerk of the Senate, obviously, who chose to engage herself very actively.

Under severe pressure, Bercow announced a 'modest pause' in the recruitment process on 1 September and renewed his call for the role of Clerk to be split. His climbdown was seized upon in the Chamber. Bercow had angry exchanges with Michael Fabricant, who exclaimed 'Ha!' when the Speaker announced the news and cut short Tory MP Chris Pincher during a point of order. Pincher later approached the chair and had what was described as a 'furious' conversation with Bercow. 'He said: "Go away." There was no impoliteness in that respect, he was just very aggressive and angry,' Pincher told a reporter.[7]

A Tory MP says:

> What we were trying to do was trying to make it very clear that we would not accept the selection of an entirely inappropriate Clerk in order that John Bercow would then be able to manipulate even more than he subsequently has done the rules of the House of Commons.

Bercow also faced opposition to his calls for the role of Clerk to be split. A former Deputy Speaker who opposed the move says: 'The issue was whether or not we could divide the role and how it would work, and how you could manage that split while keeping the importance of the senior clerk of the House of Commons. It was a process point.'

MPs voted to create a new committee to examine whether the role of Clerk should be broken up to sit alongside a chief executive. The committee, chaired by Jack Straw, was also tasked with considering Mills's appointment. In the Chamber, Lansley, who was no longer Commons Leader, said it was 'particularly regrettable' that Bercow sought to 'water down' the job description of Clerk so that detailed knowledge of procedure was no longer required. Eagle disagreed and said the process was 'open and fair and came to a conclusion which was by consensus'. Hodge said that the post had been advertised as a role for both a clerk and a chief executive. 'It proved impossible to find a single individual capable of fulfilling both roles ... A number of members of the panel thought that

Carol Mills was the only candidate who was appointable to the job,' she said. Though the panel agreed by consensus, four of the six members were said to have been in favour of Mills, and two against.

At the end of September, Bercow gave a speech in Canberra on 'Representative democracy in the digital age: fact or fiction?' He met Mills briefly during his trip. 'We had a short discussion and he was apologetic of how things had gone in terms of the backlash,' says Mills. 'I don't recall having any further contact with the Speaker after that.'

Straw's committee concluded the appointment of Mills should be terminated with immediate effect. MPs also recommended that the Clerk should remain 'head of the House Service' and that a new post of Director General of the House of Commons should be created. Mills received a letter from human resources in Westminster to let her know that the position would not proceed.

That was not the end of the fallout. That same month, a parliamentary committee in Canberra found that Mills may have provided misleading evidence to Parliament over what she knew about the investigation into one of her employees by CCTV.[8] She had also faced questions after her department awarded a $30,000 contract for photography services to a person she allegedly knew.[9] On 21 April 2015, Mills lost her job.[10] 'A number of different things happened, but it was all linked in a way,' she says. 'It became unmanageable. I continued, I believe, to behave very professionally. But obviously there were severe issues with the way the Clerk of the Senate had behaved. I did learn one lesson: clerks have much more influence than chief executives.'

The scars of the experience still weigh heavily on Mills. 'I had fantastic support from ex-ministers, premiers, friends, all sorts of politicians from both sides of the Houses. Personally, extremely supportive, but publicly you got hung out to dry. That's life.'

When asked whether she wished she had not been approached for the role of Clerk, Mills says: 'It waxed and waned between "I wish I had never been approached" and "I wish I had never been offered the job". I couldn't decide which it was. It had very severe personal consequences and professional consequences.'

Mills's career in the civil service came to an end after twenty-five years. She now works as a director for the Institute for Public Policy and Governance at the University of Technology, Sydney. Despite the experience, Mills has no ill feeling towards Bercow himself. 'I haven't got anything bad to say about Bercow or the process,' she says. A former official says: 'She was shafted by him. He couldn't care less. He was utterly ruthless once people are no longer useful to him. He has no conscience at all.'

The appointment of the Clerk was Bercow's first major defeat as Speaker. A former Commons staff member says of the events: 'The consequence of that for other senior colleagues, and you've seen this now go on for some years, is the message is: if the Speaker doesn't like you, your career's over, mate.'

The saga entrenched suspicions among some Bercow critics that he no longer saw himself as reliant on the advice of a senior clerk, and was seeking to preserve his power. 'He didn't require somebody else to be the last word on House rules – he would do it ... We thought he was wrong about that,' says a government source.

The episode also illustrated the ruthless nature of politics. Mills, traduced in the UK and Australian media, had become collateral damage for competing agendas.

Natzler, who had been acting Clerk since Rogers stood down, was formally appointed in March 2015. Ian Ailles took up the post of Director General of the Commons in October of that year.

Bercow said of the saga:

> I ran into trouble. In the end, we got the split in roles, but it was done in a rather messy way. If I look back, although I'm very pleased with the outcome and I've no fundamental regrets, did I handle it as well as I could have done or I should have done? I didn't. But I learned something from it.[11]

CHAPTER TWENTY-TWO

TWO DAYS IN FEBRUARY

'Personally, I voted to remain.'

John and Sally Bercow were having dinner with Labour peer Michael Levy and his wife, Gilda, at a restaurant in central London. It was March 2016, and the EU referendum campaign was in its relative infancy. David Cameron had returned from Brussels with a renegotiated deal ready to put to the British people. After meeting with his Cabinet, the Prime Minister had announced on 20 February that the vote would be held on Thursday 23 June.

In a year of landmark events, interest was also being paid to what was taking place across the pond. In November, Americans would elect either Hillary Clinton or Donald Trump as their next President. Clinton had shored up the Democratic nomination, and Trump had shocked many when he won the Republican candidacy. In another surprise election, Jeremy Corbyn had secured the Labour leadership the previous September.

After the personal tumult of 2015, during which time he survived the coup to remove him as Speaker and patched things up with Sally after a highly public breakdown of their marriage, Bercow was looking forward to a fresh start. He had faced questions in the media over his expenses: in the summer of 2015, a freedom of information request by the Press Association revealed that he had racked up a £172 bill in 2013 by taking a car to Carlton House Terrace, just 0.7 miles from the Commons. A car to

Margaret Thatcher's funeral that year cost the taxpayer £158, and £367 was spent on travel to Luton to deliver a speech on how MPs were restoring their reputation after the expenses scandal.[1] In February 2016, a separate freedom of information request found Bercow had expensed £1,954 for a dinner in honour of former Australian Speaker Bronwyn Bishop, among other claims. A spokeswoman for Bercow said: 'The Speaker is committed to cutting costs wherever possible, and the overall expenditure of the Speaker's Office has fallen during his tenure from £626,029 in 2009/10 to £504,737 in 2014/15, representing a reduction of 19.4 per cent since he was elected to the role.'[2]

On the domestic front, the Conservative government was seeking to push through its agenda after unexpectedly winning a small majority at the 2015 election. But after Cameron announced the start of the historic referendum campaign, all focus in Westminster concentrated on Britain's future relationship with the European Union.

Levy, a successful businessman who worked as Tony Blair's special envoy to the Middle East, wanted to know how Bercow thought the two major political events in the UK and the US would turn out. 'Well, John, what's going to happen?' he asked. 'Oh, Michael, the British people will vote to Remain, and Hillary will be the next President,' Bercow responded confidently. 'John,' Levy began. 'I want both of those things and I expect neither.'

Bercow, of course, was not alone in failing to predict the outcome of those two seminal events. Nor was he aware of how much they would come to influence his legacy as Speaker of the House of Commons.

Reducing ten years of Bercow's Speakership to two days in February 2017 is to over-simplify his contribution to the chair. But his interventions, first to students at the University of Reading on 3 February, and three days later to the House of Commons, would shape much of how Bercow's subsequent decisions were viewed.

* * *

The seismic result of the EU referendum cast uncertainty over Westminster. British politics was already in turmoil. One week before the referendum, Labour MP Jo Cox was brutally murdered in her constituency of Batley and Spen. Bercow led the tributes in the Commons to the much-loved politician, who had been elected only a year earlier. 'Above all she was filled with and fuelled by love for humanity,' he said. On the morning after the referendum, David Cameron announced his resignation and, following a brief leadership election, Theresa May took over as Prime Minister on 13 July, after Andrea Leadsom pulled out of the race.

It quickly became clear that the referendum would strain the UK's representative democracy. The government found itself in an ugly legal battle in the Supreme Court over whether ministers had the unilateral right to trigger Article 50 of the Lisbon Treaty, the two-year process by which a country leaves the European Union. In a major blow to the new Prime Minister, judges ruled that Parliament must sanction the exit process, as argued by businesswoman Gina Miller, who had brought the case.

MPs were determined to ensure that Parliament, which had become more of a force under Bercow, was going to be a key player in the Brexit drama. On 3 February 2017, speaking to students at the University of Reading, Bercow said that he was 'conscious that I am in office at a momentous time'. In an unprecedented move for a sitting Speaker, he shed light on how he voted at the referendum, saying:

> Personally, I voted to Remain. I thought it was better to stay in the European Union than not, partly for economic reasons, being part of a big trade bloc, and partly because I think we're in a world of power blocs. For all the weaknesses and deficiencies of the European Union, it's better to be part of that bigger bloc in the world, than thinking you can act as effectively on your own. There are a lot of supranational and multilateral and global challenges which I think we're better placed to try to address as part of a wider group.

The comments, which were reported in the press more than a week after the event, amounted to one of Bercow's biggest gambles. Though sources argue that such events are usually carried out under Chatham House rules – i.e. off the record – many of Bercow's university talks, including his address in Reading, are later uploaded to YouTube. The comments would always have been made public.

It also illustrated how far Bercow's politics had moved. In August 1999, Bercow had called for a renegotiation of Britain's relationship with the EU, which should begin from the premise that the UK would stay in if it could strike a deal 'and pull out if we cannot'. His campaign leaflet for the 2001 election included ten good reasons to elect John Bercow, no. 7 of which was: 'John Bercow believes in fighting for the interests of Britain in Europe, not the interests of Europe in Britain. He wants free trade and cooperation, not a single currency and rule from Brussels.'

Bercow also allegedly had links with a well-known anti-EU group on the Conservative benches. When Daniel Hannan left his job as researcher for the European Research Group to become an MEP in the summer of 1999, Bercow found himself on the panel to find his replacement. 'There were five or so MPs on the interview committee, of whom John Bercow was one,' says one of those to interview for the role. 'Given his subsequent fallings-out with Eurosceptic MPs, it's quite something that he was then interviewing people for that role.' The source claims that Bercow was a member of the ERG at the time.

Intriguingly, Bercow was once full of praise for Dominic Cummings, a former director of strategy for the Conservatives, who had called on the party to take a backseat role in a referendum campaign on the euro. 'I think Dominic Cummings is a brilliant man. I think he's got many good ideas. He's hired to give his advice,' said Bercow in June 2002.[3] Cummings would go on to play a key role in the Brexit-backing Vote Leave campaign and subsequently work in No. 10 for Boris Johnson.

In outing himself as a Remainer, Bercow left himself open to the charge of bias. Professor Vernon Bogdanor of King's College London says:

He's the first Speaker, I think, ever to have expressed a view on a controversial public issue, and I think that's tainted his Speakership. His procedural judgements may be right or wrong, but they've been tainted by the fact that people think they're influenced by political opinions. The Speaker should be neutral like the Queen.

Julian Lewis, his best man and close friend, was also taken aback. 'I've had to accept the fact that John has become overcommitted on this,' he says. 'He did not consult me before taking that fateful first step – which I think he should never have taken – namely, to reveal to those students that he voted Remain. That, as far as I'm concerned, was a Rubicon.'

*   *   *

Theresa May had taken a hands-on approach to Donald Trump after his election in November 2016. The following January, she became the first foreign leader to visit the newly elected President. On the visit, she was pictured holding Trump's hand (he is rumoured to have a fear of staircases) as they walked through the colonnade at the White House. As part of her strategy, May had offered Trump a state visit to the UK.

Speculation turned to whether Trump would be invited to address Parliament in Westminster Hall. The process by which a dignitary is invited to speak involves a green light from the Lords and Commons Speakers as well as the Lord Great Chamberlain, who represents the Queen. In January, Trump had imposed a controversial migrant ban on travellers from seven predominantly Muslim countries: Chad, Iran, Iraq, Libya, Somalia, Syria and Yemen. An Early Day Motion opposing Trump addressing Parliament during his stay had been signed by more than 170 MPs.

Asked about Trump's visit by students at Reading University, Bercow hinted that he was not in favour: 'If that visit takes place, so be it. No doubt, if there is a visit to Parliament, I would be expected to do my duty.'

Three days later, without consulting the other two stakeholders in the decision, Bercow unilaterally ruled that Trump would not be allowed to address Parliament in Westminster Hall. Arguing that an address by a foreign leader was an 'earned honour', not 'an automatic right', Bercow cited Trump's migrant ban as one of the main reasons for his opposition. To applause from opposition benches, he said: 'I feel very strongly that our opposition to racism and to sexism and our support for equality before the law and an independent judiciary are hugely important considerations in the House of Commons.'

A Tory minister says: 'The Trump thing really pissed me off. Surely you don't simply on your own volition decide the US President isn't going to come and address the Houses of Parliament in Westminster Hall because you don't like him.'

Bercow's failure to inform Norman Fowler, the Lord Speaker, of his intentions – let alone discuss them with him – was a great discourtesy. It illustrated a propensity for the limelight and a disregard for the conventions of the House. The Lord Speaker was distinctly unamused. Bercow reached out to Fowler to apologise, which he accepted. In a statement released the next day, Fowler said: 'The whole purpose is to seek consensus ensuring both Houses have an opportunity to consider a request.'

Tories including Nadhim Zahawi – an Iraqi-born Briton who had spoken out against Trump's migrant ban – urged the Speaker to 'reconsider' his position on the President. Others pointed out that Bercow had allowed Xi Jinping, President of China, which has a poor record on human rights, to address Parliament in the Royal Gallery in 2015. Bercow later conceded there could be some merit in this argument: 'Was it necessarily the right decision? No, not necessarily, and I'm absolutely open to the idea that maybe I should have come to a different view.'[4]

James Duddridge, one of the Speaker's leading critics, lodged an Early Day Motion expressing no confidence in Bercow, but only five Members supported it. Friends of the MP say a two-week recess period scuppered the momentum of the move, which Duddridge was initially hopeful would be supported by 100 of his colleagues. Sources say Bercow was surprised by the backlash against his intervention and was concerned about the EDM while on a trip to Israel, fearing it could lead to the end of his Speakership. Many MPs had supported Bercow's decision, however. In a point of order after the Speaker's announcement, Labour veteran Dennis Skinner said: 'Two words: well done.'

The unilateral decision on Trump was Bercow's most public grandstanding since he became Speaker. In the space of three days, Bercow had shifted the direction of his Speakership. He had taken two strategic gambles that further endeared him to one side of the political ledger and isolated him from the other.

The issue of Trump addressing Parliament is separate from the way in which Bercow conducted himself. A Westminster Hall address is an honour afforded to few foreign dignitaries. Given the US President's penchant for controversy, a strong case can be argued that bestowing upon him such a privilege would have been wrong. It was, however, a decision to which three parties were privy, and it was an issue that went beyond the musings of one man. Bercow circumvented the usual channels and acted unilaterally, in turn receiving days of media coverage on both sides of the Atlantic Ocean. Too often in his Speakership, he left himself open to the charge that this was a driving factor in his decision-making.

Brexit and Trump would continue to dominate the news agenda until Theresa May made the boldest decision of her premiership and called a snap election. The consequences of that decision would be played out in the subsequent parliament, which proved to be one of the most contentious in living memory. A hung parliament, with the Tories forming a confidence and supply arrangement with the Democratic Unionist Party, further enhanced the importance of and focus on the Commons.

Against this backdrop, Bercow would play a key role. But a storm, which had been brewing for some time, threatened to derail his Speakership.

CHAPTER TWENTY-THREE

NIGHT AND DAY

*'There must be zero tolerance of sexual harassment
or bullying here at Westminster.'*

Journalists at BBC *Newsnight* were gathered for an editorial meeting on the third floor of Broadcasting House in Portland Place, central London. It was the final day of October 2017, and a member of Theresa May's Cabinet had become the most senior politician to face accusations of sexual harassment. The #MeToo scandal that had engulfed Hollywood following successive allegations against film producer Harvey Weinstein had reached Westminster.

That morning, *The Sun* had splashed on a story that Michael Fallon, the Defence Secretary, had admitted to inappropriately putting his hand on the knee of a female journalist, Julia Hartley Brewer. Fallon would resign a day later following further allegations of inappropriate behaviour towards women, including from the journalist Jane Merrick, who reported to Downing Street that Fallon had lunged at her and attempted to kiss her on the lips after they had lunched together in 2003. Fallon's resignation letter acknowledged that his past conduct had fallen short of the standards expected of the UK armed forces.[1]

Though the Westminster harassment scandal was in its relative infancy, there was a palpable tension in Parliament. Mark Garnier, a minister in the Department for International Trade, was accused of calling his secretary 'sugar tits' and asking her to purchase sex toys.[2] A dossier of offences alleged to have been committed by MPs was circulating, and more victims were coming forward.

John Bercow had sought to intervene early on. 'Let me make it clear,' he began in a statement to the Commons on 30 October. 'There must be zero tolerance of sexual harassment or bullying here at Westminster or elsewhere, whether that involves Members, their staff, parliamentary staff or those working on or visiting the estate. If there have been assaults, they should be reported to the police here, as anywhere else.'[3] Bercow invited backbenchers and women's rights campaigners Jess Phillips, Anna Soubry and Stella Creasy to address a meeting of the House of Commons Commission on how Parliament should respond to the scandal. 'These women are going to talk and we're going to listen to them. We're going to do what they ask,' he said.

Amid the perpetually fluid news cycle, *Newsnight* was undergoing some changes at the top. Ian Katz, who had served as editor since September 2013, was leaving to become director of programmes at Channel 4. While a longer-term replacement was sought, deputy editors Jess Brammar and Daniel Clarke were appointed as acting editors. Lizzi Watson took on the position of executive producer to support both Brammar and Clarke.

Lucinda Day joined the BBC in 2011, working as a researcher and producer at Radio 5 Live. She moved to Radio 4's flagship *Today* programme in January 2015, before joining *Newsnight* in February 2017, where, as planning editor, she was responsible for shaping the editorial direction of the nightly show.

Watson pulled Day aside after the editorial meeting and headed for a sofa. She was adamant that *Newsnight* should not only expand its coverage of the Westminster harassment scandal but do a better job of it than the national newspapers. Expecting the project to take around a fortnight, Watson asked her colleague: 'Can you have a look at Westminster?'

Day spent the next week calling around predominantly female backbench MPs. The off-the-record conversations would often go the same way. 'Yes, there's a massive problem with harassment,' the respondent would say. 'But I can't help you.' Day would be directed elsewhere, including to the then Parliamentary Commissioner for Standards, Kathryn Hudson, who oversaw breaches of MPs' code of conduct. However, her enquiries bore little fruit at this stage.

The harassment scandal had exposed the fundamental flaws in the antiquated system for dealing with complaints. As MPs employ their staff, they were in turn responsible for any HR concerns. In other words, if a staff member had a complaint to lodge against their MP, they would raise it with the very person they had an issue or grievance with. Theresa May convened a meeting with Jeremy Corbyn and other party leaders in Westminster, after which they agreed to introduce new safeguards for parliamentary staff, including a new grievance procedure and an upgrade from the existing complaints hotline to a face-to-face human resources service.

Writing in *The Guardian*, Hannah White, deputy director of the reputable Institute for Government, cast doubt on whether the proposals would go far enough to challenge the culture at Westminster. The picture White painted was of a complaints and grievance procedure that was not fit for purpose, and a problematic power imbalance between MPs and staff in the House of Commons Service. Unlike MPs' staff, Commons staff in theory had the power of recourse through a newly created HR policy known as Respect. But, White wrote, there was an 'impossibly high bar for the incident to be investigated in a way that could lead to any repercussions for the MP involved'.[4]

The article pricked Day's interest. It seemed to suggest a culture of bullying as well as sexual harassment. Realising she was onto something bigger than perhaps she had initially envisaged, Day went back to her editors. 'There's definitely a story here because everybody's telling me there's a story but they can't talk about it. So, I'm going to need more time,' she asked. Watson and Brammar responded: 'OK, have a month off rota, see what you can find.' During this period, Day managed to convince

Zelda Perkins, a former employee at Harvey Weinstein's Miramax Films, to break her non-disclosure agreement and speak to *Newsnight* about allegations of sexual assault against Weinstein. In 1998, Perkins left the company after a colleague alleged that Weinstein had tried to rape her. Perkins signed a confidentiality agreement, which prevented her from speaking out about the alleged sexual assault on her former co-worker. The sensitive way in which *Newsnight* handled Perkins's story would catch the eye of potential whistle-blowers in Westminster.

The first breakthrough came when a former clerk reached out to Day over email. The two arranged to meet in person, where the source advised Day that she needed to look into the experience of House of Commons staff. 'Actually, bullying and harassment is really widespread with that group, and nobody has ever spoken about it,' they said.

Given there was an existing infrastructure in place, Day felt she could prove there was a systemic problem if, despite this, bullying and harassment were still prevalent. For the rest of the year, she met current and former staff, building up a wealth of sources. After weeks of interviews, several names kept cropping up. One of those was the Speaker, John Bercow. Another was a former clerk by the name of Emily Commander.

* * *

Emily Commander first joined the House of Commons Service in 2003. A self-professed parliamentary geek, her dreams of working in Westminster had come to fruition. Commander, who studied English at Cambridge before completing a master's at Oxford, was a standout performer. 'She could have been Clerk of the House easily. She was that capable,' says a former colleague.

In March 2011, Commander was promoted to the position of clerk to the Culture, Media and Sport Committee, chaired by Conservative MP John Whittingdale. It was a fascinating time to be joining the team: MPs were carrying out an inquiry into phone hacking at the *News of the World*, and the high-profile nature of the committee's work drew interest not just from the media but also from senior management. Commander had to brief John Bercow and Robert Rogers, the most senior clerk in the Commons, on updates relating to the inquiry, as the House's reputation was potentially at stake.

On Tuesday 19 July, in one of the most talked-about committee sessions in modern times, Rupert Murdoch, the head of News International, arrived to give evidence alongside his son, James. Rebekah Brooks, a former editor of the *News of the World*, would follow. Watching was Jonathan May-Bowles, a protestor, who rushed from the public gallery and threw a paper plate of shaving foam at Murdoch, whose wife, Wendi Deng, leapt to his defence. Commander, sitting next to Whittingdale, instructed him to suspend the session and called for the cameras to be cut, as per protocol. Bercow, who was watching from his study, rang Lawrence Ward, the Serjeant-at-Arms, to express his shock at what had taken place. 'I cannot believe what I just saw,' he said. On 2 August, May-Bowles was sentenced to six weeks in jail, of which he would serve three, and ordered to pay a £15 victim surcharge and £250 costs at Westminster Magistrates' Court.

As one might expect on a subject of such controversy, individuals on the committee held strong views. Tom Watson, a long-standing critic of the Murdoch empire, was one of these, as was fellow Labour MP Paul Farrelly, who had represented Newcastle-under-Lyme since 2001. Farrelly and Commander first worked together when she served as second clerk to the Science and Technology Committee, of which he was a member. During a trip to Italy in November 2004, Farrelly treated her 'appallingly in front of everyone', according to a witness on the trip. 'He was very aggressive,' the source said.[5] Farrelly, who says he had witnesses who 'would have attested' to this claim being false, responds: 'This allegation is untrue and fabricated by [an] anonymous source in the BBC *Newsnight* programme.'

Rebekah Brooks was being investigated by police at the time of the inquiry. The committee had evidence about the former journalist and was being leaned on by justices, the Crown Prosecution Service and the police not to use it: to do so could have prejudiced a future court case. This, according to multiple sources, agitated Farrelly, who wanted the committee to make the evidence public. According to a former staff member, he then began to 'manipulate and bully' Commander to try to get his way. Farrelly categorically denies the claims, saying: 'This is wholly untrue and I have also not heard this before. Committee members were also very careful, as ever, with respect to material that might be prejudicial to a criminal trial.'

Commander drafted a report on the committee's inquiry, which was agreed and signed off by the Speaker's Counsel, Michael Carpenter, before being returned to Whittingdale for approval.

Sources claim that Farrelly would seek to 'undermine' Commander's report by inserting amendments and querying her sentence structure and use of grammar. A former staff member says: 'It was horrible. It was kind of relentless. It seemed like everything she said he had to criticise or push back. It was pretty constant.' Farrelly rejects this version of events, arguing that there was evidence emerging from outside the committee, such as via civil cases brought in the courts, that needed to be considered. 'We asked that transcripts and copies of court judgments be obtained. This was not an "unreasonable demand" and Ms Commander, I'm afraid, did not undertake this work. To assist the committee, it eventually fell to me, with the chair's assent, to do this.' He continues: 'It is not, of course, a committee's job simply to rubber-stamp a draft report without any amendments.'

Sources claim that Farrelly was grandstanding as he felt the report did not come down hard enough on the Murdochs. 'The fact is, there simply wasn't a smoking gun with Murdoch – there just wasn't. The report couldn't say what Farrelly and Watson wanted it to, which is that Murdoch was up to his eyes in it,' says an insider. A source present adds: 'If anything, she was facilitating him probably more than she should have done, but it was very difficult to say no. It wasn't a pleasant experience when he was in the room; it could put everyone on edge.'

While MPs would approach Commander after meetings to console her, there were only a 'handful' of occasions when they called out Farrelly in person, says a source. 'They'd say, "Oh Paul, enough now," or something like that. I don't remember anybody really taking him to task saying, "For God's sake, what are you doing?"' A clerk at the time says they tried to encourage other MPs and Whittingdale to support Commander. 'In most committees, if you have problems with one member treating staff badly, the chairman will intervene and say, "I won't have this,"' says the source.

Clerks were there to assist MPs, and there was an unspoken culture of staff keeping quiet about their experiences. This was 'deemed to be a trait of a successful clerk', one female member of staff would later tell *Newsnight*. Over time, Commander became physically ill from the levels of stress and pressure she was facing both inside and outside the committee. The situation also took its toll on her staff, some of whom ended up in tears.

After a particularly difficult session, Commander returned to her office, shut the door and cried. She would spend the next two weeks off sick and was moved to the Public Administration Committee on her return. The Speaker, according to multiple sources, knew of what was taking place, given his interest in the work of the committee. In a letter to her bosses, seen by *Newsnight*, Commander said she had 'trouble falling asleep at night … I have been anxious about encountering Mr Farrelly … After particularly unpleasant meetings I have lost my appetite and have on several occasions been physically sick.'

In February 2012, Andrew Kennon, the clerk in charge of select committees, who had stepped in for Commander on the committee, decided to lodge a complaint under the new Respect policy, which had been in place since the previous June. It was agreed that the complaint, which according to *Newsnight* called for Farrelly to write a public apology and be removed from the committee, would be made in his name rather than Commander's to give her as much protection as possible. Farrelly also lodged a complaint against Kennon, whom he accused of telling him to 'shut up' in front of other committee members. House managers found no 'serious misconduct' and resolved the issue by giving Kennon 'informal' guidance on how to deal with MPs.

Two days before the committee was due to publish its report, the *Mail on Sunday* revealed that Farrelly was the subject of an investigation into bullying allegations. A member of the committee told the paper that Farrelly had been making demands of Commander 'that should be done by a team of librarians – not one clerk'. When asked if he had been rude to Commander, the MP replied: 'He was placing high expectations on the clerk in a forthright manner. I think Emily found it difficult to contend with.' Another source said they found 'some of it uncomfortable' but did not believe that Farrelly 'has ever been impolite'. Commander, who had journalists and cameras on her doorstep, refused to comment.

In a statement, Farrelly said:

> I am aware that (anonymous) allegations have been made, which are completely false. I have denied any wrongdoing whatsoever and requested further particulars. I am greatly concerned by this leak and its timing, coming as it does on the eve of the publication of the Select Committee report into phone hacking. I consider it is clearly intended as an attempt to discredit me and to undermine the report in advance.[6]

The committee, whose report was due to be published on 1 May, was split over whether James Murdoch was responsible for misleading Parliament over his knowledge of phone hacking. Sources claim that Conservative MPs concerned with the language used in the report briefed out the story. A leak inquiry was set up in response to the *Mail on Sunday* report, though the source was never found.

Edward Wood, an official in the House of Commons Library, investigated the claims against Farrelly. Two other women were asked to give evidence about previous incidents involving the Labour MP. However, a ruling was made that only instances that had taken place since the adoption of the Respect policy in June 2011 could be considered, as Farrelly had argued for, rendering the additional accounts inadmissible. The House authorities told *Newsnight* that this decision was taken on the basis of legal advice.

Wood interviewed MPs and staff about the case. In a submission, a member of the committee pointed to 'external pressures' on Commander at the time coupled with the high-profile nature of the inquiry as being 'an unfortunate combination'. '[Paul Farrelly] was not responsible for any one of those things,' the MP said. In broad terms, some MPs did not believe bullying had taken place, while members of staff did. Wood's report did not come to a conclusion on many of the issues raised in the complaints against Farrelly. In the few cases where he had been able to make a determination, he found that Farrelly had bullied Commander, reported *Newsnight*. Though he could not prove that Farrelly had intended to be a bully, he said that the Labour MP's behaviour amounted to an 'abuse of power or position, unfair treatment and undermining a competent worker by constant criticism ... The conduct was offensive and insulting.' Farrelly appealed the ruling.

Rosie Winterton, Labour's Chief Whip, was informed of the findings, but the party took no action against Farrelly. 'They categorically refused to do anything,' says a source. The matter was then escalated to the House of Commons Commission, chaired by Bercow.

The group convened on 26 November 2012 and sat in private to consider the complaint. They were unable to come to a conclusion. To arrive at some sort of resolution, the commission pursued various measures. At one point, they even summoned Commander and Farrelly to appear at the same time, until the First Division Association, a union that represents staff in the Commons, intervened. The session went ahead, but with Kennon going in Commander's place. It was communicated to him that the commission could not deal with the complaint.

The Advisory, Conciliation and Arbitration Service was brought in to mediate, and Commander met them twice. Farrelly says that claims he refused to engage are 'wholly untrue' and 'another fabrication'. In response, Farrelly says that he suggested ACAS were brought in 'as an experienced professional body' in July 2012. He states that he met with them in the first week of February 2013, before it 'all went rather quiet and I continued to chase progress for a resolution'. On 21 March, Farrelly says he was informed that Helen Eames, the Speaker's Assistant Counsel, had decided that 'ACAS involvement is unnecessary at this stage'. After months of the process dragging on, Bercow wrote to Commander to explain that the commission could not come to a view. Responding, Commander said that a finding had already been made, and the commission was simply being asked to apply a sanction.

Seeking to break the deadlock, the Speaker invited Farrelly for drinks in his office and encouraged him to write a letter of apology. Commander was not satisfied that the note she subsequently received amounted to one. Bercow acknowledged that the apology might not have been as effusive as Commander had wanted but added that he hoped she would consider the matter closed. The two had worked together in a previous incarnation in Parliament and had cordial relations. The case, which highlighted the deep flaws in the Respect policy, went no further at the time.

A member of the commission says the impasse was due to the position taken by Conservative and Labour whips. 'Both sets of whips, equally, were determined not to give what they regarded as a group of officials in the House the ability to exercise a disciplinary panel over MPs,' the source says. 'Constitutionally they regarded it unacceptable and inappropriate for officials to sanction members.' They add: 'There was a government and opposition blot on going any further. To be fair to John, I don't think he was the blot.'

But in February 2020 it was claimed that Bercow had been more dismissive of the case than previously alleged. Speaking to *The Times*, Robert Rogers said that Bercow had told him 'he was not going to have the case proved "on the word of any fucking clerk"'. Bercow responded: 'Lord Lisvane's statement doesn't accord with my recollection ... I was concerned to ensure that there was an independent process and ACAS – the independent Advisory, Conciliation and Arbitration Service – was invited to attempt to resolve the matter. As I recall, Lord Lisvane was supportive of the approach.'[7]

Following Commander's case, the commission voted to look again at the Respect policy, with the revised guidelines coming out in 2014. Investigations would now be conducted by third parties and decisions taken by the Standards Committee, comprising MPs and lay members.

Farrelly unequivocally denies all allegations of bullying. 'In 2012 allegations were made about me having bullied a clerk to the committee during the compilation of the phone-hacking report. These allegations were investigated and not upheld,' he told *Newsnight*. 'Despite this, I apologised if I had inadvertently upset the clerk who had suffered stress. The policy under which they were investigated was considered to be so unfair to those complained about that it was immediately withdrawn and replaced by another policy.'

He says now: 'I think, over eight years, that I have said all I have to say about this allegation. I never bullied Ms Commander, have never bullied anyone in my life, and have always stood up to bullies and encouraged and fought for others to do so too.'

Based on the experience with Commander, clerks felt that if they did complain, their case would eventually present itself before the commission. Given the body was composed of MPs and was chaired by Bercow, few clerks had faith in the system. Rumours also abounded about the Speaker's own record on bullying.

Commander stayed in the House for another year before taking a career break in France. Her story remained confined to the walls of Westminster until the spring of 2018.

*   *   *

By the turn of the year, Day had spoken to more than fifty sources, and Chris Cook, policy editor at *Newsnight*, who had been working on stories relating to several MPs, joined her formally on the investigation. Brammar, who continued to protect their time to work on the project, decided that the two should collaborate.

A major breakthrough came in early February, when a staff member who had initially been reluctant agreed to speak to Day and Cook. The source proved crucial: they provided the route to uncovering a broader pattern of behaviour. Namely, that the staff members who complained were moved to different positions or left the organisation altogether, rather than action being taken against the MPs in question. Instead of a series of isolated incidents, a discernible link could be made to the stories they had heard. That's when Cook and Day realised they had evidence of a systemic problem. It was around this time that specific allegations against Bercow also began to emerge.

After five months of investigation, the story was ready to go. Three MPs were going to be accused directly of bullying: Conservative MP Mark Pritchard, Farrelly and Bercow. Cook and Day had spoken to upwards of seventy sources, and Cook issued the right of replies more than a week before the story was going to launch. First would come a news feature on the BBC website, followed that evening by a twenty-minute report on *Newsnight*, presented by Cook. With Watson now on loan to *News at Ten*, it would fall to Brammar to give the final sign-off.

Late afternoon on Tuesday 8 March, a report carrying Day and Cook's byline was published. It began: 'There is a bullying and sexual harassment problem at the House of Commons.'

CHAPTER TWENTY-FOUR

'BULLY'

'He creates a climate of intimidation and fear.'

After thirty years in the Royal Navy, Angus Sinclair was looking for a new career. He found an advertisement for a job in the House of Commons. The year was 2005, and Michael Martin, the Speaker of the Commons, was recruiting for a private secretary.

The term 'Speaker's secretary' first appears in parliamentary records from the 1660s. As the role has developed over the centuries, those who hold the position have been responsible for preparing the Speaker's papers and briefs. They act as a channel of communication between the Speaker and the House of Commons, and, since the eighteenth century, secretaries have been responsible for organising official dinners at Speaker's House. In a tradition set by Sir Ralph Verney, who served from 1921 to 1955, secretaries have stood by the Speaker while he or she is in the chair. The role is appointed at the sole discretion of the Speaker.

By the early summer of 2009, Sinclair and the rest of Martin's team had endured a torrid time. The Speaker was forced out over his handling of the expenses scandal, and many members of staff had worked long days and nights responding to the crisis. When John Bercow was elected on 22 June 2009, Sinclair was in position next to Speaker's chair. He remained in the role until the following May. In fewer than twelve months, their relationship had deteriorated.

Sources say the hostility began from the moment Bercow took office. One former official says: 'He treated Angus as his enemy from the start.' Another says: 'As soon as he arrived, he did not speak to Angus as he should do to a private secretary. It was just extraordinary.'

Two months after *Newsnight* broke its bullying and harassment story, Sinclair told the programme: 'Our problem was that he would not communicate. It was as if we had to best guess what he wanted. And that will always lead to mistakes.' He added: 'The Speaker responded in a way that I can only say is a form of bullying, and that is to show anger and to thump the table.' Bercow would mimic Sinclair and put him down in front of members of his team. 'Sometimes, he would say in front of somebody who was working for you that "your boss had failed". That is quite hard,' he recalled.

Tim Hames, a former leader writer at *The Times*, had offered advice to Bercow during his campaign for the Speakership. In September, news emerged that Hames was being appointed as a special adviser to the Speaker, on a salary worth between £87,000 and £107,000 a year.[1] Hames's role – the first of its kind for a Speaker – was to spend a third of his time dealing with the media, while also assisting Bercow on his work to promote Parliament externally.

Sinclair, sources say, was not informed in advance about the appointment, which overlapped with his own. Sinclair went to meet Hames soon after he started. According to a parliamentary source, Bercow subsequently told Sinclair: 'You are doing separate things and I do not want you meeting with him.' Other members of the Speaker's Office were taken out to lunch by Hames. The appointment left Sinclair feeling isolated and vulnerable.

While this was taking place, Sinclair was also allegedly experiencing episodes of bullying. One day, he was working at his desk when Bercow came in, angry that some information he had asked for from another part of the House had yet to reach him. Sinclair had urged for an earlier resolution, and, as a result, Bercow held him responsible for the hold-up. He told *Newsnight*:

There was a tirade of how I had let him down, it was quite the worst thing; a lot of bad language. Suddenly, his mobile phone, which he had been holding, was flung on the desk in front of me and it broke into a lot of bits. It was a pretty dramatic moment, and he left the office shortly afterwards. It's an anger, a visible frustration. I don't say it was thrown at me; I got hit with bits of it.

On a separate occasion, sources say that Sinclair and another member of staff had to 'pick up the pieces' of Bercow's mobile phone after he had once more thrown it in anger. The pair were not in the room at the time he threw it, but 'they had heard the fracas', says the insider.

Sinclair alerted Malcolm Jack, the Clerk of the House, to what was taking place. He later recounted:

On a number of occasions, I went to him and explained what had happened, and I revealed to him that I didn't think I was producing the goods. But, on the other hand, I thought the Speaker's behaviour – the bullying in particular – was way over the top, and it was making things difficult.

However, as the Speaker appoints his personal staff, there was no available route to lodging a complaint, other than with Bercow himself.

Sources claim that Bercow would test Sinclair on his views about various political matters. In one instance, he asked his private secretary whether he went to church. When Sinclair said he received communion from Westminster Abbey on Sundays, Bercow allegedly cast aspersions about his views on gay marriage and other matters, despite not knowing what they were. In another incident, Bercow talked about Sinclair's time in the Navy, and asked: 'I suppose you use your rank?' He added: 'I suppose you like rugger as well?' A source explains: 'Immediately, a shutter would come up and you had been cast in a particular area that either he didn't like or didn't agree with.'

After a difficult first half of 2009, Sinclair insisted that staff in the Speaker's Office were allowed to take leave over the summer recess. During his own two-week leave, Bercow is alleged to have rung him on several occasions. After a week, he called and 'demanded' that Sinclair return to Westminster from Scotland, according to a former official. On his arrival, Sinclair found that there was nothing specific that he had been asked to do.

Bercow called Sinclair into his office shortly after the general election in May 2010. Bercow was initially 'very charming and gracious', Sinclair would later recall. 'Look, I'm going to redesign the office and make some changes. I don't have a part for you in that change,' the Speaker said. Sources close to Sinclair say he was 'absolutely finished and exhausted' from working for Bercow.

Despite press reports that Sinclair had resigned, he had in fact agreed to a compulsory early retirement, part of which included a £86,250 payment package, after turning down another internal post said to be at an equivalent level. In return, he had to sign a non-disclosure agreement, known internally as a compromise agreement, pledging to 'refrain from instituting any complaint against the Employer', and to make 'no public statement or comment relating to the Employee's service with the House of Commons'. As to why he had been asked to sign, Sinclair told *Newsnight*: 'I can only think it was because of the detail of what had happened. The bullying and the manner of my leaving.'

At the time, a friend of Sinclair's hinted about him and Bercow not seeing eye to eye. 'Angus is a highly principled man and felt that some of the changes in his job were unacceptable,' the friend told the *Mail on Sunday*.[2] A source in the Commons countered: 'Angus has done a good job, but we must move with the times. The demands of the job have changed.'

Two months after his departure, a source close to Sinclair went further in suggesting friction between the two. 'Bercow gave no proper explanation for his decision,' said the source.[3] 'He said he needed his own people in and wanted Angus out. He was treated appallingly. Angus believes that customs and tradition are as important as being up to date. The Speaker has different priorities.' Speaker Martin, Bercow's predecessor, also described Sinclair as 'the best Speaker's secretary there has ever been'.

Malcolm Jack signed a letter of reference that stated that Sinclair 'acted with a very high degree of professionalism. He showed discretion, loyalty, assiduity and efficiency … There were no disciplinary issues affecting him.' A source with knowledge of events says: 'There was an incompatibility there. Angus got on very well with Martin, but not with John. So, it was bound sooner or later to come to an end. That's what happened.' Responding to the claims in the *Newsnight* report, a spokesperson for Bercow said: 'Mr Speaker strenuously denies that there is any substance to any of these allegations. Mr Speaker has a superb team of dedicated, effective and long-serving staff – five of whom have worked for him very happily for a combined total of over forty years.'

In February 2020, Sinclair became the third person – after Robert Rogers and David Leakey – to lodge a formal bullying complaint against Bercow. Bercow told an audience in 2020:

> One characteristic that so far several of the detractors have in common, and they are now going public, briefing, smearing, trying to use the media to prosecute the case against me … is that they are institutionalised. They are change-resistant, and they are people who are very long accustomed not just to having their say but to having their way.[4]

Approached about the comments, Sinclair says: 'I just feel he's been dishonest about this from the beginning. My issue is he shouldn't really have exposed any of that at all. I would say, of course, that he's got me wrong and always has done.' For Sinclair, Bercow's decision to speak about various members of staff – both in his memoir and in public – is in breach of the confidence that should surround a Speaker's impartiality even after he has left office. 'If, in future, Speakers do as he has done and issue, in whatever form, a resumé of what they think of people then the successful working of procedure will suffer. I think it distasteful that a trust has been broken,' he argues.

Sinclair kept contemporaneous notes of some of his experiences with Bercow, but revisiting them would prove too difficult. 'He tried to shut that door, but I'm afraid these things played on his mind,' says a friend. The first time he looked again at the various instances of alleged bullying was when Lucinda Day came to visit him in his home in Scotland.

Sinclair's name did not feature *in Newsnight*'s original report from March 2018. It was only after hearing about the fate that befell his successor that he decided to speak out publicly two months later.

'When I heard what had happened with Kate Emms, I was absolutely horrified that yet again the leopard had not changed its spots,' he says. 'I just thought, "No, it's the same cards that are being played and the same brutality. It's not on." That's why I thought I'm going to speak out despite this NDA and get on with it.'

* * *

Kate Emms is a rare unifying figure in Westminster and Whitehall. You would be hard pressed to find anyone who has a bad word to say about her. One civil servant says she is 'as good as they possibly come'. 'It is hard to be anything but full of admiration at this cheerful, positive, fantastic person,' they say. A government source says: 'She is a very professional, robust character, and someone who can stand up to pressure.' Politicians of all colours have described her as a highly able, clubbable, effective clerk. A former Tory MP adds: 'She is very competent, decent and honest.'

While a permanent replacement for Sinclair was sought, Emms, along with John Benger, a future Clerk of the Commons, acted as Bercow's private secretary. The recruitment process, however, was in difficulty. A source says there were only four people who applied for the position. 'That offended Bercow hugely, but people knew what an awful job it was,' they say.

One of those to apply was Emms, who had worked in the House for sixteen years. Unlike many of her predecessors, Emms, a mother of three, was not from a military background, had not worked as a clerk throughout her Commons career and was a woman. She appeared to embody the type of modernising change Bercow was seeking to instil across the House. A former official says: 'All these things would make her a really, really good secretary for the Speaker.' The reality could not have been starker. 'She was properly traumatised by working for him.'

Those in the know say Emms was the standout candidate. 'We gave him the best person we could find in Kate Emms,' says an insider. Emms volunteered her candidacy willingly and, despite a limited field, competed with enthusiasm to secure the job.

Bercow was seeking to modernise and felt that the established elements were resistant to his reforms. Staff say that Bercow 'resented' that he had been advised to appoint Emms. 'He seemed to regard Kate as the basis of a plot with the clerks to take over his office,' says one. House authorities were looking to shake up some of the most arcane practices and, according to an insider, they were considering implementing a rotational scheme for working in Speaker's Office. 'In retrospect, I wish that I had known that this pitch by the clerks effectively to run the Speaker's office was not the first such attempt,' wrote Bercow in his memoir, *Unspeakable*. 'The Clerks wanted both to exert greater influence and to add to the career opportunities for Clerks.'[5]

In June 2010, Emms was appointed Bercow's new private secretary. She understood that she was going in with a mandate to modernise. 'The ways of working haven't changed since Betty Boothroyd's time. It was so labour-intensive and inefficient,' says a source. 'Part of her remit was to shake it up and work out what the systems should be. It was never to compromise its separateness, but in a positive way to enact reform.' Among her proposed reforms was the introduction of two deputies to the Speaker's secretary, one to look after House matters and one to pursue outreach and engagement.

But reform hinged on personnel change. Peter Barratt, the long-standing assistant Speaker's secretary, was scheduled to be swapped out in a re-shuffle. At the last minute, however, Bercow told Emms that Barratt was to stay. The assistant secretary informed a stunned Emms that he had told Sally that he and the Trainbearer, Ian Davis, didn't want to move. A family member says: 'Kate felt that massively undermined her position. From that moment on, she was dealing with a team that she was perceived as trying to get rid of and was expected to just work around it.'

With her innovations rejected, Emms offered to tender her resignation, saying: 'Clearly, you will want me to go.' Bercow replied: 'No, no, nothing could be further from the truth.' According to multiple sources, there was residual animus against Emms from Barratt and Davis. A member of Emms's family explains: 'They just froze her out. They knew they had this line to his wife, Sally.' Both men, particularly Barratt, divide opinion. Some Commons staff accuse them of being blindingly devoted to the Speaker. Others say this is an oversimplification of a complicated issue, with the role of Speaker, not the individual, commanding allegiance. Some point to the unique perks, privileges and allowances of the existing jobs and say it is hardly surprising that incumbents might fight tooth and nail for the status quo. Some dispute any criticism entirely: 'Peter was a lovely guy and very laidback,' says an ex-Bercow staffer. Barratt and Davis continued to work for Bercow until he stood down as Speaker. Both were approached to contribute to this book but declined.

Bercow states that he did not warm to Emms.[6] A former official says: 'I don't think Bercow ever really trusted her. From his point of view, this was being imposed on him by "the clerks" and she was a clerk. Why he chose to go into confrontation, I don't know.'
A family member adds: 'She did definitely start out by thinking she could fix it. She's a very good person at developing personal relationships with people.'

Those close to Emms say the trouble began when she started travelling with Bercow on overseas trips. 'They were stressful because they were one-on-one for so much of it. That's the truth,' says a family member. On consecutive September weekends in 2010, they went to Ottawa and then Nairobi. The second trip followed Pope Benedict's Westminster Hall address. Emms had worked hard on the event, helping with Bercow's speech and the organisation. However, Bercow's mood was unlikely to have been calm after Sally criticised the Pontiff on Twitter.[7]

After the event, Emms and Bercow departed swiftly for the airport. According to friends and family of Emms, she then had to inform Bercow that his bag, which contained large-size toiletries, would have to be checked in. This reportedly provoked an outburst from Bercow – said to have been particularly intimidating in the back seat of a car – including reference to Emms's 'presumption' in making such a judgement, and denigrating her competence. Other sources recall a similar incident while travelling when Bercow was found with toothpaste in his carry-on luggage at airport security. A family member says: 'He was absolutely outraged that his toothpaste had been confiscated. He thought that was profoundly disrespectful. He didn't talk to Kate for the whole of a nine-hour flight, which was ridiculously out of proportion.'

Insiders claim that Bercow was consistently demanding. During one tirade, a source claims Bercow called Emms a 'jobsworth'. As with testimony we will hear in subsequent chapters, Emms was never sure what mood she would find Bercow in, those close to her say. On occasion, he could be charming, effusive and gracious. Other days he would be 'totally irascible', finding fault with every decision or action taken that day, or suddenly placing the highest priority on the smallest task that had yet to be completed. 'She never knew what she was going to get. The worst was pretty bad, and the best was all sunshine and marvellous,' says a former colleague. Friends recalls the impact this unpredictability had on Emms, including one occasion during a trip to Poland when she anxiously chased down the hotel chambermaids' bins to fish out Bercow's conference scribbles, in case he would ask for them later. A family member says: 'I do remember thinking towards the end before she left that she couldn't be expected to manage in the current circumstances.'

According to multiple sources, there were three or four incidents of bullying by Bercow, which included 'in-your-face unpleasantness'. 'In between all that was the low-key intimidation, punctuated by over-the-top thanks or praise,' says one. Friends of Emms recall confidences about Bercow being 'vile', 'unpleasant', 'inappropriate' and 'appalling' one day and then apologising to her the next, insisting it would never happen again. One former colleague likened Bercow's consistent sweeping denials of bullying as 'gaslighting'.

Something of a milestone was passed after a meeting of the House of Commons Commission, which took place in Bercow's office. Emms and Bercow's press officer were sitting in the corner of the room while the Commission met for its monthly gathering. The Speaker, according to Commons sources, kept staring at Emms as conversations went on around him. During the day, Emms had passed on advice she had been given, but the source was giving different advice in the meeting. 'It was chilling but ludicrous. He may have felt she had misled him or just got it wrong because she had told him one thing and now someone else was telling him another thing. He took this as some kind of personal affront,' a friend of Emms says.

According to family and a former colleague, after others had left, Emms sought to clear the air and asked: 'Are we all right?' The answer reportedly was a firm 'no' followed by a furious tirade, 'very much in Kate's personal space'. Emms's colleague said Bercow 'grew into a rage and there was abuse about her personally and her abilities; he insinuated that she was a lazy person who didn't really care about standards; it was intense and frightening'.

For the first time, Emms 'put her foot down' with Bercow, a family member recalls. She is believed to have banged the table and asked him to stop talking. She then left the room. Emms emerged from this confrontation 'dazed' and 'massively shaken', says an associate. She went to see colleagues, including Robert Rogers. They could see that she was not in a good way. 'What's happened?' they asked, directing her to sit down.

'When someone accuses you of being lazy, incompetent and sneers about you, and you emerge from that conversation having been fairly robust, it must have been a very shaking experience,' a source in the House of Commons Service says. A family member remembers: 'She came back that evening and said, "I think I may have lost my job." It was because of the way he degraded her.'

Emms slept poorly that evening. However, on this occasion she arrived in the office to find a voicemail from the Speaker. He was 'hugely apologetic' and said he had been 'completely inappropriate, overstepped the mark and crossed boundaries'. 'It won't happen again,' he is alleged to have vowed. Bercow followed up with a face-to-face apology that same morning.

The role of Speaker's secretary should have been one that Emms excelled at, insiders argue. Instead, within months, she was dreading returning to her accommodation in Westminster as a new week loomed. 'It would make your hair curl the kind of abuse he would give to people who were just trying to do their job,' says a government source. A former Conservative MP says: 'The way he treated Kate Emms was literally awful. She was absolutely delighted when she got the job, but for one reason and another, he does have this thing where he has this way of behaving that you either sign up for or you don't. Most people wouldn't.'

A member of her family recalls feeling powerless. 'I could be a listening post and a sounding board. It was dreadful to watch.'

In February 2011, seven months after taking on the role, Emms was signed off sick with stress. She texted Lawrence Ward, then an Assistant Serjeant-at-Arms, who had been working in Speaker's Office. 'Over to you,' she said, according to Ward.

Not everyone around at the time knew of what had been taking place. Ward, who had also been seconded to the Speaker's Office to review how operations in the department could improve, says he 'never got a whiff' of anything related to bullying. On Emms, he says: 'I think she was finding it quite difficult – the hours, living in that old creaky house on Parliament

Street is not easy, she had a family. I know how she felt because I fell into that when I became the Serjeant.' Ward took over as the Speaker's private secretary while a longer-term solution was sought. He stresses that he did not experience bullying or bullying behaviour from Bercow during his short tenure in the role.

Eliot Wilson, who was working as private secretary to Lindsay Hoyle, the most senior of the three Deputy Speakers, went for lunch with Emms soon after she was appointed. The only clues Wilson had were when Emms would roll her eyes or pull faces and say things were 'a bit difficult' as their paths crossed. 'She was professional enough to know that if it was going to be a serious problem, she needed to be slightly circumspect about it,' he says.

Emma Macey worked in Bercow's constituency office at the start of Emms's time as secretary. 'To begin with I think they had a good relationship. I don't know what went wrong. I wondered, retrospectively, whether she was very keen to do what John wanted – she was definitely keen on John's reform agenda – but maybe didn't know how to achieve it,' Macey says.

Emms has never spoken out publicly about her time working with Bercow. Many colleagues, both past and present, are categorical about her experience. Her story is one that continues to circulate in the House of Commons Service.

The Speaker's official portrait was commissioned when Emms was still his private secretary. As opposed to previous Speakers' paintings, Bercow's featured him standing in the chair, with his private secretary in view. Emms, the first female Speaker's secretary, posed for the artist while in the role. However, when the portrait was unveiled in September 2011, she had been replaced by her successor, Peter Barratt. 'I remember that happening. That was the most vindictive and petty thing,' says a family member. Bercow says that the painting was in progress when Emms left the office and so it was updated accordingly.[8]

Bercow has consistently denied any and all allegations of bullying in very absolute and forthright terms, as well as accusing potential victims and complainants of bad faith. After the *Newsnight* broadcast in March 2018, a spokesperson for Bercow said: 'The Speaker completely and utterly refutes the allegation that he behaved in such a manner, either eight years ago or at any other time. Any suggestion to the contrary is simply untrue.' Bercow himself has stated: 'For the record, I categorically deny that I have ever bullied anyone, anywhere at any time.'[9]

In his memoir, Bercow named Emms directly and recounted aspects of their relationship and the reshuffle of his existing staff. This prompted the House of Commons, who had been strategising over how to respond to the book for weeks (no advance copy was made available to them, sources say), to take the extraordinary step of publicly censuring Bercow. In a statement, the House said it was 'unacceptable' for the former Speaker to have named current and former parliamentary staff without their permission for 'financial gain'. 'A crucial element of the work of House of Commons staff is to provide confidential, impartial advice to MPs. Breaking this confidentiality undermines this important principle and also places staff in a position from which they are unable to respond.'

In response, Bercow's spokesperson said: 'Given there is a small but highly vocal group of people consistently seeking to blacken his name, it would be odd if Mr Bercow did not comment on their unfounded allegations and the reasons behind them.'[10]

A staff member in the Commons comments: 'If someone who worked under me was signed off with stress, it would make me think about my own behaviour and whether or not the way I treat people is up to what is expected. The fact it has not [for Mr Bercow] speaks volumes.' Another former colleague put it more plainly: 'Bullying is not about intent; it is about impact. How can anyone say they haven't bullied anyone without pausing to ask, to find out.'

By May 2011, Emms was appointed clerk in charge of Private Members' Bills. Her path did cross on a couple of occasions with Bercow over subsequent years. She remains a member of the House of Commons Service.

When news emerged of Bercow's nomination for a peerage by Jeremy Corbyn in January 2020, Emms was 'very upset', a source close to her says. 'She had been genuinely convinced that he would not be around the place after retiring. Also, it would be a complete travesty; it would reward bad behaviour that we all know about.'

*   *   *

Emily Commander was working in France while on leave from the House. A fortnight after *Newsnight* reported her story, she decided to go on the record. She walked into a hotel in Lyon, where she was greeted by Chris Cook. 'How do you feel about doing your resignation letter on national TV?' he asked.

Commander had still hoped to return to the House of Commons Service and the job she loved, and her relationship with senior colleagues remained cordial, even after the *Newsnight* programme aired. However, she knew that it would be difficult for her to work with MPs again. She has subsequently left, and it is not known whether a settlement took place.

The last of the Bercow accusers to come forward was David Leakey, the former Black Rod. He spoke of his encounter with Bercow over the Westminster Hall address by Aung San Suu Kyi, when the Speaker allegedly called him an antisemite. 'He creates a climate of intimidation and fear amongst a whole group of people,' he told *Newsnight*. In a statement, the Speaker's spokesperson said: 'Mr Speaker refutes all the allegations levelled by Mr Leakey. John Bercow and David Leakey are two very different people with very different backgrounds, perspectives and ideas. They had fundamental disagreements in 2011 and 2012 but interacted adequately after that.'

Newsnight's investigation continued in August, when Jenny Mc-Cullough, a former clerk, accused Labour MP Keith Vaz of bullying her when he was chair of the Home Affairs Select Committee – accusations he denies. Cook would win Reporter of the Year at the Royal Television

Society, and *Newsnight* would be nominated for a Bafta and an RTS prize for investigative journalism.

Bercow's bullish responses to accusations of bullying have left a sour taste for many in the House of Commons Service. For some, it has given them a reason to speak out.

CHAPTER TWENTY-FIVE

COMING FORWARD

*'You shouldn't have to go to work feeling like
you're about to enter a warzone.'*

In the course of researching this book, accounts of alleged bullying
by John Bercow have emerged in relation to three other people, all
of whom have yet to make allegations or be associated with complaints
against him. Of those, two have spoken for the first time about their experiences, under strict anonymity. Their reasons for requesting anonymity
range from the position they currently hold through to not wanting the
media spotlight that would follow from going public. The third person
declined the opportunity to contribute. Their story has been pieced together from other sources. To preserve their respective rights to anonymity, they will be known henceforth as Person A, Person B, and Person C.
Their pronouns have been changed to 'they' or 'them'.

For those who knew of Person A, who turned down the opportunity to
speak, the *Newsnight* report did not come as a shock. 'I've always known
that [Bercow] is a bully and nasty,' says a clerk who was previously friendly with Person A.

A Conservative Party source explains:

He did have a bit of a reputation for not being nice to a member of his
staff. I've heard that he made [them] cry on a number of occasions after

shouting at [them]. I got the sense that [they] felt that he was demanding a lot and may not have been that understanding.

A former aide to a Tory MP recalls answering a call from someone on the parliamentary estate. It was Person A, who was attempting to contact a colleague to talk about Bercow. 'He's a shit, he's a shit!' Person A said down the phone. The source, who has been friendly with Bercow, explains: 'I like him as a person; he's genial, his heart is in the right place, he's good company. I also believe in all the bullying stuff, actually.'

Person A would continue to defend Bercow, however. An ex-government source explains: 'There are some very, very, very difficult people in life who can also still be very interesting, rewarding, funny and enjoyable people to work for. If you're the sort of person who wants an interesting life, they can be more interesting to work for than other MPs can be.'

Person B worked in the House with Bercow when he was Speaker. After years of cordiality, things soured, and they increasingly found themselves in conflict with Bercow. 'It was almost like he became a completely different person,' they say. 'What became really difficult with him was there was a big element of shoot the messenger. In my role I was giving him news he would rather not hear.' Person B gives the example of raising a query that had come through to the office that Bercow took issue with. 'He started shouting an answer at me as if it was me asking it.' When angry, 'his lip would curl, he would be sneery, snarling, his brow would drop', they add.

The fortunes of Bercow's favourite sports stars would often dictate how he would behave on a given day. 'If you heard that Arsenal or Federer had lost, you'd know what you would be walking into that morning. That is not normal,' Person B says. 'The only way I could describe it is he would throw a paddy – stamping, slamming doors, screaming. It would never ostensibly be about Federer losing; it would be about procedural advice he didn't agree with or something. It was pretty aggressive.' Other warning signs would be if anything had 'kicked off' in the Chamber.

Mondays were usually the worst days for being summoned to his study, as Bercow may have spent the weekend arguing with Sally or a sports result may not have gone his way, according to Person B. 'In the moment, it would always be like he started off cross and then the more he went on the more he riled himself up, and the worse it got. He was quite vicious in his language and his tone,' they explain. It would take an enormous amount of energy and resolve to push back against Bercow in these moments. 'You shouldn't have to go to work feeling like you were about to enter a warzone.'

Person B also recalls Bercow hurling phones, car keys or stationery when angry. 'More than one person in the office would have to fix his phone after he broke it. He would throw it into the fireplace and then ram the battery in the wrong way round. We would have to pluck it out.'

Bercow, according to Person B, would get especially tense around the time he was preparing to deliver a speech. 'He never really understood that it takes time to gather and collate information and would often have a massive fit if he thought it was taking you too long. He always got nervous on the day of the speech itself and would take it out on other people.' On one occasion, 'he was a complete thug to me all day', says Person B. 'I was weary, not upset. I was fairly used to it by that point.'

They conclude:

> I did feel bullied. I felt that I was being targeted for things that weren't my fault. I thought that if he was in a bad mood it would largely be taken out on me irrespective of who was to blame, if anyone. I think he got worse as he went on.

Person C worked with Bercow when he was Speaker. 'He is the most appalling human being I have ever met. He is that bad. He is a truly, truly despicable and loathsome man in my view,' they say. Person C had several encounters with Bercow that they characterise as 'rages, tantrums and bullying-type episodes', adding: 'He behaved absolutely appallingly.'

Describing the exchanges, Person C says if they tried to speak or interpose during one of Bercow's rants, he would pounce on it and say: 'I'm sorry, you find that funny, do you? Oh, that's very interesting.' They say that sarcasm and belittling were the tools he employed. They continue: 'He is a practised shit. He is really good at it; he is really, really good at being unpleasant. It is quite an odd skill to have in life, and Bercow has it in abundance.'

Person B and Person C both say that Bercow had the capacity to be charming and personable. That dual personality made the anger more pronounced, they say, and left them more on edge. 'He could be emollient, but it was sometimes with this horrible, maudlin, gushing sentimentality, which was the other side of the same coin,' Person C explains.

A consistent thread running through the experiences of Person B and Person C, and others we have discussed in earlier chapters, is that Bercow was not shy of people observing his anger. 'He does enjoy an audience, which was never really that sensible as it does create witnesses,' says Person B. Person C explains: 'It was as if somehow by having witnesses to it, it wasn't therefore inappropriate behaviour. That's how he justified it.'

Officials claim that Bercow would often summon individuals without notice. 'The Speaker wants to see you. I'm afraid he's not very happy,' Peter Barratt, the Speaker's private secretary, would say. Sometimes Bercow would ask Barratt to sit in on some difficult meetings.

Person C says they too were bullied by Bercow. 'Definitely. It takes quite a bit to bully me. I had never had sleepless nights caused by the behaviour of a member, other than in contact with him. That was quite a shock.'

Person B and Person C have decided not to lodge formal complaints against Bercow. Both are determined to retain their anonymity, having seen others who have come forward be talked about consistently in the media.

Remarkably, some of the experiences recounted to me occurred after the *Newsnight* investigation and the publication of the inquiry into bullying and harassment by Dame Laura Cox. 'He didn't really moderate his behaviour at all. He never learned that lesson. It's just astonishing,' says one former senior official.

Someone who has met Bercow on several occasions says:

> I know an awful lot of clerks who as soon as you've given them one pint are absolutely scathing about his personal conduct in private. When dealing with him, I've always thought you didn't have to scratch the surface very hard and you could see the slightly angry man lurking beneath.

Julian Lewis has staunchly defended his close ally against accusations of bullying. Central to understanding Bercow's character, Lewis explains, is to realise that he 'cannot and will not tolerate being bullied by anybody'. He says when you get into an argument with Bercow, the 'very worst thing you can do is threaten him'. 'Because a) he is very capable of defending himself, and b) even if he were not, even if he were up against something that was obviously a superior force, he would never submit to pressure or bullying,' he continues.

> If you want to get John to do something, it is far better to lead him to it gently – and preferably to encourage him to suggest it himself, so that he thinks it's his own idea! If anybody tries to coerce John, he will strike back, even if it's against his own interests. That's why many of his friends, knowing that he has a bit of a temper, have always had to say to him: 'Do not explode. Do not lose your temper. Do not "flip". Calm, calm, calm!' He's taken that expression from us, and he has often used it himself to quieten people down in the Chamber.

Benedict Rogers, who has known Bercow for sixteen years, says the bullying allegations do not 'chime with the person I know'. He adds:

> From my own experience, I can't fault him. I always feel very sad and

a bit annoyed when I hear some of the really nasty and really extreme criticism. No human being is perfect and I'm sure some of his critics have valid criticisms. But I also think those who are so hostile to him haven't seen the John that I know.

Emma Macey ran Bercow's constituency office from 2009 to 2010. She enjoyed a decent working relationship with Bercow. 'He was a good boss, he was a kind man,' she says. As part of her job, Macey would organise surgeries, events and correspondence related to Buckingham. As Bercow 'never used a computer', Macey would print everything off and leave letters, emails and queries for him to go over on his desk at the end of the day. 'I'd come back the next morning and everything would be signed, and he was incredibly diligent at going through the boxes I'd left out for him every night,' she says.

As part of his constituency staff, Macey was based in an office next to Speaker's apartment. She says she does not believe Bercow is a bully. 'John is actually a very sensitive man. He's very empathetic, hugely empathetic, actually. I've never come across a bully who is particularly empathetic. So, for me, the two characteristics don't go together,' she argues. She adds: 'That isn't to say he doesn't have a temper – he does. I think that's fine. I heard him shout – he never shouted at me. He's more likely to shout about a situation than at a person.'

Macey left her role in 2010 due to the volume of work.

When you're working in that kind of environment, it's more like family than a normal working relationship. So, you see a broader range of emotions and what not, as I'm sure you do in somewhere like Downing Street or wherever else. I never came across behaviour that I would say was unreasonable.

However, Macey notes that there could be a contrast in experience depending on your role. 'There was a potentially a difference between how he may have treated constituency staff, who are literally just there to support him, whereas I suspect when he came in he may not have 100 per cent felt that all of the Speaker's Office was pulling wholeheartedly in the right direction.'

This observation seems to cut right to the heart of the matter. Those who worked in his constituency office had fewer interactions with him each week. They were often dealing with far less contentious issues. There were fewer occasions when they would run up against him. Insofar as those who accuse him of bullying are concerned, the main issue was when they had to tell Bercow things he might not want to hear. The bullying was also directed towards 'the people on whom he needed to impose his will', says Person C.

Robert Rogers, Angus Sinclair and Kate Emms were all clerks at the time of the alleged bullying. David Leakey was an official in the House of Lords. At various points, all had to deliver news or views contrary to what Bercow wanted to hear. Often, they were simply messengers.

His run-ins with Lindsay Hoyle seem based on a perception that the former wanted his job. The public disagreements with Andrea Leadsom, to be considered in later chapters, came in part because she pushed back against him. His alleged encounter with George Young came over an issue in which he felt resistance.

For Bercow, reform was totemic. To him, clerks were obtrusive to that overall aim, and presented obstacles to his plans. He often felt them resistant and innately conservative. It appears that he felt the ends justified the means.

'Clerks are not conservative by nature; they're quite radical by nature. If you look at the procedural chicanery of the 2017–19 parliament, all of those things were suggested by clerks,' says one well-placed source. 'The idea that clerks are fuddy-duddy old farts who block everything is a very convenient fiction for him.'

As for Bercow's continued denials, some accusers say they are sincere. 'He genuinely believes he didn't bully anybody, as he has to,' says Person

B. To think otherwise would be to address a fundamental character flaw, and perhaps delve into an area he would not wish to explore.

Many take the view that you do not need to have seen behind closed doors to draw the conclusion that his behaviour amounted to bullying. Often flashes of what many had seen in private were there for all to see. After all, Bercow did not mind if there were witnesses. 'Just look at the Chamber. It was in plain view,' says a Commons source. 'In small and big ways, he showed it even in public.'

CHAPTER TWENTY-SIX

FALLOUT

'I've never bullied anyone, anywhere, at any time, in any way.'

By the time *Newsnight* aired on Thursday 8 March 2018, Lucinda Day had broken her arm. She was in the hospital for a check-up the following Monday when she caught wind of what had taken place in the Commons. Andrea Leadsom, the Leader of the House, had just announced an independent inquiry into bullying and harassment in Westminster.

In Parliament, the temperature was running high. John Bercow had awarded an Urgent Question on the *Newsnight* report and was overseeing the debate. He had temporarily stood down as chair of the commission to allow for a probe into the allegations. Leadsom had already been working with MPs on forming an independent complaints and grievance policy in the wake of the sexual harassment scandal. Announcing the news of an inquiry into bullying, Leadsom said: 'It is right that everyone working for or with Parliament regardless of position or seniority should have the same rights and protections and should be held to the same high standards.'

Among those to speak in the debate was Paul Farrelly, the Labour MP accused of bullying Emily Commander, who urged colleagues not to rush to judgement over the 'very one-sided, selective BBC broadcast', adding: 'Finally, may I ask the House to consider why old, historical allegations like this are being selectively recycled now, and by whom, because whatever is at play this is not a game for reputations or families?'

The reaction of the House of Commons authorities to *Newsnight*'s reporting left some staff with the impression that they were in denial about the scale of the problem. Officials had dismissed as a 'grotesque exaggeration' that a 'culture of fear' had persisted in the institution, as alleged in the programme. In a follow-up letter to staff, David Natzler, the Clerk of the Commons, said there was 'no doubt' that there are unresolved issues of bullying and harassment. 'I acknowledge we got it wrong in giving the impression we were in denial,' he wrote.

In the days after the original report, staff in the Commons reached out to journalists at *Newsnight*. However, producers on the show had a difficult time getting politicians to come forward to discuss the allegations. 'We felt like we couldn't get any Labour MPs to speak on the record because of Brexit and the fact that Bercow was very useful to the Labour Party on that front,' says a BBC source. According to the insider, there was also an element of tribal behaviour, with MPs protecting their colleagues. Many would open up off the record, but few wanted their words to be attributed to them.

On 23 April, the commission announced that Dame Laura Cox, a High Court judge, had been made chair of the bullying inquiry. Her objectives included establishing the nature and extent of the claims, examining how complaints had been handled and advising how procedures could be improved. 'It is not the purpose of the inquiry to reopen past complaints of bullying or harassment or to investigate new ones against particular individuals,' the commission said in a statement. In other words, the inquiry would not investigate specific allegations of misbehaviour.

Angus Sinclair spoke out at the beginning of May. Soon after, Andrew Bridgen, Conservative MP for North West Leicestershire and noted Bercow critic, asked Kathryn Stone, the Parliamentary Commissioner for Standards, to investigate whether the Speaker had breached the MPs' code of conduct. As the allegations against Bercow went back more than seven years, Stone sought the opinion of the Standards Committee – composed of MPs and lay members – to decide whether an investigation should take place. Only MPs could vote on the matter, and one – an SNP MP – was away. The chair of the Standards Committee, Sir Kevin Barron, was not allowed to vote.

The MPs decided by three to two to block an investigation. A source with knowledge of the events says that Barron was furious at the 'deeply damaging' result, believing it to have been made to 'protect the Speaker'. Barron subsequently took the highly unusual decision to publish how MPs had voted. It transpired that Conservative MPs John Stevenson and Christopher Chope and Labour MP Kate Green had voted against allowing Stone to conduct the investigation. Labour MP Bridget Phillipson and Tory Gary Streeter had voted in favour.

Stevenson, a former lawyer, says:

On the evidence in front of me, there was an allegation which came from a particular MP whose judgement I find questionable; it was about an allegation of many, many years ago, supported by an ex employee of Parliament who had signed a confidentiality agreement. Therefore, I felt on balance that there was insufficient evidence for something to go ahead.

Chope felt that if there was a 'regular pattern of conduct' to Bercow's behaviour, then more recent claims against him would be made. The backbencher, who also took into consideration the non-disclosure agreement signed by Sinclair, felt that a probe into the Speaker would be problematic. 'The mere starting of an investigation into the Speaker is itself very damaging. I didn't think that that was justified,' he says. 'I thought that his position as Speaker – OK, he would be subject to an investigation – but the mere fact that he was being investigated for something going back more than seven years would be undermining the position of Speaker.'

As for the decision to publish how MPs voted, Chope says: 'That was an example of Kevin Barron wanting to pander to what he saw was the populist opinion on this and to insulate himself against the criticism forthcoming from various members of his own party and some of the media.'

'My view was that if the Commissioner wanted to investigate it, then we shouldn't seek to stop her from doing so,' Phillipson says. 'I thought that whatever the merits of it, serious allegations had been made and should be considered. If I was the person that was being complained about, I would want the opportunity to put forward my version of events.' Green and Streeter did not respond to requests for an interview.

Though Bercow had been spared being subject to an independent investigation, he would soon find himself once more in hot water.

* * *

Bad blood had been brewing between Bercow and Leadsom. After the 2017 election, the minority Conservative government had taken a less-is-more attitude to parliamentary scrutiny. As part of this approach, ministers had refused to contest votes during opposition day debates on non-binding motions, to limit the damage of a defeat. In successive weeks, the opposition won votes on social care funding, the roll-out of universal credit, and NHS pay, among other areas. Amid the mounting backlash, Leadsom said that ministers would provide a written response within twelve weeks of a defeat. Whereas previous governments had, on occasion, felt compelled to act after a loss of this kind, Theresa May's administration took a different view.

The Labour Party became creative in response. It began to deploy an antiquated procedure known as a Humble Address that compelled ministers to acknowledge the will of the House. Sir Keir Starmer, the shadow Brexit Secretary, used the device to force the publication of sectoral analyses on the impact of leaving the EU. Members of the government suspected that the use of such a unique and historical parliamentary tool was first suggested to Labour frontbenchers by Bercow, who they argue is far more au fait with parliamentary procedure. A former No. 10 aide says: 'We are given to understand the Labour Party only used it because the Speaker told them, "This is how to do it."' One Tory minister argues: 'I don't think humble and John Bercow are words you would normally associate with each other. But certainly, the address part of it, yes. I am sure he prompted that suggestion.'

However, insiders say the suggestion came from one of the clerks, who are available to every MP to offer guidance. One official says: 'It arose from a conversation between one of the anti-Brexit crew and one of the procedurally adept clerks.'

The failure to contest non-binding motions was not the Labour Party's only bugbear. They also felt that the government was breaching convention by using up time reserved for opposition debates with statements in the House. Nick Brown, the party's Chief Whip, raised a point of order on the matter after Prime Minister's Questions on 16 May. Staring at Leadsom, Bercow said: 'This is an undesirable state of affairs, and if it were to happen on further occasions, a great many honourable and right honourable Members, not to mention interested parties in the opposition day debates outside the Chamber, would view it, frankly, as an abuse.'

Resuming his seat, Bercow was reportedly heard by an MP mouthing 'stupid woman' and, allegedly, 'fucking useless' or 'fucking outrageous'. The comments, which went against Bercow's perception as a progressive, were passed on to the *Daily Telegraph* by the MP.[1] Bercow admitted to using the word 'stupid' in a 'muttered aside' but stopped short of apologising. 'That adjective simply summed up how I felt about the way that that day's business had been conducted. Anyone who knows the Leader of the House at all well will have not the slightest doubt about her political ability and her personal character,' he told MPs.

At the end of 2018, a furious row broke out in the Commons after Jeremy Corbyn appeared to mouth 'stupid woman' at Theresa May during PMQs. MPs picked up on the footage, which had circulated on social media, and the atmosphere in the Commons began to heat up. At the end of proceedings,

Corbyn had made it out of the Chamber before Bercow had selected a point of order. Initially, Bercow said that points of order should be raised after statements, with Sajid Javid, the Home Secretary, due to address the House. After eventually accepting a query from Sir Patrick McLoughlin, Bercow said he had not seen what was alleged to have taken place. 'It is incumbent upon all Members of this House to operate in accordance with its best conventions and to follow the conventions and courtesies. If a Member has failed to do so, that Member has a responsibility to apologise,' he added.

Leadsom signalled that she would like to intervene. 'I would just like to ask, after your finding that individuals who are found to have made unwelcome remarks should apologise, why it is that when an opposition Member found that you had called me a "stupid woman", you did not apologise in this Chamber,' Leadsom asked.

A wall of noise came up from the backbenches. As Leadsom resumed her seat, a number of Tory MPs could be seen with their mouth agape. 'I dealt with that matter months ago in remarks that I made to the House of Commons, to which the right hon. Lady in our various meetings since has made no reference, and which requires from the chair today no elaboration whatsoever,' Bercow said.

The episode was damaging for Bercow. His reticence over allowing points of order, despite perhaps being procedurally sound, jarred with his previous approach from the chair. In Leadsom, Bercow had yet another public enemy. Anna Soubry says: 'That's where John Bercow really lets himself down. The moments where he can't help himself.' Corbyn returned to the Commons soon after and insisted he had said 'stupid people'.

Leadsom, like Bercow, refused to back down. When Bercow urged Conservative backbencher Sir Peter Bottomley to 'grow up' and for MPs to 'raise the level', Leadsom interjected: 'Mr Speaker, may I just say that your response does not raise the level? I will leave it there.' On another occasion, Bercow chastised Leadsom for 'playing with her electronic device'. Apparently unable to help himself, he attacked Chris Pincher, the Deputy Chief Whip, who previously had been spotted in the Chamber calling Bercow a 'bully': 'I did not include him in the category of very senior people in the House, but I readily grant that that is a debatable proposition.'

A source close to Leadsom says she felt compelled to speak out: 'I said a couple of times, "We don't want it to backfire, we just need to be a bit careful". She said, "The thing with bullies is that if you don't stand up to them, they get away with it. I don't want to, I have to."'

The public confrontation reflected what was taking place behind the scenes. 'Anyone who has seen them in a room together will understand there is a mutual wariness which reflects the fact that they have been political antagonists,' says a government source. 'Their relationship was the worst between a Leader of the House of Commons and a Speaker in modern times.' Leadsom, a Brexiteer who had been runner-up in the race to succeed David Cameron before withdrawing from the contest, was appointed Leader of the House in June 2017. For the initial period of her time in the role, Kate Emms, Bercow's former private secretary, worked in her office as parliamentary adviser to the Leader of the House. As a result, a government source suggests the Cabinet minister became 'emboldened' to take Bercow on over accusations of bullying.

The animosity also played out on the commission, which would meet once a month to discuss matters pertaining to the House. Sources say that Bercow did little to hide his disdain for Leadsom. On one occasion, the tensions between them were so great the non-executives present at the end of the meeting noted for the record that they had witnessed un-acceptable behaviour.

A source with knowledge of the interactions says:

He was very aggressive towards her. He would get quite close to her and if she would disapprove of anything he would say, 'Can I finish? Does the Leader mind if I finish?' Patronising, quite aggressive, quite intimidating. He would stay on the right side of being able to say it was all debate or it was a heated discussion. He knew what he was doing.

At another meeting, John Benger, the Clerk of the House, told Bercow that he would leave the room if the conversation was not conducted in a more reasonable fashion, a Commons source says.

Benger took over from Sir David Natzler as Clerk of the House of Commons on 1 March 2019. He had served as the Clerk Assistant and managing director of the Chamber and Committees team prior to his appointment. In total, Benger had been a member of the House of Commons Service for nearly thirty-three years.

According to multiple sources, Bercow sought to intervene in the recruitment process. His preference was Sarah Davies, a more junior clerk who served as a Principal Clerk of Select Committees. Bercow was clearly undeterred by the backlash that greeted his involvement with Carol Mills's botched appointment. 'Rather than being careful and playing this one straight, he was back at it,' says an official with knowledge of events.

Sources say that Bercow did not have a personal issue with Benger, whom he rated highly. Instead, he wanted to install Davies to become the first woman to serve as Clerk of the Commons. 'If he can get a positive diversity message out of it, he would,' says an insider. However, the committee in charge of assessing candidates, which included Janet Gaymer, a leading employment lawyer, had sifted her out. 'He was cross about that and via Rosie Winterton tried to have it reopened. She was a key agent of Bercow,' alleges a source. A female candidate was considered in the final shortlist.

Benger was appointed Clerk and took over from Natzler in March 2019. A month later, Davies was promoted to Benger's old position of Clerk Assistant and MD of the Chamber and Committees team. She is one of the three clerks to sit in front of the Speaker in the Commons at the start of each day's proceedings.

Natzler's relations with Bercow are said to have been an improvement on those the Speaker maintained with Robert Rogers. Described as a calm, deeply intelligent and reserved man, Natzler held dear the principles surrounding the relationship between the Clerk and the Chair. 'He would think it inappropriate for him to tell you his conversations with the Speaker, so he never would,' says a government source.

While they held similar ideals, sources in Leadsom's office sensed that Benger's relationship with the Speaker was at times problematic. One says: 'He was better placed than his predecessors to push back.' Such was the atmosphere on the commission that Tom Brake, the Liberal Democrat representative, visited Leadsom in her office. According to multiple sources, he asked Leadsom to address her relationship with Bercow, which he said was becoming uncomfortable. 'What would you like me to do, Tom? Should I just let him bully me? Should I let him sit and shout at me?' Leadsom replied.

Brake says: 'That relationship I think in all aspects was a very poor relationship. I think you can draw your own conclusions as to whether it went beyond what you saw publicly in the Chamber.' Asked about the alleged incident with Leadsom, he replied: 'I think I'd better say, "No comment" to that.' As for Bercow's wider approach to the commission, Brake adds: 'He has perhaps strong views on many aspects of what the commission is responsible for.'

Angela Eagle says Bercow was anxious to pursue change. 'He wanted to get rid of the wigs for everybody and the stuffiness. He was prepared to ride roughshod over some traditions like that if they were being a bit silly, while obviously glorying in some others.' When Eagle took the lead on opposing zero-hour contracts, Bercow ensured that no member of staff in the House of Commons Service was employed under the arrangement. 'He was very good on things like that.'

Bercow's running of the commission, particularly during Leadsom's time as Commons Leader, has come in for criticism. 'The behaviour was just unimaginably bad. It was horrible,' says a Commons source. 'He's an intimidating presence even in there, but she did stand up to him.'

According to insiders, Bercow would talk 'non-stop' during meetings, which would often be cancelled due to his 'obsession' with being in the Chamber at key moments. 'It wasn't a priority for him. When we did have the commission, he would do these ridiculous monologues and pose rhetorical questions to himself,' says one. A government source says: 'It was mainly a forum through which the Speaker would just pontificate as much as he felt the need to.'

Leadsom resigned as Commons Leader in May 2019. After returning to the backbenches, she was invited to an awards ceremony on diversity and equality for her work on the steering group reviewing sexual harassment claims in Parliament. Unbeknownst to her team, the Speaker was due to present some of the awards.

'He started off at the beginning with this great long speech that went on for what felt like hours,' says a witness.

> Andrea does this thing that really annoys him where he will be talking, and she will be looking elsewhere and just won't engage him. I was trying to watch for this and he's constantly looking at her. He's desperate for her to be engaged with him, to be almost approving of him.

Bercow told an interviewer in February 2020 that Leadsom had wanted to be 'Secretary of State for the Commons' and accused her of 'weaponising' the issue of bullying. 'She rushed to judge me without evidence, and I think that is bigoted,' he said.[2]

Staff behind the scenes in the leader's office speak of Bercow's inconsistent temperament, and that he would often 'blow hot and cold'. 'People don't often associate it together, but it is very much the hallmarks of bullying; the uncertainty of what you're dealing with that day,' says an insider. A government source says: 'You never know what side of him you're going to get.'

* * *

On 15 October 2018, seven months after *Newsnight*'s first report on bullying and harassment in Westminster, Dame Laura Cox published her findings. The 155-page report was devastating. The High Court judge had identified a culture 'of deference, subservience, acquiescence and silence, in which bullying, harassment and sexual harassment have been able to thrive and have long been tolerated and concealed'.

More than 200 people had come forward to provide testimony. After quoting several contributors who said that meaningful change to the culture at Parliament would take 'several generations', Cox argued: 'On this basis, I find it difficult to envisage how the necessary changes can be successfully delivered, and the confidence of the staff restored, under the current senior House administration.'

The conclusion was interpreted as a call for Bercow and other senior House of Commons staff to step aside. Among those to urge the Speaker to consider his position were Maria Miller, the Women and Equalities Committee chair, and Sir Kevin Barron. The most controversial intervention came from Dame Margaret Beckett, who said in public what many had suspected some Labour MPs felt in private.

Speaking to the *Today* programme, Beckett said that the question of Brexit superseded that of allegations regarding bullying:

> Abuse is terrible, it shouldn't happen, it should be stopped, behaviour should change anyway, whether the Speaker goes or not. But yes, if it comes to it, the constitutional future of this country – the most difficult decision we have made not just since the war but certainly in all our lifetimes and possibly for hundreds of years – yes, it trumps bad behaviour.[3]

The remarks caused widespread upset, including among staff who worked for Labour MPs, and the broader House of Commons Service. 'The Labour Party is pretty complicit,' says a Tory minister. A Labour MP says: 'I didn't agree with that rhetoric, I have to say.' Another Labour backbencher says: 'I was very disappointed by that because it's a false choice. This could have all been considered long before the crucial decisions that the Speaker was going to have to take around Brexit.' A Commons official says: 'That's what we've battled with for years, which is why the staff stuff has never been taken seriously.'

Bercow had already irked Tory MPs by not following through on his pledge to stand down after nine years in the chair. He had argued that the 2017 election changed the calculation, and that an experienced hand was needed in the Chamber at a time of such constitutional significance. But under pressure by the findings of the Cox Report, friends of Bercow said he would step down in the summer of 2019.

Cox put forward three main recommendations in her report: the removal of the previous complaints procedures; the introduction of an entirely independent process to handle complaints; and the inclusion of historical allegations. The House of Commons Commission voted at the end of October to implement all three of the recommendations. In February 2020, it finally backed the creation of an independent expert panel for determining bullying or sexual harassment complaints against MPs.

The *Newsnight* investigation and subsequent independent inquiries, including a report by QC Gemma White into bullying and harassment of MPs' parliamentary staff, should have shocked senior management into taking action. But for staff in the House of Commons Service, there was still a sense that the upper echelons had failed to come to grips with the issue. This feeling was compounded by an interview David Natzler gave to *The House* magazine in February 2019, shortly before stepping down as Clerk. The Clerk criticised the BBC for its own record, citing the findings of an inquiry into the paedophile former presenter Jimmy Savile. 'Although we've nothing as grave as that, it is a good thing that a public organisation is subject to public scrutiny in this way,' he said.

Natzler accepted the findings of the Cox Report and conceded that 'there probably still is bullying and harassment'. Asked whether the Commons could be seen to be taking the allegations seriously while Bercow remained in the chair, he responded:

> There's accusations and accusations. If he had been found to have done something wrong and was irremovable in some way, that would be damaging to the organisation. But I'm afraid this isn't a benign environment, and you have to differentiate between people who are accused by the press or anybody else of stuff and people who have been found to have done something wrong. The old-fashioned phrase, you can't believe everything you read in the newspapers.

Of course, the problem with this argument is that the accusations against Bercow had not, at this point, been investigated. (MPs voted in July 2019 to allow the parliamentary complaints scheme to investigate historical allegations of bullying and harassment.)

Lucinda Day had just landed back in the UK when she looked at her phone to find a number of messages from House staff upset at Natzler's comments. One says they felt 'utter fury' at the article. 'It was a bit like Prince Andrew's interview. They just don't know what to say,' they add, referring to the Duke of York's car-crash interview on Jeffrey Epstein. A government source says Natzler's heart 'is always in the right place'. They continue: 'On bullying and harassment, he would have wanted to deal with it in completely the right way. But because of the magnitude of the situation and him never having dealt with anything like that before, he didn't really have the tools at his disposal to deal with it.'

Bercow is unequivocal in his denial of the claims. 'I've never bullied anyone, anywhere at any time in any way,' he says. 'Some working relationships don't work. They might break down or be unsatisfactory in some way. The fact that that happens doesn't prove that one person maltreated another person.' He noted that two members of the Speaker's

Office – Peter Barratt and Ian Davis – had worked alongside him through-out his tenure in the chair, adding:

> But that of course is of no interest to what I would call the bigot faction
> … If the bigot faction want to go on for ever and a day saying 'bully boy
> Bercow', then no doubt they will do so, and they're perfectly entitled to
> their opinion, however bigoted it is.[4]

The lack of finality over the allegations was in nobody's favour: not the alleged victims', nor Bercow's. 'One thing I feel quite strongly about, and I'd be critical about, is I do know he genuinely did bully members of his staff quite badly,' says a former Cabinet minister who held good relations with Bercow. 'It was pretty clear there was substance to the allegations. That is something he does need to explain. He's always denied it, but it is true.'

By the end of 2018, the end of Bercow's career was looming. Shrouded in controversy in the wake of the Cox Report, his legacy was at stake. After nearly two years of negotiation, Theresa May had just signed a deal with the European Union. It set the scene for Bercow's final act.

CHAPTER TWENTY-SEVEN

GOING NUCLEAR

'Members do have to take the rough with the smooth.'

Dominic Grieve, the former Attorney General, visited John Bercow in the Speaker's apartment. The Tory MP for Beaconsfield, one of the Speaker's constituency neighbours, had become a vocal opponent of a no-deal exit from the European Union. That day, 8 January 2019, he had taken steps to try to prevent such an event from occurring.

MPs were supposed to have been given the opportunity to vote on Theresa May's withdrawal agreement in December. A series of strategic blunders had allowed opponents on both sides of the Brexit divide to rubbish the contents of the deal, and a large-scale defeat looked likely. It marked a fractious period for the Prime Minister, during which time her government was found in contempt of Parliament after failing to produce in full the legal advice provided by Geoffrey Cox, the Attorney General, on the new agreement. Labour had once more used the Humble Address device en route to compelling ministers to publish the documents.

Facing certain defeat, the Prime Minister decided to pull the vote in the Commons on 10 December. To further consternation, ministers turned down Bercow's request for MPs to decide on the matter. 'This whole proceeding has been extremely regrettable. I think that is manifest, palpable, incontrovertible,' Bercow told the House. May went on to win a no-confidence motion in her leadership of the Tory Party two days later by 200 to 117, after Conservative MPs acted prematurely in trying to remove her from Downing Street.

For months, if not years, friction had been building between the government and the House of Commons. Brexit had tested the UK's constitution in unprecedented ways, and MPs had to fight to have their say in the Brexit process. Under the plans initially pursued by May's government, Parliament was not going to have a vote on triggering Article 50, nor on the final divorce deal.

Major policy announcements on Brexit also took place outside of the Chamber. The most consequential speech of May's premiership was made not to MPs in the Commons Chamber, but at Lancaster House. Under the plans unveiled by May – the most significant in generations – the UK was set to leave the single market and end freedom of movement. Its membership of the customs union was in doubt. Ken Clarke says: 'If the government would have had its way, the House of Commons wouldn't matter.'

With a Speaker so preoccupied with the rights of the Commons, a clash between Bercow and the minority Conservative government was inevitable. Denying MPs the ability to vote on the deal greatly irritated the Speaker, whose patience was wearing thin. No. 10's main gripe with Bercow up to this point was the length of time he would keep May at the despatch box for statements in the Commons, with sources noting that the Prime Minister suffered from type 1 diabetes. Aides also took issue with the way in which Bercow would select MPs to question the Conservative leader, arguing it would largely alternate between senior Eurosceptics in the European Research Group – a band of predominantly Brexiteer MPs – and members of the Labour Party. 'He would call Labour hardliner, ERGer, Labour hardliner, ERGer, so that it would be an hour before the PM had done anything other than play defence,' says a No. 10 insider.

With the Cox Report still fresh in the mind, a former No. 10 aide believes Bercow made a cool calculation:

A cynic would suggest he had a choice to make, which is: do you want to be the guy who went down in history as a reforming Speaker, but also treated his staff badly and was rude and boorish, or do you want to go down as the guy who did everything they could to try to haul the government over the coals in terms of Brexit and to play to a very particular audience?

At the turn of the year, Bercow would make the most high-profile intervention of his Speakership.

*   *   *

When Dominic Grieve tabled an amendment to a government business motion detailing the timetable for the Brexit debate, few eyebrows were raised. The expectation, based on centuries of precedent, was that the motion was unamendable, and the amendment would therefore not be selected. MPs had approved the business motion for the original vote on the Brexit deal back on 4 December. Paragraph 9 of the motion stated: 'No motion to vary or supplement the provisions of this Order shall be made except by a Minister of the Crown; and the question on any such motion shall be put forthwith.'

An almighty row over the interpretation of 'forthwith' was about to ensue. A parliamentary expert explains: 'Forthwith effectively means, in Commons parlance, no amendments and put straight away.'

Grieve knew he was chancing his arm. 'I knew very well what I was doing when I tabled the amendment and I thought he would reject it. But as a lawyer I know that if you want to argue for something which you think important, you must not be deterred by the difficulties with your argument,' he says. Bercow asked to see Grieve in his study. 'This is a very interesting amendment, and I just wanted you to know that I ordered for it to be put on the order paper because otherwise it couldn't be considered and I will need to reflect on it overnight,' he said. Surprised, Grieve told the Speaker: 'You do realise it is controversial?' Bercow responded: 'Of course I know it's controversial. I will make up my own mind.'

Grieve, who stresses that Bercow did not behave improperly, explains:

> As I had a concern for him, I certainly did not want to lure him into doing something improper. I actually went out of my way to point out that there were good arguments that could be made for rejecting the amendment. John took no decision and expressed no opinion at the meeting.

Bercow selected Grieve's amendment, which called for Theresa May to announce within three days details of her Plan B for Brexit if MPs rejected her deal on 15 January. The decision would have widespread consequences: it meant all future government 'Brexit next steps' motions could be amended. A former Cabinet minister says: 'That changed everything. Nobody was warm to [Bercow] up to that point ... That was when he really stepped into the fray and tried to redo things in a way that he had no real authority to do.'

Suspicions mounted that Bercow had ignored the advice of the clerks of the House. Sources in the leader's office say they were privy to the same guidance Bercow had received, which went against his ruling. 'The bottom line is he did ignore the clerks' advice,' says one source. Another says: 'The clerks were appalled. It went against all their advice.' Peter Bone, a Eurosceptic Tory MP who is favourable towards Bercow, told the House that he had also approached the clerks about tabling an amendment, which he was told 'would be totally out of order and that no other amendments had been tabled'. In an interview with *The House* magazine, David Natzler, the Clerk of the House, said: 'I will never reveal what I say to [the Speaker] in private.'

An insider who spoke to one of the clerks involved says:

There was this massive row where the Deputy Speakers and the clerks in the Speaker's conference said, 'You can't allow this.' Bercow said, basically, 'I don't give a fuck, I'm going to do what I want,' and stormed out. That's why there was a lot of pressure from Tory MPs to ask, 'What did the clerks say?'

The decision triggered a spectacular set-to between irate Tory MPs and Bercow. Over the course of an hour, the Speaker defended his decision, taking successive points of order from upset backbenchers. 'I have been here for eighteen years and I have never known any Speaker to overrule a motion of the House of Commons,' said Mark Francois, a Brexiteer and former member of the FCS. After Bercow replied: 'We are not treating here of a motion but of an amendment to a motion,' Francois exclaimed: 'That's ridiculous,' and accused the chair of 'utter sophistry'. Crispin Blunt, a Eurosceptic, said that many MPs now had an 'unshakeable conviction' that the Speaker was 'no longer neutral'.

Setting out his defence, Bercow said that he was 'not in the business of invoking precedent, nor am I under any obligation to do so'. The Speaker said he interpreted the 'forthwith' instruction to mean that there can be no debate, adding: 'I must advise the House that the terms of the order do not say that no amendment can be selected or moved.' Defiantly, Bercow declared: 'If we were guided only by precedent, nothing would ever change.'

In his pitch for the Speakership, Bercow had said he would not be bound by precedent. He had proved that multiple times, not least when he allowed a backbench amendment to the Queen's Speech in 2013, to the benefit of Brexiteers. Christopher Chope highlighted this fact in the Chamber: 'Let nobody suggest that you, by your actions, have been undermining Brexit. It would seem to me to be an absolute own goal for this House if we started undermining your position in the chair.' Bercow had also defended UKIP's right to run a candidate against him at the 2010 election, despite it contravening convention. The issue for Bercow would arise when he would invoke precedent to make certain decisions but not others, as we shall discover.

A Tory minister says: 'He has no care for the consequences of what he's doing. He's doing it because he's motivated by dislike of the government … And he does it because it's all about him.'

Tory MP Adam Holloway referred to press reports that a 'Bollocks to Brexit' sticker had been placed on one of Bercow's cars. 'This is a serious point about partiality. Have you driven that car with the sticker there?' he asked. Bercow responded:

> That sticker on the subject of Brexit happens to be affixed to, or in the windscreen of, my wife's car … I am sure the hon. Gentleman would not suggest for one moment that a wife is somehow the property or chattel of her husband. She is entitled to her views.

Towards the end of his Speakership, Tory staffers began distributing 'Bollocks to Bercow' stickers around the Houses of Parliament.

Not everyone took issue with the move to overturn precedent. Hilary Benn, the Labour MP and chair of the Brexit Select Committee, says:

> His decision on the Grieve amendment in particular was not John saying, 'I have a view on this particular proposition.' It was John saying, 'I think the House of Commons should be allowed to express its view.' He has come down on the side of the House of Commons being able to debate something, to consider a proposition, then it's up to the House to decide whether to pass it or not.

Labour MPs Jess Phillips, Yasmin Qureshi, David Lammy and Angela Smith were among those to call for calm. Julian Smith, the government Chief Whip, however, confronted Bercow in the chair, calling his ruling 'totally out of order'. 'You are overturning precedent, defying the advice of the Clerk of the House and trying to overturn the referendum result,' he said. A No. 10 aide says Smith 'bore the brunt of the difficulties' in the relationship between the government and Bercow: 'Every now and again, he'd come into the PM's Commons office when she was preparing for a statement and his eyes were glazed because he'd just had another difficult evening with a recalcitrant Speaker who had been determined to ignore the government's point of view.'

Seventeen rebels voted in favour of the Grieve amendment, which was passed by 308 to 297. The vote showed that Bercow had a sense of the mood of the House. May expressed her 'surprise' at Bercow's decision, saying: 'Members of Parliament need to know that there is a set of rules in the House of Commons; they need to know that there will be consistent interpretation of those rules so that they know how they can operate within the House.' A source who worked for May says: 'Her main quarrel with it was always about procedural impropriety. She is a very by-the-book person.'

Charles Walker, Bercow's close confidant, also took issue with the ruling. As chair of the Procedure Committee, Walker wrote to the Speaker a week later and asked if the same interpretation of 'forthwith' would be used in the future. 'You would probably discover that was the first time that such a letter had ever been written by a chair of the Procedure Committee to a Speaker,' Walker says. Asked for his views on Bercow's rulings on Brexit, Walker answers: 'Interesting. We'll leave it at that.' When pushed, he adds: 'I think John has stretched the envelope.'

Julian Lewis also wrote to his old friend. He told the Speaker that his legacy had centred on being on the side of Parliament against the executive, but he now risked being on the side of Parliament against the people. 'I've left you a letter with my views on this. I don't require or want a reply, I just wanted to put one point forward for your consideration,' he said when he notified Bercow. Lewis says his role during Bercow's Speakership has been

a little bit like a therapist, in the sense that I'm someone to whom he's always felt able to pour out his heart politically … Often, when you're wound up about something, or you're too close to something and you're thinking: 'Should I do this or should I do that?', it is enormously valuable to be able to confide in a trusted ally.

Given that Bercow had revealed how he voted at the EU referendum, many Tory MPs felt his decision on the Grieve amendment confirmed his bias. A Tory MP says: 'The Speaker is there to referee the match. He can decide whether or not to award one side a penalty, but he can't change the rules of Association Football. The House can do that.' A former Cabinet minister disagrees: 'I understand the point that is made about bias, but I do not recognise it.'

Bercow's actions would now be subject to renewed scrutiny. On the day of the first meaningful vote, 15 January 2019, Bercow overlooked two amendments from Tory backbenchers – Hugo Swire and Andrew Murrison – that sought to address perceived shortfalls in the backstop element of May's Brexit deal. The mechanism, which was in place to avoid a hard border in Northern Ireland, had proven to be the most controversial aspect of the agreement. In March, Bercow did not select an amendment that called for a second referendum to be ruled out, despite it being supported by 127 MPs – more than any other amendment chosen – with representatives from the Tories, the DUP, Labour and an independent. Sir Bernard Jenkin, chair of the Public Accounts Committee, asked: 'What are we to conclude from your own views on these matters?' Bercow said that the amendment did not have enough support from different parties in the House, and argued: 'Members do have to take the rough with the smooth.'

In explaining to the public how he selects amendments, Bercow says he considers a number of factors. First of all, he decides if it is in order and related to the motion or bill that it is seeking to amend. He also takes into account how much support an amendment has: 'Does the amendment or new clause have cross-party support? Is it, perhaps, backed by the chair of a select committee? Does it help the House to reach a conclusion that

I suspect that the House might want to reach in relation to a particular motion or piece of legislation?'[1]

On 15 January, the House defeated May's withdrawal agreement by 230 votes, the largest parliamentary defeat of a British Prime Minister in the democratic era. She survived a vote of no confidence in the Commons a day later.

Bercow's intervention had further heightened his profile overseas. Radio France Internationale named him European of the Week. But his ruling led to reports that the government would not send him to the House of Lords after he stepped down as Speaker, a time-honoured convention for departed chairs. 'I can't imagine we would look favourably on those who've cheated centuries of procedure,' said a Cabinet source. Bercow has long been an advocate of an elected House of Lords, and in September 2017 he called for the number of peers to be cut by half to around 400.[2]

Abiding by the Grieve amendment, the government set out its Plan B in a neutral motion, which was amended by MPs. Two of the votes were passed by the House: one, put forward by Sir Graham Brady, which called for 'alternative arrangements' to be pursued in place of the backstop; and a second, tabled by Dame Caroline Spelman and Jack Dromey, which expressed the Commons' desire to avoid no deal. The Prime Minister embarked on a tour of Europe to try to achieve concessions on her Brexit deal over the vexed issue of the backstop.

*   *   *

Following his meeting with Grieve, a lot more interest was paid to Bercow's relationships. The *Sunday Express* had a picture of the Speaker dining with Clarke at the Kennington Tandoori in south London, known as 'KT' to insiders, which was Bercow's curry house of choice. The paper branded the rendezvous 'the poppadom plot'.[3] Describing the reporting as 'gullible', Clarke says he often visits the KT with Bercow: 'I don't deny it, we're both very political animals, we spend a very high proportion of the time talking about politics, but it's not in any purposeful plotty way … It's just very enjoyable, long political chat between two fairly obsessive political addicts.'

Now that he had broken his pledge of serving for nine years, unofficial campaigns to replace him were already underway behind the scenes. In February 2019, Dame Eleanor Laing, one of the three Deputy Speakers, became the first MP to publicly announce their candidacy. 'I will try to become Speaker when he finally decides to go,' she told *The House* magazine. Labour's Chris Bryant, the SNP's Pete Wishart and Tory back-bencher Sir Edward Leigh would also put their names forward before Bercow had set out his departure date.

After her efforts to secure vote-winning concessions to her Brexit deal fell short, May suffered another major defeat at the second meaningful vote on 12 March, losing by 149 votes. Labour MP Angela Eagle was concerned that ministers would continually bring back the same deal before MPs. Bercow said a ruling on the matter 'might at some point in the future be required', noting: 'There are historical precedents for the way in such matters are regarded.' This was a clear hint from Bercow that he would not allow ministers to continually pose the same question to the House.

On 18 March, Bercow made a statement. Referencing Erskine May, the parliamentary bible on rules and procedures, the Speaker cited a precedent, dating back to 2 April 1604, that a motion or an amendment which is the same 'in substance' as one that has already been ruled upon during a session, 'may not be brought forward again during that same session'. Bercow argued that the second meaningful vote did not breach this rule as it was a sufficiently different proposition that MPs were voting on as a result of May's renegotiation.

The reaction in the House was fairly muted in comparison to Bercow's call on the Grieve amendment; those in favour of no deal welcomed the ruling, while Remainers were also happy. It was a different story inside No. 10. 'There was frustration at, on a matter of such importance, not being able to think we can bring back the meaningful vote,' says an aide. Bercow's invocation of precedent in one instance, and rejection of it in another, was inconsistent.

The House had also rejected two attempts for MPs to take control of the order paper. This was the tactic being pursued by opponents of no deal in light of the Grieve amendment. They wanted the chance to schedule business in the Commons and allow for a process of indicative votes, where a number of Brexit outcomes would be voted on by MPs, such as a Norway-style Brexit (which would involve remaining in the single market) and a second referendum.

Brexiteer MPs wanted clarification that, given the Commons had voted against such moves, Bercow would apply the same logic if another effort was made. The Speaker said it would depend on 'context and circumstance'. On 25 March, Bercow selected an amendment by Sir Oliver Letwin, the Tory former minister and linchpin of the anti-no dealers, calling for a series of indicative votes. MPs voted in favour by 329–302. The process took place over two rounds, which fell either side of a third defeat of May's Brexit deal. However, MPs failed to reach a consensus on a Brexit outcome. Parliament had failed to break open the Brexit impasse.

* * *

Standing orders are the codified written rules of Parliament that are agreed upon by the House. Standing Order 24 allows any MP the opportunity to apply for an emergency debate at short notice. SO24 had never been used, however, to allow the Commons to enact legislation or express a formal opinion. A parliamentary expert says: 'There has never been an instance where a motion has been moved under Standing Order No. 24. It's always been on a "take note" basis.'

This changed on 3 April 2019, when Oliver Letwin and Labour's Yvette Cooper used the third day tabled for indicative votes to bring forward a bill. Known as the Cooper–Letwin Bill, the legislation sought to compel ministers to seek MPs' consent for any or no extensions to the date the UK would leave the European Union. In just six hours, MPs debated the bill's second reading, committee stage and third reading before it went to the House of Lords. An extraordinary tie took place on an amendment put forward by Hilary Benn, which sought to secure an extra day for more indicative votes. In the event of a tie, the Speaker has the casting vote. 'In accordance with precedent and on the principle that important decisions should not be taken except by majority, I cast my vote with the noes,' Bercow said. 'That is the proper way in which to proceed.'

With the Commons blockage unresolved, the EU agreed to extend Article 50 until 31 October. May resigned as Prime Minister in early June, after her attempts to change her Brexit deal was met with incredulity among Conservatives.

Malcolm Jack, the former Clerk of the House, says Bercow's two most 'egregious' interpretations of procedure came on SO24 and the Grieve amendment, but he adds:

> He has departed from precedent, there's no doubt about that. But there are moments in history when precedent has to be departed from. I'm not impressed by the last two governments' attitude toward Parliament. Therefore, John's actions have to be seen in that context. Once more, they have been endorsed by the House. If the House didn't like what he was doing, that would have been the end of it.

Another Commons official argues: 'Although he definitely manipulated, ignored and contradicted advice, I do think any Speaker would have struggled in that parliament.'

An independent MP says: 'In some ways, he's terribly brave, because he's prepared to be drummed out of office, he's prepared for all the brickbats, to be condemned by history because he will not allow our country to be treated in the way that certainly the Conservative government has.'

A Labour MP who voted Remain says: 'On the issue of Brexit he is not even-handed, far from it, and he has in part created this bloody impasse and mess that the country's in now.'

Lewis explains:

His long-time friends have to decide whether or not the fact that he sometimes takes positions with which they disagree is more important than the value of having his personal friendship. Most of us would say, 'No, it isn't,' even though some of us have been flummoxed, if not frustrated, by some of the positions he adopted towards the end. Nevertheless, that's not a reason that outweighs the value of the friendship.

Grieve argues: 'I don't think any of his actions can be criticised as being a conspiracy to stop Brexit. In a sense, Brexit wasn't stopped and it wasn't because there was never a majority will in the House of Commons to do it.'

Bercow's procedural creativity came about as a reaction to successive governments' approach to the House of Commons. Procedures in the Commons are designed to allow the House to conduct itself in the way in which it chooses. Usually, that is entirely congruent with the way government wants Parliament to conduct itself, because it is in a majority. In truth, both the May administration and that of Boris Johnson prior to the December 2019 election acted as if they had a majority government, and cried foul when the Commons pushed back.

A former clerk argues: 'Bercow is trying to read what might be the will of the House … I don't think he's fundamentally done anything which undermines the role. Certainly, [he's been] much more interventionist than what we've been used to.'

Bercow's rulings undoubtedly did the government no favours – but it was not only the Speaker who was contravening expectations. In normal times, a Prime Minister would have resigned after losing three major votes, a Cabinet minister would have stepped down after being found in contempt of Parliament, and opposition MPs would have supported an early general election, which the Labour Party and others subsequently resisted in order to gain greater assurances on Brexit. The Fixed Term Parliaments Act, which required two thirds of MPs to support a call for a general election, allowed a zombie parliament to prevail. Bercow was not the only stakeholder guilty of aberrations or of testing the UK's unwritten constitution.

Usual conventions have been despatched in this time of turmoil for British politics. Bercow reacted to that and allowed Parliament to take control. It was not his failing that MPs, who were well versed in what they were against on Brexit, were unable to agree on what they were for.

CHAPTER TWENTY-EIGHT

THE BACKBENCHERS' BACKSTOP

'If the Speaker doesn't speak up for Parliament,
it's hard to know who does.'

John Bercow was enjoying his morning at Club Med Palmiye, in Turkey's Antalya province, where he was spending his summer holiday with his family. The break offered a welcome, albeit brief, period of calm amid a tumultuous year. In July, Boris Johnson had become Prime Minister, after defeating Jeremy Hunt in the race to succeed Theresa May as Conservative leader. The former London Mayor, who had played a pivotal role in the EU referendum, had won on a platform of pledging to leave the EU on 31 October 'come what may, do or die'. The UK now had a Prime Minister who, on the face of it, was prepared to take the UK out of Europe without a withdrawal agreement in place.

Parliament was scheduled to reconvene in early September, before departing again for the party conference season. Just over three weeks would remain when they came back in October to prevent the UK from crashing out. Anti-no dealers were torn between pursuing legislative routes or backing a no-confidence motion in the government and trying to form an alternative government in its place, with various MPs suggested as would-be Prime Ministers, with Bercow's name among those to be floated.

Over the summer, various reports emerged of how Downing Street planned to neutralise resistance in the Commons. Among the myriad of options being considered was the idea of proroguing Parliament. The act brings an end to a parliamentary session, which usually takes place once a year, leading to a short break and a Queen's Speech at the start of the new session, setting out the government's legislative agenda. The current session had been running since the election in June 2017, marking only the second time since 1945 that Parliament had sat for a period of two years. The question of prorogation had featured during the Tory leadership contest, with candidates such as Matt Hancock, the Health Secretary, railing against it.

On 28 August, Johnson confirmed the rumours. The Prime Minister announced that Parliament would be prorogued from 10 September until 14 October. 'We've got to be bringing forward new and important bills and that's why we are going to have a Queen's Speech,' he said. Three Conservative privy councillors, including Jacob Rees-Mogg, the newly appointed Leader of the Commons, took the request to the Queen's residence in Balmoral for her approval.

Despite being on holiday hundreds of miles away to the east, Bercow released a statement within an hour: 'This move represents a constitutional outrage. However it is dressed up, it is blindingly obvious that the purpose of prorogation now would be to stop Parliament debating Brexit and performing its duty in shaping a course for the country.' He added: 'At this early stage in his premiership, the Prime Minister should be seeking to establish rather than undermine his democratic credentials.'[1]

The strength of Bercow's words was considered unconstitutional by his critics. 'That annoyed some: they said it wasn't for me to pronounce. But if the Speaker doesn't speak up for Parliament, it's hard to know who does,' he told an interviewer later that year.[2]

The prorogation plans narrowed the timeline available to MPs to rein Johnson in, and Bercow had been in conversation with Sir Oliver Letwin and Hilary Benn about the implications. 'Look, throughout history, Members have talked to the Speaker about what's going on. That's part of the job; that's not something new as far as John is concerned,' says Benn.

Letwin applied for an emergency debate on a bill, known colloquially as the Benn Bill, under Standing Order 24. The legislation sought to compel Johnson to write a letter to the EU asking for an extension to Article 50 if MPs had not approved a deal by 19 October. MPs supported the motion by 328 to 301 and agreed to debate the legislation the following day. The twenty-one Tory MPs who voted in favour, including former Cabinet ministers Dominic Grieve, Philip Hammond and Ken Clarke, had the party whip removed. On 4 September, MPs passed the bill by 329 to 300.

Johnson maintained in public that he would find a way around the legislation. Having renegotiated the withdrawal agreement, he called for a special Saturday sitting of Parliament to be held on 19 October. Letwin, who did not trust the government to abide by the law of the Benn Act, tabled an amendment that would withhold Parliament's approval for the deal until the legislation implementing the agreement had been passed. After MPs supported the move, Johnson pulled the vote on the main deal. Bercow refused a government request to hold a vote on the deal two days later, citing this decision. Johnson was forced to send a letter to Donald Tusk, the outgoing President of the EU Council, asking for an extension of Article 50 to 31 January. EU leaders agreed.

The strength of Bercow's condemnation of the prorogation, and his actions in granting SO24 debates, had been his last throw of the dice. On 8 September, Andrea Leadsom, the Business Secretary, who had served as his sparring partner for the previous twelve months, confirmed that the Tories would run a candidate against him in Buckingham at the next general election. 'Bring back an impartial Speaker,' she said.[3]

*　*　*

Sally was the giveaway. Her presence, along with Oliver, Freddie and Jemima, sitting in the viewing gallery above the Commons Chamber, meant that the game was up. The longest-serving Speaker since the Second World War was about to step down. 'Colleagues, I would like to make a personal statement to the House,' Bercow began.

Sally had wanted Bercow to step down the year before, but by the time of the summer of 2019, she was willing him to stay on. But Bercow had run out of road. With the Tories planning to run against him in Buckingham, he would have faced an almighty battle to be re-elected an MP, let alone as Speaker. To leave on his own terms, he would need to act.

Even his resignation was confrontational. He announced that, bar an election being called prior to this date, he would stand down on Thursday 31 October – the day the UK was due to leave the European Union. This would allow the current parliament to choose his successor.

'Throughout my time as Speaker I have sought to increase the relative authority of this legislature, for which I will make absolutely no apology to anyone, anywhere, at any time,' he said. 'To deploy a perhaps dangerous phrase, I have also sought to be the backbenchers' backstop.' Breaking into tears, Bercow looked up at the viewing gallery. 'I could not do so without the support of a small but superb team in Speaker's House; the wider House staff; my Buckingham constituents; and, above all, my wife Sally and our three children, Oliver, Freddie and Jemima. From the bottom of my heart, I thank them all profusely.'

He concluded: 'This has been – let me put it explicitly – the greatest privilege and honour of my professional life, for which I will be eternally grateful. I wish my successor in the chair the very best ... Thank you.'[4]

More than an hour of points of order followed, during which MPs from across the House paid tribute to the Speaker, including Jeremy Corbyn, who held decent relations with Bercow. 'Whatever you do when you finally step down from Parliament, you do so with the thanks of a very large number of people, and as one who has made the role of Speaker in the House more powerful, not less powerful,' he said. Eleven other Labour

MPs spoke, and six Conservatives. Among them was Michael Gove, who said Bercow's 'energetic efforts' are appreciated by 'those of us who may not always be the best behaved in class'. MPs from the DUP, Plaid Cymru, the Lib Dems and the SNP all expressed their gratitude.

While being lavished with praise, Bercow also began to shoot from the hip. He claimed that elements of the media were not interested in the plight of Nazanin Zaghari-Ratcliffe, a British-Iranian dual national jailed in Tehran. 'It is about time, if they have any sort of moral compass, that they took an interest,' he said.

Chris Leslie comments: 'When he laced into the media ... I was thinking, "John, you don't need to actually say that." But he was a bit demob happy.'

A source in the Commons says Charles Walker was 'upset' that he had not been told in advance about Bercow's decision to step down. Indeed, Walker was in conversation with me in his parliamentary office when news broke that Bercow was about to resign.

Farcical scenes followed into the early hours, as the Queen's representative arrived to shut down the Commons, as per the rules of prorogation. MPs, some brandishing pieces of paper with 'Silenced' written on them, gathered round Bercow to prevent him from witnessing the prorogation in the Lords. Bercow condemned what was about to take place: 'This is not a normal prorogation. It is not typical. It is not standard.' Earlier in the proceedings, he had lambasted Tory MP Graham Stuart for heckling from the backbenches. 'Mr Stuart, if you do not like it, you are perfectly entitled to your view. I could not give a flying flamingo what your view is!'

When the Supreme Court came to the unanimous verdict late in September that Johnson's prorogation was unlawful, Bercow felt vindicated. 'It was declared illegitimate. Ultra vires. Not *proper*. And, crucially, void. I repeat: void. Void. *Void.* Invalid. It didn't happen ... I am glad about it,' he said.[5] In a rare jaunt outside of the Commons, Bercow gave a statement to confirm that Parliament would resume as normal.

On 29 October, after the House had rejected three times Johnson's call for a general election, MPs passed a bill calling for a vote to be held on 12 December 2019.

Bercow's last day in Parliament would follow a similar theme to that of his resignation. Among those to champion Bercow's legacy during the two-hour debate was Jacob Rees-Mogg, who had proposed him for the Speakership in 2015. The pair's unlikely relationship had been strained since Rees-Mogg joined the government, with the eccentric Brexiteer taking issue with Bercow's rulings from the chair. 'His recent mistakes have, to my deepest regret … damaged the standing of the House in the eyes of the British public to the lowest point in modern history,' he told Tory conference in September. But in saying farewell, Rees-Mogg told MPs: 'The ultimate, most important, highest duty of the Speaker of the House of Commons is to be the champion of our House and its Members, and to defend our right to freedom of speech in defence of our constituents. Mr Speaker, you have done that.'[6]

The cordiality in the Chamber was unceremoniously shattered when business moved on to Keith Vaz. MPs were being asked to endorse a call from the Standards Committee that Vaz be suspended from the House for six months for offering to buy drugs for sex workers, as revealed by the *Sunday Mirror* in 2016. The complaint had been lodged by Andrew Bridgen, Bercow's long-standing foe. They had clashed over the Leicester East MP before, during a debate on Vaz's appointment to the Justice Select Committee, which came soon after he had stood down as chair of another committee in the wake of the allegations. Sensing that Bridgen was now using the platform to make accusations against the MP, Bercow ruled him out of order. In heated exchanges on Bercow's last day, the Speaker intervened on Bridgen for the contents of his speech, which he ruled were an 'ad hominem attack' on Vaz. Bridgen shot back:

It is clear to me, and it will be clear to the public, that to the fag-end of your tenure in that chair you are defending the indefensible, and your very close relationship with [Mr Vaz]. The House can come to its own conclusions. The Standards Committee has come to its own conclusions. And, Mr Speaker, the public will come to theirs.

Bercow countered: 'He can try to smear me; he will get the square root of nowhere ... I am friendly with a great many Members, having served in this place for twenty-two years. I do not get involved in matters appertaining to standards.'[7]

It would not have been a suitable tribute to Bercow if his last day did not contain some controversy. His tenure came to an end at 5.30 p.m. on Thursday 31 October, as he called his last 'Order, Order'.

CHAPTER TWENTY-NINE

LEGACY

'In Europe, most people absolutely love John Bercow.'

By virtue of a televised Commons, and being in the chair during a re-markable period of British political history, John Bercow was always likely to become well known. But his eccentricities also helped make him a household name. By 2019, as much of the world was gripped by the Brexit saga, Bercow became a global figure.

'In Europe, most people absolutely love John Bercow,' says Antonello Guerrera, the UK and Ireland correspondent for Italian newspaper *La Repubblica*. 'Just as they love British and English theatre, they consider the English Parliament to be very theatrical. In this context, John Bercow was the most recognisable man, as he was the host of the House.' Europeans would rejoice in Bercow's use of language, Guerrera says, which 'is something between Shakespeare and Monty Python'.

Guerrera has interviewed Bercow twice, the first time in March 2019. Versions of the interview were also run in *El País* in Spain, *Le Soir* in Belgium and *Die Welt* in Germany. 'He was surprised by this mega audience that he had across the Channel,' Guerrera says. 'He was really honoured and pleased. Maybe he hadn't realised yet how famous he was on continental Europe.'

Cátia Bruno, a journalist for Portuguese website Observador, says Bercow cut through the more mundane aspects of Brexit. 'He lit up a debate that would seem boring at first,' she says. In Portugal, there is a perception that Bercow was the man who encouraged politicians out of the deadlock. 'Most readers here don't know so much of the finer details, and there is an idea here of him being more impartial than he might be in truth,' she explains.

Ellen Barry, a journalist at the *New York Times*, wrote a profile of Bercow in January 2019, when she served as the paper's London-based chief international correspondent. 'As a writer, what was magnetic about John Bercow is it seems like a case where historical events and personality, personal character, are in confluence to propel processes forward,' she says. 'Because he was the Speaker at this moment in British history, that has led Brexit in a different direction. It's just interesting to look at when the person in a role really matters, when that person's character matters, and this does seem like one of those moments.'

Like their European counterparts, the American audience was taken in by Bercow's unconventional style. 'The way he weaponises prolixity and almost archaic nineteenth-century presentation, they love it. It's catnip. He's an object of fascination,' Barry says. On Brexit, he was perceived as someone who made a 'fairly muscular challenge to executive power and asserting a role for Parliament in Britain'. For US residents, witnessing a Speaker push back against the executive was nothing new. 'He emerged from the sometimes-stultifying Brexit hamster wheel as a very vivid and somehow comprehensible actor.'

The accusations of bullying against Bercow, which perhaps plague his standing in the UK, have not made their way overseas. 'Looking at the different parts of his career and his reputation, most American readers don't get that far,' Barry explains. Guerrera adds: 'People don't know much about that. What has more impact in this era are images, videos, sounds. Of course, this has a more powerful impact on people's minds, especially when they're not particularly into British politics.'

In December 2019, Bercow appeared on *Che tempo che fa*, a popular Italian talk show. The hosts asked him to repeat his patented phrase

– 'Order' – in Italian. *'Ordine!'* Bercow bellowed at the camera.[1] His appearance came soon after the general election, when Bercow appeared as a star guest on Sky News. Friends of Bercow say he wants to pursue more television opportunities in the future. Chris Leslie argues that Bercow, with all his English idiosyncrasies, will also be in high demand as an after-dinner speaker.

Having moved to Battersea after leaving Speaker's House, Bercow will continue to support his beloved Arsenal Football Club. Lawrence Ward used to go to matches with Bercow when his eldest child, Oliver, could not attend. 'We would go for a few beers before or after the game,' he says. Bercow has an 'encyclopaedic' knowledge of the entire Arsenal squad. However, his grip on the machinations of a football match leave a little to be desired, says Ward. When they travelled on the Underground, Ward would become nervous for the Speaker's safety. 'From one end of the Tube to the other, everyone was shouting "Order!" and "Mr Speaker!",' he recalls. However, Bercow would always be relaxed in the environment, and 'revel' in meeting members of the public. 'He was totally at ease with that. He never gave a second thought to his own personal security.'

Ed Balls once invited Bercow and Oliver to watch a game at Norwich City, the football club where he served as chairman. He recalls Bercow, an adopted fan for the day, leaping off the ground when the home side scored a last-minute winner. 'Nobody, including Delia Smith or any of us, came anywhere near the exuberance of the Speaker when the final Norwich goal went in. The guy was at least two feet of the floor,' Balls recalls. 'There is an enthusiasm, an enjoyment of sport and a love of a good comeback story, which is part of his personality.'

The world of tennis is another potential avenue for Bercow to pursue after retiring from frontline politics. Barry Cowan, a friend and former tennis player who commented for Sky Sports, says: 'I don't see how you can be that passionate about something and not [get involved in some way].' In 2019, Bercow had been put forward for membership of the All England Club, only for the person to change their mind after 'disapproving' of decisions he had made on Brexit. 'Do I bear any ill will towards this person? No. Am I bothered about it? No, I'm not. Am I losing any sleep over it? No, I'm not.'[2]

During his time as Speaker, Bercow accrued a number of free tickets to sporting events, including to Wimbledon finals over consecutive years. In December 2018, the *Daily Telegraph* reported that he had received more than £70,000 worth of freebies since he took on the Speakership.[3] The majority of the gifts were tickets to sporting events, though these weren't his only indulgences. The *Daily Mail* reported that Bercow spent £1,003 on a 250-mile trip from Westminster to Nottingham to give a speech in his final year (aides said he had been advised it was safer for him to travel by taxi rather than by rail). In total, his travel bill amounted to £13,627.[4] Though he has passed his test, former staffers say Bercow is a 'hopeless' driver.

With his memoirs published, friends also say Bercow would like to continue writing. At fifty-seven, he still has plenty of time left to pursue political causes. Benedict Rogers, the human rights activist, says Bercow will continue campaigning on countries such as Burma and Hong Kong: 'He is looking to do something in this field as part of a portfolio of activities.'

At his leaving do in Speaker's House on 23 October 2019, Bercow praised Rogers as 'one of the finest human beings I've ever met anywhere at any time'. After thanking Sally and his three children, he became emotional as he praised Emil Kirchner and David Sanders, two of his professors at university, who were also in the room. Dame Margaret Beckett also spoke, saying Bercow's Speakership had been 'exciting, controversial' and 'full of achievement'.

Arguments will rage for years about Bercow's legacy. At constituency level, reports are favourable. 'The typical thing you hear locally is he is a very, very good local MP. He'll turn up to anything,' says one constituent. During the 2017 election, even some Tory supporters who did not approve of Bercow's political journey promoted 'Vote Bercow' posters, the source adds.

Bercow, like many in the constituency, is a vehement opponent of HS2. Emma Macey, who ran his constituency office between 2009 and 2010 from Speaker's House, said Bercow would have resisted the project from the chair. 'If push came to shove and he would get the deciding vote over whether HS2 happened or not, John always said that he would break parliamentary convention and would vote against it, for the sake of his constituents,' she says.

Bercow would often visit journalists at the *Buckingham Herald* in their offices for a catch-up. Hayley O'Keeffe, content editor at the *Herald*, says Bercow would always provide a comment to the paper when asked. 'No one can deny he is not a present and good constituency MP,' she says. Bercow once invited a reporter down to Westminster. 'He is open in a way you wouldn't necessarily expect,' the journalist says. However, Bercow did snap at a *Herald* reporter when they asked him a question during a World Book Day event at a school, says O'Keeffe. Bercow, who perceived that the *Herald* had misrepresented him on an issue, bristled: 'This is what the press is like.'

Bercow was noted for his charity work, auctioning an annual game of tennis against a member of the public, and taking part in local swimathons for Brain Tumour Research, a charity for which he is a patron. Hugh Adams, a constituent who works at the charity, reached out to Bercow when they were struggling to find specialist provision for their son, who has special educational needs. 'It was quite extraordinary. We had a number of email and written letter communications which always came back very promptly,' says Adams. While Speaker, Bercow met Adams and his wife in person. 'What was amazing about it was the fact that it was him, my wife and myself and no one else in this small village hall.'

Brain Tumour Research hosted an annual event in Speaker's House during Bercow's tenure. 'I've always found him charming, friendly, impressive ... I don't have a word against him,' Adams says. Benedict Rogers adds: 'He is an incredibly generous and generous-spirited person. So many times over the years that I've known him, he has gone the extra mile, he's done things that he was under no obligation to do.' Friends also describe Bercow as amusing company. 'He's good fun. He's got a great sense of humour,' says Rogers.

By dint of his being Speaker, however, Bercow did suffer some unrest at constituency level. Many voters spoilt their ballots in anger at being disenfranchised. (Convention sees none of the major parties stand against an incumbent Speaker. Constituents also do not get a voice in the Commons, though Bercow would argue that he was more able to effect change by summoning ministers to discuss casework.) 'There is an element of dissatisfaction about the Speaker convention. People feel really aggrieved they can't vote Tory and Labour at an election. It's not to do with him; it's to do with rules,' says O'Keeffe.

Though there is broad agreement around his constituency work, the wider picture is far more muddied. The Speakership election that followed his departure from the Commons saw his potential successors distancing themselves from his platform. Most candidates, including Eleanor Laing, Harriet Harman and Rosie Winterton, vowed to lower the temperature in the Commons, while many pledged to cut back on the number of Urgent Questions granted each day. After he was elected Speaker, Sir Lindsay Hoyle announced that any break with existing parliamentary conventions by a Speaker would be accompanied by a statement from the Clerk of the House outlining why they disagree. The move was interpreted as a riposte to Bercow in the wake of his rulings on Brexit.[5]

The election result also sullied things for Bercow. With the Tories returning to Parliament with a majority of nearly eighty, Brexit was a foregone conclusion. Speaking prior to the vote on 12 December, Julian Lewis pondered whether Bercow's endeavours on Brexit would be worth it:

If Labour wins the election, then John has altered the course of history by blocking Brexit. If, however, Boris wins, then I'd say it's largely been a wasted effort and it has, to some extent, detracted from what was otherwise an admirable Speakership which brought up to date and strengthened the power of the House of Commons to hold the executive to account.

On Bercow's legacy, Sir Malcolm Rifkind says: 'He will be remembered as a one-off, as an extremely smart, clever, tough, courageous Speaker, but one whose flaws were as evident as his virtues.' Ken Clarke argues: 'I think he's been an excellent Speaker and probably the best Speaker in my time in the House of Commons.' George Osborne agrees: 'He's one of the biggest and most important Speakers in our history.' The SNP's Tasmina Ahmed-Sheikh adds: 'He offered opportunity for proper challenge and proper scrutiny.'

'His legacy is that he enabled Parliament to find its voice and to express its view,' Labour MP Hilary Benn says. 'That is why I have no doubt at all that history will record him as a great Speaker.' Professor Vernon Bogdanor disagrees: 'I think he's the worst [Speaker in history], frankly. I can't think of any previous Speaker who's been publicly partisan.' Professor Philip Cowley argues: 'UQs alone would give him a more beneficial impact on Parliament than almost any other Speaker in my lifetime. It's just that you then have this stuff on the other side of the ledger which is more problematic.'

Nick Robinson, Bercow's former sparring partner, says: 'He genuinely will go down in history as a Speaker who put a huge emphasis on outreach, changed the procedures to ensure that news would be made first in the Chamber, but he was also self-absorbed, vain and infuriating in the chair.' A Tory critic argues: 'We need to be very careful to avoid having another John Bercow.'

Labour MP Jess Phillips says: 'I would say John Bercow's legacy will be good and progressive. The thing that he always wanted to be known for, he will certainly be known for: the idea of holding the executive to account and being the friend of the backbencher.' Gillian Keegan argues: 'This has been not easy constitutionally. It has tested all of our institutions and he's been one of the people who's had to step up and deal with things that are unprecedented.'

Dominic Grieve concludes: 'At a time when a government did not have a majority, he will be remembered as having fearlessly stood up for the right of Members of the House of Commons to express a dissenting view from the view that the government itself wanted to promote.'

In January 2020, Jeremy Corbyn nominated Bercow for a peerage. The news reignited the accusations of bullying against him, spurring former colleagues to action. Former Clerk of the House Robert Rogers, now Lord Lisvane, was the first person to lodge a formal bullying complaint against Bercow. David Leakey, the former Black Rod whom Bercow had clashed with over Westminster Hall, followed, as did Angus Sinclair, his former private secretary. Sources say others are contemplating coming forward.

Among those to come to his defence was Diane Abbott, who suggested in a tweet that as a former military man, Leakey could not have been bullied by Bercow. Dawn Butler, a candidate in the Labour deputy leadership race, claimed Bercow could have been the victim of bullying himself, as a result of the apparent refusal of Tory bosses to give him a peerage.[6]

In a combative appearance on Sky News, Bercow dismissed Leakey as 'utterly ignorant' and called Andrea Leadsom 'untrustworthy'. He once more categorically denied the bullying claims against him.[7] In a subsequent interview, he claimed there was a 'conspiracy' against him entering the House of Lords.[8]

*　　*　　*

A Speaker's role is to chair debates in the Commons Chamber, keep order and be a symbolic representative of the institution. They are also required to be impartial. Against these measures, it is worth considering Bercow's legacy.

Many of his contributions to Parliament should be credited. His uncompromising pursuit of reform saw some progressive and important developments, such as the creation of a crèche and the education centre. Through his use of Urgent Questions and emergency debates, he rejuvenated the House of Commons as a place of scrutiny. He was more willing than many of his predecessors to exert Parliament's authority over the government. Thrown a hospital pass by the Fixed Term Parliaments Act, his procedural creativities helped impose the authority of the Commons against a minority government that behaved as anything but. His outreach work extolling the virtues of a parliamentary democracy should not go unremarked. His unique character sparked an interest in the UK Parliament from all corners of the globe.

There is always a double edge to the sword, however. Many reforms – such as the use of UQs and the creation of the nursery – originated somewhere else. Though they still needed a champion – a role he performed zealously – Bercow would rarely credit the originators of such ideas, who often were clerks. While so-called established elements can be a hindrance to change, Bercow's treatment of clerks often fell well short of the mark. Being a reforming politician does not give you carte blanche to treat people in the way that many in this book have recalled. The best politicians know that achieving reform is a balancing act of leadership and bringing people with you. Determination is a prerequisite; being indecent to colleagues is not.

His personal utterances make it difficult to conclude that Bercow was not prone to bias in the chair. He has argued that his only bias is towards the House of Commons itself, over any particular party or cause. But if he were able to contain his views on Cameron, or indeed Brexit, it would be easier to defend him. In a perfect illustration of this argument, just days after stepping down as Speaker, Bercow described Brexit as 'the biggest foreign policy mistake in the post-war period'.[9] Few were surprised – but for those who had defended Bercow against charges of bias, such proclamations undermined the cause. While his forceful approach as Speaker could keep in check dissenting MPs, his divisive manner often exacerbated existing tensions in the Chamber, particularly during the final twelve months of his time in the chair.

The most concerning aspect of his personality relates to bullying.

While Labour MPs defended him, those on the receiving end were coming forward to talk about their experiences. There are two sides to every story, but the number of people mentioned who had experiences of this nature with Bercow is truly notable. There is a consistency across the accounts that speaks for itself.

The fact that the bullying allegations were put on ice in the name of Brexit is of great shame to the Labour Party and many of its MPs. Bercow was able to survive for as long as he did simply because of the nature of politics. Those who defend him still have their heads in the sand, certain that such a 'progressive' figure could not be capable of bullying. Their relentless pursuit of modernity clouded their own judgement. At the very least, these members of staff were owed a duty of care, due process or a proper hearing. The realpolitik was they were not many MPs' priority.

Likewise, his detractors on the Conservative benches did themselves and the victims no favours by using the accusations for their own ends. For too many of them, the protection of members of staff wasn't the motivating factor. For their own reasons, they hated Bercow and would appropriate anything negative as part of their personal vendetta. This sullied the waters and created doubt where there should have been empathy and concern.

Love him or loathe him, Bercow was undeniably one of the most talented politicians of his generation. In a crude way, he was 'box office'. At a time of huge political intrigue, he was a fascinating character to have right at the heart of it.

Every story needs a hero and a villain. John Bercow's unique attribute is that he could play both at the same time.

His friend Charles Walker concludes: 'He was either going to be a hugely talented Secretary of State, senior minister, maybe more, but wherever he ended up, he was going to be noticed. He ended up in the Speaker's chair, and my word he's been noticed, hasn't he?'

NOTES

CHAPTER ONE: DON'T CALL IT A COUP

1 John Bercow speaking event, Mile End Institute, 9 November 2017

CHAPTER TWO: PLANTING SEEDS

1 Philip Webster, 'Bercow v Boris', *Tortoise*, 29 August 2019
2 Ibid.
3 John Bercow speaking event, University of Reading, 3 February 2017
4 Iain Dale, 'In conversation with... John Bercow', *Total Politics*, issue 19 (January 2010)
5 'Now John Bercow's mother steals the limelight', *Evening Standard*, 23 September 2013
6 Alastair Campbell interview with John Bercow, *GQ*, 7 November 2019
7 Ibid.
8 Ann Treneman, 'John Bercow and Sally Bercow: Westminster's odd couple', *The Times*, 13 March 2010
9 Quoted in Hannah Crown, 'MPs tuck in to Jam Roly Poly as school celebrates its 70th birthday', *Hendon & Finchley Times*, 22 November 2009
10 Simon Hoggart, 'A plague on Hirst's latest art concept', *The Guardian*, 11 July 2009
11 'Tail-gun Charlie has pot at Brown', *Mail on Sunday*, 29 November 2009
12 John Bercow, *Tennis Maestros: The Twenty Greatest Male Tennis Players of All Time* (Biteback Publishing, 2014), p. 109
13 Dominic Midgley, 'My love match with tennis: John Bercow reveals the sporting path that he almost took', *Daily Express*, 5 June 2014

CHAPTER THREE: BULLIED

1 Richard Kay, 'Mellor lies into age at customs', *Daily Mail*, 3 August 2010
2 Pandora, *The Independent*, 6 September 2001
3 Jemima Khan, 'Jemima Khan meets John Bercow: "I've never liked little cliques"', *New Statesman*, 13 September 2012
4 John Bercow responding to Seumas Milne, 'Pale Rider', *The Guardian*, 12 October 1999
5 Jemima Khan, *New Statesman*, op. cit.
6 Hansard, vol. 667, col. 513
7 'Study reveals shortcomings in men of modest stature', *Toronto Star*, 23 January 1999
8 Ibid.
9 Charlotte Edwardes, 'John Bercow: The former Speaker on bullying, Brexit and Boris', *Sunday Times*, 2 February 2020
10 Stuart Jeffries, 'The Saturday interview: John Bercow', *The Guardian*, 22 July 2011

11 Stefanie Marsh, 'What I've learnt: John Bercow', *The Times*, 5 July 2014
12 Rachel Cooke, 'John Bercow: "I may be pompous and an irritant. But I am completely authentic', *The Observer*, 10 November 2019
13 Bobby Friedman, *Bercow, Mr Speaker: Rowdy Living in the Tory Party* (Gibson Square, 2011)
14 John Bercow speaking event, University of Leeds, 3 November 2017

CHAPTER FOUR: THE MONDAY CLUB

1   Alastair Campbell, *GQ*, op. cit.
2   Philip Webster, Tortoise, op. cit.
3   Jemima Khan, *New Statesman*, op. cit.
4   Ibid.
5   Stuart Jeffries, *The Guardian*, op. cit.
6   Anne McElvoy, 'The New Statesman Interview: Tory Boy', *New Statesman*, 13 November 2000
7   Gordon Rayner and John Bingham, 'Speaker John Bercow called for "assisted repatriation" of immigrants', *Daily Telegraph*, 26 June 2009
8   Interview with Gregory Lauder-Frost
9   Anne McElvoy, *New Statesman*, op. cit.
10 Martin Hannan, 'Far-right group VP Gregory Lauder-Frost fined for racist abuse', *The National*, 27 July 2019
11 Jemima Khan, *New Statesman*, op. cit.
12 Marie Woolf, 'John Bercow: "I have been to Sudan … seen the poorest people on the planet. They need our help', *The Independent*, 2 August 2004
13 John Bercow speaking event, Cambridge Union, 12 October 2015
14 Alastair Campbell, *GQ*, op. cit.
15 John Bercow speaking event, Mile End Institute, 9 November 2017
16 Jemima Khan, *New Statesman*, op. cit.
17 *Jewish Chronicle*, 18 July 1986, republished in Jenni Frazer, '"Aggressive and defensive": the JC's interview with John Bercow, 23, in 1986', *Jewish Chronicle*, 9 September 2019
18 John Bercow speaking event, Mile End Institute, 9 November 2017

CHAPTER FIVE: FRESH START

1   'Rt Hon. Dr John Bercow MP, Essex graduate and Speaker of the House of Commons, University of Essex', YouTube, University of Essex, 21 October 2014
2   Ibid.
3   Ibid.
4   'John Bercow – My first week', YouTube, University of Essex, 5 December 2017
5   Ibid.
6   Ibid.
7   'Pint-size surprise: Getting lairy with Bercow', Popbitch, 31 October 2019
8   'John Bercow – My first week', YouTube, op. cit.
9   *Jewish Chronicle*, 18 July 1986, op. cit.
10 Ibid.
11 Simon Hoggart, 'Simon Hoggart's diary: Gordon Brown and other planets', *The Guardian*, 4 July 2009
12 'John Bercow – Graduation day', YouTube, University of Essex, 5 December 2017
13 'Rt Hon. Dr John Bercow MP, Essex graduate and Speaker of the House of Commons', YouTube, op. cit.

CHAPTER SIX: THE FED

1   Paul Johnson, 'Tory students join Loyalist poll fight against Dublin deal', *The Guardian*, 9 January 1986
2   Andrew Moncur, '"Red Scum" gibe inflames students', *The Guardian*, 10 December 1984
3   David Rose, 'Is the party over for the Tory fringe? / Background report on extremism in the Federation of Conservative Students', *The Guardian*, 4 April 1985
4   Letters, *The Independent*, 11 July 1996

5   Anne McElvoy, *New Statesman*, op. cit.
6   'Conservative Party Conference: Union power pricing workers out of jobs – Lawson speaks on the economy', *The Guardian*, 11 October 1984
7   'Conservatives at Blackpool: Enterprise units boost for small firms, tourism / Employment debate', *The Guardian*, 11 October 1985
8   Alan Travis and Peter Hetherington, 'Conservatives at Bournemouth: Tebbit claims the centre ground / Party policy', *The Guardian*, 11 October 1986
9   James Naughtie and David Rose, 'Gummer stops party funds for Tory "vandals"', *The Guardian*, 3 April 1985
10 Ibid.
11 David Rose, 'Right wing tightens grip on students and scorns inquiry', *The Guardian*, 3 April 1985

CHAPTER SEVEN: CUTTING TIES
1   United Press International, 5 September 1982
2   Alan Rusbridger, 'Guardian Diary', *The Guardian*, 22 August 1985
3   David Rose, 'Tory students face rift over "war crimes"', *The Guardian*, 20 August 1986
4   'Conservative Gets Injunction Against Magazine', Associated Press, 19 August 1986
5   James Naughtie, 'Tebbit muzzles student attack on Stockton', *The Guardian*, 20 August 1986
6   'FCS renews assault on Stockton record', *The Guardian*, 8 September 1986
7   *The Times* Diary, 11 September 1986
8   David Rose, 'Tebbit's axe falls on right-wing Tory students', *The Guardian*, 14 November 1986

CHAPTER EIGHT: ELECTIONEERING
1   Bobby Friedman, *Bercow, Mr Speaker*, op. cit.
2   Brendan Carlin and Glen Owen, '"MPs should be paid £100,000 a year", says favourite to become Commons Speaker John Bercow', *Mail on Sunday*, 21 June 2009
3   Ibid.
4   *The Times* Diary, 'Lambeth line-up', *The Times*, 1 October 1987
5   Hansard, vol. 007, col. 524
6   Tom Shields, 'New angle on Glen's', *The Herald*, 14 January 1992
7   Bobby Friedman, *Bercow, Mr Speaker*, op. cit.
8   'John Bercow's 1995 CV: tennis coach with a record for sticking it to the lefties', ITV, 31 December 2019
9   Andrew Martin, 'Young Guardian: New kids in the House', *The Guardian*, 18 January 1991
10 Bobby Friedman, *Bercow, Mr Speaker*, op. cit.
11 'Huge support for Thatcher', *Sunday Times*, 18 November 1990
12 Andrew Martin, *The Guardian*, op. cit.

CHAPTER NINE: WORKING MAN
1   Steve Bevan, 'Four promoted to Rowland board', *PR Week*, 27 January 1994
2   'John Bercow's 1995 CV: tennis coach with a record for sticking it to the lefties', op. cit.
3   David Reed, 'Business Initiative: Ex-minister chairs new Saatchi outfit', *Campaign*, 17 July 1992
4   *Private Eye*, Issue 881, 22 September 1995
5   *The Guardian*, 10 April 1995
6   David Pallister and Christopher Elliott, 'Aitken issues writ against Granada TV', *The Guardian*, 28 April 1995
7   Hansard, vol. 301, col. 323
8   Matthew Norman, Diary, *The Guardian*, 30 August 1995

CHAPTER TEN: JULIAN
1   Rebecca Dowman, 'Westminster Strategy gains Bercow expertise', *PR Week*, 19 April 1996
2   Hansard, vol. 667, col. 551
3   Hansard, vol. 667, col. 520

CHAPTER ELEVEN: ROTTWEILER

1   Melissa Kite, 'Labour MPs buttonhole Blair over parliamentary hours', *The Times*, 28 June 2000
2   Black Dog, 'Brown in a battle royal', *Mail on Sunday*, 14 June 1998
3   BBC *Newsnight*, 10 June 1997
4   'Bitter divisions as Tories reach the final round', Press Association, 18 June 1997
5   David Cracknell, Press Association, 19 June 1997
6   Hansard, vol. 300, col. 585
7   Jo Dillon, 'Redwood steps up attack on ministers', Press Association, 1 December 1997
8   Martin Hickman, 'TV chief unsuitable to head BBC, claims Tory', BBC, 22 April 1999
9   Michael Brown, 'The week in Westminster: resurrection shuffle sends ministers into a cold sweat', *The Independent*, 10 July 1999
10   'Ground gaffe in Commons', *Derby Evening Telegraph*, 28 March 2001
11   Nicholas Watt and Toby Helm, 'Commons speaker election: Tory favourite faces threat from own party in bitter race: Senior Conservatives say John Bercow, backed by at least 100 Labour MPs, could be removed if they win general election', *The Guardian*, 15 June 2009
12   Hansard, vol. 365, col. 1090
13   '"Gorbals" under fire', *Evening Standard*, 12 October 2001
14   Hansard, vol. 297, col. 564
15   Andrew Pierce, 'It's a fresh start, but a long way to recovery', *The Times*, 31 July 1997
16   Melissa Kite, 'MP's war on waste costs the taxpayer over £500,000', *The Times*, 19 April 2002
17   'The Scurra', *Daily Mirror*, 2 July 2002
18   'The Scurra', *Daily Mirror*, 10 July 2002
19   Michael Kallenbach, 'Bercow accused of compulsive disorder for asking questions', *Daily Telegraph*, 12 July 2002
20   Hansard, vol. 302, col. 161
21   Alastair Campbell, *GQ*, op. cit.
22   Hansard, vol. 304, col. 349
23   Jo Dillon, Press Association, 16 April 1998
24   Press Association, 21 January 2000
25   Black Dog, *Mail on Sunday*, 21 June 2009
26   Black Dog, 'The art of smalls talk', *Mail on Sunday*, 10 November 2002
27   Charlotte Edwardes, *Sunday Times*, op. cit.
28   Jemima Khan, *New Statesman*, op. cit.
29   John Bercow speaking event, University of Reading, 3 February 2017
30   Interview with colleague of Nicholas Soames
31   'Parliamentary Quotes of the Day', Press Association, 5 March 2001
32   Hansard, vol. 344, cols 455–86

CHAPTER TWELVE: BACK TO FRONT

1   Philip Thornton and Paul Waugh, 'Blunkett: We aim for full employment', *The Independent*, 12 August 1999
2   Bob Roberts, 'Tories to accuse Labour of "educational vandalism"', Press Association, 20 October 1999
3   James Landale, 'Backlash grows at decision to sack Redwood', *The Times*, 3 February 2000
4   Anne McElvoy, 'Dyke is a "vulgar, uncouth oaf", says frontbench Tory', *The Independent*, 13 September 2000
5   Steve Doughty, 'Cherie Blair has Hillary syndrome, say Tories', *Daily Mail*, 8 August 2000
6   Andrew Woodcock, 'Hague condemned over attack on Cherie Blair', Press Association, 8 August 2000
7   Philip Webster, 'Cherie attack sanctioned by Tory chiefs, critic insists', *The Times*, 9 August 2000
8   Anne McElvoy, *The Independent*, op. cit.
9   Ibid.

10   Tom Baldwin and Alice Miles, 'We have failed ethnic minorities', *The Times*, 3 October 2000

11   Anne McElvoy, *New Statesman*, op. cit.

12   Ibid.

13   Ibid.

14   Ibid.

15   Gavin Cordon, 'Will she – won't she: Ann to take support soundings', *Birmingham Post*, 11 June 2001

16   Londoner's Diary, *Evening Standard*, 22 August 2001

17   James Landale, Tom Baldwin and Melissa Kite, 'Duncan Smith wins backing of far-right club', *The Times*, 17 August 2001

18   Paul Waugh, 'With a spring in his Hush Puppies, Ken takes on the Right brigade', *The Independent*, 22 August 2001

19   Michael Prescott and Dipesh Gadher, 'Duncan Smith pledges purge on far right', *Sunday Times*, 26 August 2001

20   Paul Eastham, 'Tory wants purge of far Right', *Daily Mail*, 28 September 2001

21   Andrew Sparrow, 'Duncan Smith orders Monday Club to suspend Tory links', *Daily Telegraph*, 19 October 2001

22   Interview with Simon Richards, Freedom Association chief executive

23   Benedict Brogan, 'Tories "could have first gay PM"', *Daily Telegraph*, 11 October 2001

24   Tom Baldwin, 'We have never looked worse, says top Tory', *The Times*, 17 January 2002

25   Matthew Tempest, 'Duncan Smith: the party I lead is a decent party', *The Guardian*, 18 January 2002

26   Rachel Cooke, *The Observer*, op. cit.

27   Paul Waugh, 'How a tactical error by Duncan Smith led to a bad call', *The Independent*, 5 November 2002

28   Greg Hurst, 'Portillo speaks out against party's hard line on adoption vote', *The Times*, 5 November 2002

29   Joe Churcher, 'Rebel Bercow hits out at "arrogance and ignorance"', Press Association, 4 November 2002

30   Nicholas Watt, 'The ghost of conferences past returns: "Offensive" Tebbit faces calls for his expulsion', *The Guardian*, 10 October 2002

31   Andrew Pierce, 'People', *The Times*, 7 November 2002

32   *GMTV*, 6 January 2003

33   Gavin Cordon, 'IDS "facing leadership challenge sooner rather than later"', Press Association, 23 February 2003

34   Simon Walters and Jonathan Oliver, 'IDS "will quit if MPs force ballot"', *Mail on Sunday*, 26 October 2003

35   Rachel Sylvester, 'No going back, says the diehard moderniser', *Daily Telegraph*, 8 November 2002

36   *The World at One*, BBC Radio 4, 22 July 2004

37   *GMTV*, 23 February 2004

38   Charlie Methven, 'Bercow follows which leader?', *Daily Telegraph*, 23 July 2004

39   Marie Woolf, *The Independent*, op. cit.

40   Simon Walters, 'There IS something of the night about you Michael: Leading Tory's amazing outburst at Howard as he is sacked from the Shadow Cabinet', *Mail on Sunday*, 11 September 2004

CHAPTER THIRTEEN: THE CANDIDATE

1   Iain Dale, *Total Politics*, op. cit.

2   Ibid.

3   Vivienne Morgan, 'Tory leadership hopefuls begin to jockey for position', Press Association, 8 May 2005

4   Liam Creedon, 'Speaker "standing up to snobs and bullies"', Press Association, 28 February 2008

5   Quentin Letts, 'The vultures are already circling defiant Speaker Martin', *Daily Mail*, 28 February 2008

6   'Parliamentary Quotes of the Day', Press Association, 19 May 2003

7   Charlie Methven, 'Bercow is not going anywhere', *Daily Telegraph*, 3 November 2004
8   Anne McElvoy, 'Sally Bercow: "Two bottles a day, one-night stands, my life was out of control', *Evening Standard*, 3 December 2009
9   Brendan Carlin, 'A reshuffle without any thorns?', *Daily Telegraph*, 29 June 2009
10 Glen Owen, 'Revealed: John Bercow had secret talks to become a Labour minister for Gordon Brown – amid fresh row over "anti-Brexit bias"', *Mail on Sunday*, 24 August 2019
11 Ambitious About Autism, interview with John and Sally Bercow, 5 October 2012
12 Sian Griffiths, 'Helping my opponents for the sake of our son', *Sunday Times*, 16 September 2007
13 Ibid.
14 Benedict Brogan, 'Grassroots fury at Tory MPs lured by Brown', *Daily Mail*, 10 September 2007
15 Sian Griffiths, *Sunday Times*, op. cit.
16 Hansard, vol. 472, col. 1941
17 Hansard, vol. 478, col. 510

CHAPTER FOURTEEN: ELECTION NIGHT

1   Nicholas Watt, 'Frontrunner for Speaker's role vows to fix "broken" parliament', *The Guardian*, 21 May 2009
2   'We will vote for a Speaker they hate', *Evening Standard*, 21 May 2009
3   Gordon Rayner, 'MPs' expenses: John Bercow claims maximum allowance for £540,000 flat', *Daily Telegraph*, 22 May 2009
4   Gordon Rayner, 'MPs' expenses: John Bercow to repay £6,500 capital gains tax', *Daily Telegraph*, 23 May 2009
5   Patrick Sawer, 'John Bercow: claimed nearly £1,000 for tax advice on MPs' expenses', *Sunday Telegraph*, 21 June 2009
6   Hansard, vol. 494, col. 624
7   Bob Roberts, 'New speaker John Bercow – the Tory the Conservatives hate', *Daily Mirror*, 23 June 2009
8   Hansard, vol. 494, col. 636
9   Hansard, vol. 494, cols 637–8
10 Hansard, vol. 494, col. 623

CHAPTER FIFTEEN: SALLY

1   Anne McElvoy, *Evening Standard*, op. cit.
2   Ibid.
3   Colin Brown, 'The Conservative Party in Blackpool: Warning over new curbs on press', *The Independent*, 8 October 1993
4   Rachel Cooke, *The Observer*, op. cit.
5   Stephen Cook, 'People Diary', *The Guardian*, 6 September 1986
6   Anne McElvoy, *Evening Standard*, op. cit.
7   Ibid.
8   Ibid.
9   Ann Treneman, *The Times*, op. cit.
10 Ted Jeory, 'Crusade for better mental health: John Bercow on changing attitudes to mental health', *Sunday Express*, 15 July 2012
11 Anne McElvoy, *Evening Standard*, op. cit.
12 Sam Leith, 'Bubbling over', *Daily Telegraph*, 12 January 2001
13 Nicholas Watt, 'John Bercow says he is ready for the Speaker's role', *The Guardian*, 21 May 2009
14 Michael Kallenbach, *Daily Telegraph*, op. cit.
15 'Room for growth', *Daily Telegraph*, 9 December 2003
16 Marie Woolf, *The Independent*, op. cit.
17 Alastair Jamieson, 'Speaker's wife Sally Bercow launches Twitter poll to name Commons cat', *Daily Telegraph*, 13 February 2010
18 Charlotte Edwardes, *Sunday Times*, op. cit.

19 Anne McElvoy, *Evening Standard*, op. cit.
20 Hannah Nathanson, 'London's sexiest places... for power lovers', *Evening Standard*, 3 February 2011
21 *Celebrity Big Brother* interview, August 2011
22 *The House* magazine, 23 February 2012
23 'Speaker's wife Sally Bercow voted off Big Brother', BBC News, 26 August 2011
24 *The House* magazine, 23 February 2012
25 Josh Halliday, 'Sally Bercow tweet libelled Lord McAlpine, high court rules', *The Guardian*, 24 May 2013
26 David Churchill, 'Exclusive: "I go out and have fun but I'm not ashamed," says Sally Bercow on nightclub kiss', *Evening Standard*, 4 February 2014
27 John Stevens, 'Side by side in prime House of Lords seats, Mr Speaker's wife and her drinking pal', *Daily Mail*, 2 August 2014
28 Glen Owen, 'Bercow "to divorce Sally" after MoS affair exposé', *Mail on Sunday*, 17 May 2015
29 Rachel Cooke, *The Observer*, op. cit.
30 Ibid.
31 Charlotte Edwardes, *Sunday Times*, op. cit.

CHAPTER SIXTEEN: REFORMER

1 Andrew Sparrow, 'John Bercow abandons traditional dress as he begins Speaker role', *The Guardian*, 23 June 2009
2 Jeremy Corbyn, 'The strange journey of Mr Speaker: Bercow's election was not down to the party whips – and that can only be a good thing', *Morning Star*, 24 June 2009
3 John Bercow speaking event, University of Reading, 3 February 2017
4 John Bercow speaking event, Brookings Institution, 28 May 2019
5 Nicola Bolden, 'Global protests over Burmese regime', Press Association, 6 October 2007
6 John Bercow speaking event, Brookings Institution, 28 May 2019
7 Andrew Hough and Richard Savill, 'Row over appointment of female cleric as Commons chaplain', *Daily Telegraph*, 27 June 2010
8 Steve Hawkes, 'Commons Speaker John Bercow faces new scandal after bullying verdict against senior official he picked for the job', *The Sun*, 17 February 2019
9 *Woman's Hour*, BBC Radio 4, 16 July 2018
10 'MP Bryant's civil partnership a "first" for Westminster', BBC News, 27 March 2010
11 Statement on UK Parliament website, 13 September 2012

CHAPTER SEVENTEEN: WHIPS

1 Nigel Nelson, 'Top Tory in door rage', *Sunday People*, 18 June 2000
2 Nigel Nelson, 'Tory "vandal" in new farce over a door', *Sunday People*, 25 June 2000
3 Hansard, vol. 667, col. 553
4 John Bercow speaking event, University of Cambridge, 15 October 2015

CHAPTER EIGHTEEN: BOLLOCKED BY BERCOW

1 John Bercow speaking event, University of Reading, 3 February 2017
2 Simon Walters, 'Cameron cutie's obscene rant at Bercow after not being allowed to speak in debate', *Mail on Sunday*, 6 March 2011
3 David Hughes, 'MP's regret over Bercow comment', Press Association, 6 October 2011
4 BBC *Daily Politics*, 13 June 2018
5 Simon McGee and Marie Wool, 'A BBB – the Tory medal of honour', *Sunday Times*, 17 July 2011
6 'Speaker "ticks off twice as many Tories as Labour MPs"', *Daily Mail*, 18 July 2011
7 Brendan Carlin, 'Bercow "using Speaker role to bash Tories in Commons", *Mail on Sunday*, 29 July 2012
8 John Bercow speaking event, University of Cambridge, 15 October 2015
9 Hansard, vol. 664, col. 140
10 Ibid.

CHAPTER NINETEEN: CAMERON

1   John Bercow speaking event, Mile End Institute, 9 November 2017
2   'John Bercow: Ken Clarke is the natural leader of the Tory Party', *The Independent*, 21 May 2005
3   John Bercow speaking event, Mile End Institute, 9 November 2017
4   Matt Chorley, 'David Cameron says Theresa May ignored his Brexit advice', *The Times*, 19 September 2019
5   James Anthony and Joe Murphy, 'PM hauled to Commons over Jeremy Hunt affair', *Evening Standard*, 30 April 2012
6   Ibid.
7   Rachel Cooke, *The Observer*, op. cit.
8   Ibid.
9   Matt Chorley, *The Times* Red Box podcast, 19 September 2019

CHAPTER TWENTY: CLERKS

1   Simon Walters, 'Expenses enforcer blasts MPs who say they're forced to sleep at their desks', *Mail on Sunday*, 2 January 2011
2   Alastair Campbell, *GQ*, op. cit.

CHAPTER TWENTY-ONE: CAROL

1   John Bercow speaking event, Mile End Institute, 9 November 2017
2   Ibid.
3   *Mail on Sunday*, 20 July 2014
4   Black Dog, 'Carb offsetting at the Treasury', *Mail on Sunday*, 29 June 2014
5   Simon Walters and Brendan Carlin, 'Bombshell email accuses Bercow of secret power grab', *Mail on Sunday*, 17 August 2014
6   Joe Churcher, 'Row deepens over Commons Clerk job', Press Association, 18 August 2014
7   Christopher Hope, '"He was just very aggressive and angry": Tory MPs clash again with John Bercow over clerk appointment', *Daily Telegraph*, 1 September 2014
8   Daniel Hurst and Katharine Murphy, 'Carol Mills loses Canberra parliament job after months of criticism', *The Guardian*, 24 April 2015
9   Daniel Hurst, 'Parliamentary Services department under Carol Mills "deeply dysfunctional"', *The Guardian*, 28 April 2015
10 Daniel Hurst and Katharine Murphy, *The Guardian*, op. cit.
11 John Bercow speaking event, Mile End Institute, 9 November 2017

CHAPTER TWENTY-TWO: TWO DAYS IN FEBRUARY

1   Camilla Turner, 'John Bercow: I will only take chauffeur-driven cars when "absolutely necessary"', *Daily Telegraph*, 25 July 2015
2   Tim Sculthorpe, '£2,000 on special beeswax candles, £500 on pictures of himself and even £286 to tune his grand piano: The lavish lifestyle of Commons Speaker John Bercow is revealed', MailOnline, 12 February 2016
3   BBC *On the Record*, 9 June 2002
4   John Bercow speaking event, Brookings Institution, 28 May 2019

CHAPTER TWENTY-THREE: NIGHT AND DAY

1   Jamie Doward, 'Revealed: why Michael Fallon was forced to quit as Defence Secretary', *The Observer*, 5 November 2017
2   Heather Stewart and Haroon Siddique, 'Tory minister faces inquiry after getting female assistant to buy sex toys', *The Guardian*, 29 October 2017
3   Hansard, vol. 630, col. 577
4   Hannah White, 'I worked in parliament for 10 years. Staff need proper protection from harassment', *The Guardian*, 7 November 2017
5   BBC *Newsnight*, 8 March 2018

6 Glen Owen, 'Hacking probe MP "bullied and harassed" women at Commons', *Mail on Sunday*, 29 April 2012

7 Francis Elliott and Esther Webber, 'John Bercow accused of failing female clerk who was "bullied by an MP"', *The Times*, 6 February 2020

CHAPTER TWENTY-FOUR: 'BULLY'

1 'Speaker Bercow appoints ex-journalist as special adviser', *The Guardian*, 8 September 2009

2 Simon Walters and Brendan Carlin, 'New expenses chief "forced to quit"', *Mail on Sunday*, 13 June 2010

3 Simon Walters, 'Clash of the Speakers as sacked Secretary wins £100K pay off', *Mail on Sunday*, 4 July 2010

4 'John Bercow in conversation', Guardian Live Events, 18 February 2020

5 John Bercow, *Unspeakable: The Autobiography* (Weidenfeld & Nicolson, 2020)

6 Ibid.

7 Steve Doughty, 'Embarrassment for Commons Speaker as wife uses Twitter to join attacks on Pope hours before Benedict goes to Parliament', *Daily Mail*, 17 September 2010

8 John Bercow, *Unspeakable*, op. cit.

9 'John Bercow "categorically" denies bullying allegations', BBC News, 23 January 2020

10 'Former Speaker John Bercow naming staff in book unacceptable – Commons', BBC News, 6 February 2020

CHAPTER TWENTY-SIX: FALLOUT

1 Harry Yorke, 'John Bercow accused of calling Andrea Leadsom a "stupid woman" in foul-mouthed tirade', *Daily Telegraph*, 17 May 2018

2 Charlotte Edwardes, *Sunday Times*, op. cit.

3 BBC *Today* programme interview, 16 October 2008

4 Alastair Campbell, *GQ*, op. cit.

CHAPTER TWENTY-SEVEN: GOING NUCLEAR

1 UK Parliament YouTube channel, 5 April 2019

2 John Bercow, 'Cut the size of the House of Lords', BBC News, 14 September 2017

3 David Maddox and David Williamson, 'John Bercow "conspiring" with remainers in cosy curry house talks', *Sunday Express*, 10 February 2019

CHAPTER TWENTY-EIGHT: THE BACKBENCHERS' BACKSTOP

1 Kate Proctor, 'Boris Johnson's move to prorogue parliament "a constitutional outrage", says Speaker', *The Guardian*, 28 August 2019

2 Rachel Cooke, *The Observer*, op. cit.

3 Andrea Leadsom, 'His abuse of the rules flagrantly defied the will of the people', *Mail on Sunday*, 8 September 2019

4 Hansard, vol. 664, col. 497

5 Rachel Cooke, *The Observer*, op. cit.

6 Hansard, vol. 667, col. 510

7 Hansard, vol. 667, col. 559

CHAPTER TWENTY-NINE: LEGACY

1 Harriet Brewis, 'Bizarre moment John Bercow bellows "order" in Italian', *Evening Standard*, 16 December 2019

2 Alastair Campbell, *GQ*, op. cit.

3 Camilla Tominey, 'Speaker John Bercow has received more than £70,000 in freebies, Telegraph can reveal', *Daily Telegraph*, 25 December 2018

4 John Stevens, 'Order, order me a £1,000 taxi!', *Daily Mail*, 14 January 2020

5 Alain Tolhurst, 'Lindsay Hoyle pledges greater "transparency" in veiled attack on John Bercow', PoliticsHome, 29 January 2020

6   'Tory refusal to give Bercow peerage is "bullying too", Labour MP says', Sky News, 9 February 2020
7   Alix Culbertson, 'John Bercow: Bullying accusations against me are "total and utter rubbish"', Sky News, 5 February 2020
8   'John Bercow: Ex-Speaker says he is victim of a conspiracy in peerage row', BBC News, 9 February 2020
9   'John Bercow: Brexit "biggest post-war foreign policy mistake"', BBC News, 6 November 2019